E. CARRINGTON BOGGAN is a New York City attorney who has done extensive work in the area of gay civil rights. He serves as General Counsel for Lambda Legal Defense and Education Fund, Inc., a non-profit, tax-exempt corporation organized to seek protection of the civil rights of gay people through the legal process. He is also Chairman of the Committee on Equal Protection of the Law of the American Bar Association Section of Individual Rights and Responsibilities.

MARILYN G. HAFT has worked extensively in the areas of women's rights, prisoners' rights, and sexual privacy. She has served as Director of the ACLU National Project on Sexual Privacy, and chairs subcommittees on prostitution and victimless crimes for the American Bar Association. She is also Adjunct Professor of Law and a coordinator of New York University's Women's Prison Clinic, which teaches law to women in prison.

CHARLES LISTER is an attorney in Washington, D.C. A graduate of Harvard and Oxford Universities, he has served as a special assistant in the Office of the Secretary of the Air Force and as law clerk to Mr. Justice Harlan of the U.S. Supreme Court. He has been an associate professor at the Yale Law School, and has served as a consultant on privacy and civil liberties issues to various state and federal agencies.

JOHN P. RUE
School, and i
District of Co

Also in this Series

AN AMERICAN
CIVIL LIBERTIES
UNION HANDBOOK

THE RIGHTS OF GAY PEOPLE

THE BASIC ACLU GUIDE TO A GAY PERSON'S RIGHTS

E. Carrington Boggan
Marilyn G. Haft
Charles Lister and
John P. Rupp

General Editors of this series:
Norman Dorsen, *General Counsel*
Aryeh Neier, *Executive Director*

DISCUS BOOKS/PUBLISHED BY AVON

AVON BOOKS
A division of
The Hearst Corporation
959 Eighth Avenue
New York, New York 10019

First Discus Printing, July, 1975

ISBN: 0-380-00391-0

Printed in the U.S.A.

Acknowledgments

In the course of completing this project, we depended on the wisdom and assistance of a great many people. We wish particularly to thank Dr. Franklin Kameny, David Addelstone, Susan Hewman, Lawrence Spelman, Wayne Outten, Dee Pridgen, Bob Roth, Leonard Cohen and Michael Miller. Much of what is good in the pages that follow is attributable to their willingness to lend a hand. Any errors of fact or judgment that remain stem from our failure to rely upon our friends even more heavily than we did.

THE
RIGHTS OF
GAY PEOPLE

CONTENTS

Preface

This guide sets forth your rights under present law and offers suggestions on how you can protect your rights. It is one of a series of guidebooks published in cooperation with the American Civil Liberties Union on the rights of mental patients, prisoners, servicemen, teachers, students, women, suspects, and the poor. Additional books, now in preparation, will include volumes on the rights of hospital patients, aliens, civil servants, veterans, and the aged.

The hope surrounding these publications is that Americans informed of their rights will be encouraged to exercise them. Through their exercise, rights are given life. If they are rarely used, they may be forgotten and violations may become routine.

This guide offers no assurances that your rights will be respected. The laws may change and, in some of the subjects covered in these pages, they change quite rapidly. An effort has been made to note those parts of the law where movement is taking place but it is not always possible to predict accurately when the law *will* change.

Even if the laws remain the same, interpretations of them by courts and administrative officials often vary. In a federal system such as ours, there is a built-in problem of the differences between state and federal law, not to speak of the confusion of the differences from state to state. In addition, there are wide variations in the ways in which particular courts and administrative officials will interpret the same law at any given moment.

If you encounter what you consider to be a specific abuse of your rights you should seek legal assistance. There are a number of agencies that may help you, among them ACLU affiliate offices, but bear in mind that the ACLU is a limited-purpose organization. In many communities, there are federally funded legal service offices which provide assistance to poor persons who cannot afford the costs of legal representation. In general, the rights that the ACLU defends are freedom of inquiry and expression; due process of law; equal protection of the laws; and privacy. The authors in this series have discussed other rights in these books (even though they sometimes fall outside the ACLU's usual concern) in order to provide as much guidance as possible.

These books have been planned as guides for the people directly affected: therefore the question and answer format. In some of these areas there are more detailed works available for "experts." These guides seek to raise the largest issues and inform the non-specialist of the basic law on the subject. The authors of the books are themselves specialists who understand the need for information at "street level."

No attorney can be an expert in every part of the law. If you encounter a specific legal problem in an area discussed in one of these guidebooks, show the book to your attorney. Of course, he will not be able to rely *exclusively* on the guidebook to provide you with adequate representation. But if he hasn't had a great deal of experience in the specific area, the guidebook can provide some·helpful suggestions on how to proceed.

Norman Dorsen, General Counsel
American Civil Liberties Union

Aryeh Neier, Executive Director
American Civil Liberties Union

THE
RIGHTS OF
GAY PEOPLE

Introduction

Upon hearing that we were undertaking to write a book on the rights of gays, a wit remarked: "It must be a very short book." In fact, the book is relatively short. That is attributable, however, to how we have conceived our task and the uses to which we expect the book to be put rather than to the absence of possible subject matter. It cannot be overemphasized that we have not here attempted to set forth in exhaustive or encyclopedic fashion the unique problems that confront gay people because of their sexual orientation; rather, we have endeavored to deal with only the most commonly occurring problems and to sketch the impact of the law in those circumstances.

If there is a single, overriding lesson that emerges from the discussion that follows, it is that gay people do have a great many rights—indeed, the same rights as all other members of society—but that these rights take on significance only to the extent that they are intelligently and knowledgeably exercised. This means that at the moment your sexual orientation becomes an issue in the context of your employment, your familial relationships, housing, public accommodations, etc., you should secure the advice of counsel—either a lawyer, if a legal dispute is involved, or some other qualified person. A list of groups willing to assist you in securing qualified counsel appears in the Appendix. (See page 265.) Special note should be taken of the role of the American Civil Liberties Union (ACLU) in this respect. In the past year the ACLU formed the National Sexual Privacy Project in response to the growing needs of the gay community and others who are being persecuted because of their private sex lives. One of the primary purposes of the project is to eliminate discrimination against gays through test-case litigation. Local ACLU affiliates work in coordination with the project. Therefore, if you are being discriminated against because you are gay, or your sexual privacy is being invaded, we urge you to contact the local ACLU affiliate in your state or the Sexual Privacy Project at the national office of the ACLU. The addresses are found in the Appendix.

Your reading of this book will have been time well spent if it serves to impress on you the extent to which problems that you have are shared by others, and that the chance of successful resolution of those problems will be immeasurably enhanced if you do not attempt to go it alone.

One final caveat. The law is an ever-changing thing. It changes in responses to shared perceptions of enlightened social policy and, significantly, in response to demands placed on it by those upon whom it impacts. During the past decade the laws applicable to the activities of gay people (both judge-made and statutory law) have been undergoing a revolution of sorts. Gay people are now conceded to have rights that were not conceived of ten or twenty years ago. This revolution has been spontaneous, however, only in the sense that its time had come; it did not simply happen, but was made to happen by vast numbers of people demanding equitable treatment. We do not presume to have sufficient prescience to anticipate all future legal developments in this area. Instead, we have largely confined ourselves in this book to delineating the present state of the rights of gay people and to an occasional conjecture directed at how the laws can and, in our collective view, should develop.

We realize that there is a great deal of controversy over the nomenclature of the movement. Although we debated at length over the title of the book and the proper use of the words "gay," "lesbian," and "homosexual," we are aware that we still have not used words that will be universally acceptable. The word "homosexual" was used as infrequently as possible because many people contend that the name puts too much emphasis on the sexual aspect of gay relationships. But the courts still use the word, and consequently we must do so in describing court decisions. We have used the word "gay" to include gay men and lesbians simply as a matter of editorial necessity. We have addressed the book to lesbians and gay men, and it is our sincere hope that it will be useful to both.

Finally, we would like to dedicate the book to those people who have had the courage and the foresight to organize and speak out in defense of the rights of gay people. The progress made over the past decade in the area of gay rights is very largely attributable to their efforts, and it is to the continued efforts of like-minded people that we must look for progress in the future.

E. Carrington Boggan
Marilyn G. Haft
Charles Lister
John P. Rupp

I

Freedom of Speech and Association: The Right to Organize and Speak Out

Until the late 1960s and early 1970s, gay men and women in the United States generally feared to speak out about their sexual orientation or to organize groups to secure their legal rights. Indeed, the thought that gays even had rights that they could assert did not occur to most people—gay or straight. The few organized groups that did exist used names designed to conceal their homosexual nature so that prospective members would feel less uncomfortable about joining them. Only a very few individuals dared to speak out publicly in support of equal legal rights for gays.

In the late 1960s the situation began to change dramatically. One of the events that provided a focal point for the gay movement as it exists today was an event that has come to be known as the Stonewall Riots.[1] A gay bar on Christopher Street in New York's Greenwich Village was raided by the police—a then-common occurrence—and the gay patrons fought back in an unprecedented assertion of the right of gay people to be free from unlawful police harassment. Shortly thereafter, the Gay Liberation Front was formed in New York City. It was one of the first organizations to use the word "gay" in its name. Similar groups have since appeared across the country, both in large and small cities and towns and on college campuses, openly referring to themselves as lesbian or gay or homophile organizations. Gay men and women have increasingly been willing to speak out in public and to form groups in support of their right to be free from discrimination because of their sexual orientation. The right of gays to organize and speak out has not always been willingly conceded by society, however, and resort to the courts has frequently been necessary to redress discriminatory treatment.

Do gays have a right to join together in organizations for the purpose of securing equal treatment under the law?

Yes. Freedom of association is a right that flows from the guarantees of freedom of assembly and speech contained in the First Amendment to the United States Constitution and the guarantee of liberty assured by the due process clause of the Fourteenth Amendment. Courts have specifically acknowledged that the right of freedom of association extends to gay organizations.[2]

Do gay organizations have the right to incorporate?

There is no reason why the legal benefits of incorporation should not be available to gay organizations to the same extent that they are available to any other organization, and New York State's highest court has so held.[3] The Ohio Supreme Court, however, recently refused to incorporate a gay organization. That decision has been appealed. Gay organizations have been incorporated without problem in many other states.

May corporate status be denied a gay organization on the ground that its purposes offend "public policy"?

As long as the stated purposes of the organization do not violate any law, corporate status should not be denied to a gay organization on "public policy" grounds.[4] Such a rationale would in fact be merely a subterfuge to conceal prejudice against homosexuals and as such should not be sanctioned by the courts.[5] The New York court has so held. The Ohio Supreme Court decision mentioned above, however, is to the contrary. Hopefully it will be reversed on appeal.

For what purposes may gay organizations be formed?

Any lawful purpose, which includes advocating the change or repeal of any existing law. When the Gay Activists Alliance sought to incorporate in New York, the certificate of incorporation was initially rejected by the

Secretary of State on the grounds, among others, that "the purposes of the proposed corporation raise serious questions as to whether it may be formed to promote activities which are contrary to public policy and contrary to the penal laws of the State."[6] In rejecting this rationale, a New York court held: "Generally, they propose to allow assemblage of homosexuals to foster the repeal of certain laws which . . . discriminate against them as a class. It is well established that it is not unlawful for any individual or group of individuals to peaceably agitate for the repeal of any law."[7]

What are some of the specific purposes that have been upheld as proper and lawful for gay organizations?

The following purposes have all been upheld as lawful:[8]

1. To safeguard the rights guaranteed homosexual individuals by the constitutions and civil-rights laws of the United States and the several states through peaceful petition and assembly and nonviolent protest when necessary.

2. To speak out on public issues as a homosexual civil-rights organization working within the framework of the laws of the United States and the several states, but vigilant and vigorous in fighting any discrimination based on the sexual orientation of the individual.

3. To work for the repeal of all laws regulating sexual conduct and practices between consenting adults.

4. To work for the passage of laws ensuring equal treatment under the law of all persons regardless of sexual orientation.

5. To instill in homosexuals a sense of pride and self worth.

6. To promote a better understanding of homosexuality among homosexuals and heterosexuals alike in order to achieve mutual respect, understanding, and friendship.

7. To hold meetings and social events for the better realization of the aforesaid purposes enunciated above and to achieve, ultimately, the complete liberation of homosexuals from all injustices visited upon them as such, that they may receive ultimate recognition as free and equal members of the human community.

Does the constitutionally protected right of association extend to gay student organizations at state-supported colleges and universities?

Yes. The right of freedom of association has been held to protect student organizations at state-supported institutions from arbitrary denial of that right by school authorities, subject to certain limitations deemed necessary for the preservation of the institution.[9] The right has been held to apply to gay organizations at state-supported schools.[10] Official school recognition of gay organizations cannot be withheld by officials at state-supported schools merely because they do not approve of the organization.

To what school benefits are such gay student organizations entitled?

The same benefits as any other officially recognized student organization. The benefits include the use of campus facilities for meetings and other appropriate purposes and the right to use school media for the expression of ideas to the school community and the community at large.[11]

Are gay student organizations entitled to sponsor and participate in social functions such as dances on the college or university campus?

Yes. A state-supported school must deal with similarly situated organizations in an evenhanded manner. Thus, if other student organizations, including those committed primarily to educational and political activities, are permitted the right to hold social functions, that right cannot be denied to gay student organizations.[12]

What criteria may legally be employed by a state-supported school to determine whether recognition may be denied to or withdrawn from a student organization?

There are three criteria that may lawfully be employed by school officials to evaluate any student organization: (1) failure or refusal to abide by reasonable "housekeeping" rules; (2) danger of violence or disruption of the university; and (3) violations of the criminal law by the organization or its members at functions sponsored by the organization.[13]

Is there anything inherent in a gay student organization that would come within any of these criteria?

No. The criteria basically require factual determinations in each particular case, and there is nothing in the nature of a gay organization per se that would cause it to be in violation of any of these standards. In one case, a university contended that a gay organization's social functions were tantamount to criminal solicitation of deviate sexual relations, but the court found that there was no evidence that any unlawful activity was solicited or had occurred at any of the organization's functions.[14] (See the discussion of solicitation in the chapter of this book on "Gays and the Criminal Law.")

Does the freedom of association for gay students and gay student organizations extend to public high schools as well as to colleges and universities?

Yes. It has been held that "the relevant principles and rules [concerning students' rights] apply generally to both high schools and universities."[15] Thus, although there has not been a case dealing specifically with the rights of gay public-high-school students to organize, it can be expected that the same principles will be applied to them as to gay college or university students.

Does the constitutional guarantee of the right of association for gay organizations at state-supported schools apply equally to gay organizations at private schools, colleges, and universities?

No. The constitutional protection against arbitrary interference with freedom of association applies only to schools run by the government—federal, state, or local. This is because the protections afforded by the Constitution are against unlawful *state* action that interferes with fundamental rights, not against deprivation of those rights by private organizations. It is possible, however, that a private school might be held to have participated in, and benefited from, public programs of support such that its operations in fact become public. If this were to be found, the "private" school would become subject to the principles described above.

Do gay organizations have a right to keep the names of their members confidential?

Probably. The Supreme Court has held that where, because of community temper, disclosure of the names of members of an organization might prejudice those members, the organization is not required to disclose its membership list even if a state or local law requires it, or a governmental official demands it.[16] The reason is that to force disclosure under such circumstances would have a deterrent effect on the members' exercise of their right to freedom of association.[17] Since public knowledge of a person's homosexuality is still something that might adversely affect members of gay organizations, and since a gay person who feared that his membership in a gay organization might become known to others might not join the organization, gay organizations would probably be held to have a constitutional right to keep the names of their members confidential. It is, however, a matter on which competent legal advice should be obtained if a group confronts any official demand for its list of members.

Do gay organizations have to reveal the names of persons who make financial contributions to them or pay dues to them if required to do so pursuant to local or state laws?

No. The Supreme Court has held that governmentally forced disclosure of members and contributors to organizations that espouse unpopular views can have a deterrent effect on the associational rights of the members of the organizations, and they may not be forced to divulge such information even if required to do so by a local law.[18] The only exception to the principle is that if an organization seeks tax-deductible status, information as to the specific sources and expenditures of the funds might be relevant.[19]

Here again, legal advice should be sought in the event of any dispute.

Would there ever be a circumstance under which a governmental body or official could compel disclosure of the members of or contributors to a gay organization?

Probably not, except where, as noted above, the organization seeks tax-deductible status. In the latter case, certain information as to financial sources might be sought, although it would not necessarily mean disclosure of the names of all contributors or members to the government. Other than in that limited instance, however, the right to freedom of association for the advancement of beliefs and ideas is so fundamental to our constitutional system, especially where unpopular ideas are involved, that it requires the protection of the privacy of such association.[20] To override the right of privacy of association requires the showing of a substantial state interest.[21] The nature of the organization and the possible danger to the state involved in its covert operation determine whether its membership lists can remain secret.[22] It is highly doubtful that any danger to the state from a gay organization could be shown that would justify compelling disclosure of membership lists.

Does an individual member of a gay organization ever have a right to refuse to reveal his association with the organization to the government and to prospective private employers?

Sometimes. The Supreme Court has held that while the Constitution unquestionably protects an individual from being forced to disclose his associational relationships in some circumstances, the right is not absolute, and where there is a state interest sufficiently compelling to overcome the individual's right to associational privacy, disclosure can be required.[23] A sufficiently compelling state interest has been held to exist where the inquiry is related to the rights of Congress to investigate Communist activity in the United States,[24] and the discharge of a public-school teacher for refusal to answer a question by his superintendent about Communist activity has been upheld.[25] The Supreme Court said that a public-school teacher does not give up the right to freedom of speech, belief, or association by teaching in the public schools, but he does undertake an obligation of frankness, candor, and cooperation in answering questions by the employing board because a teacher works in a sensitive area in the classroom and shapes the attitude of young students toward society.[26] In *Acanfora* v. *Board of Education of Montgomery County,* a federal court of appeals upheld the transfer of a gay teacher from classroom to administrative duties on the grounds that he failed to reveal his participation in a gay student organization while in college in answer to a question concerning his extracurricular activities.[27] The decision was based on grounds of misrepresentation because of the teacher's failure to list his membership in the gay organization on his application form, and unfortunately did not reach the freedom of association issue.

Competent legal counsel should be sought when trying to decide whether or not membership in a gay organization must be disclosed on an application form or in an interview. Further, it is important to remember that a right not to disclose does not mean that there is a right to lie. False statements in response to official inquiries may give rise to civil liability, criminal penalties, or both.

May gay organizations obtain federal tax-exempt and tax-deductible status?

Yes. There is nothing in the tax laws or regulations that would prohibit a gay organization from obtaining tax-exempt deductible status as long as it falls within the scope of organizations that generally qualify for such treatment. Those are organizations organized and operated exclusively for one or more of the following purposes: religious, charitable, scientific, testing for public safety, literary, education, or for prevention of cruelty to children or animals.[28] One of the major disadvantages of attempting to qualify as a tax-deductible organization is that such organizations are generally prohibited from "carrying on propaganda, or otherwise attempting, to influence legislation" and from "participat[ing]" or "interven[ing]" in political campaigns on behalf of particular candidates.[29] If a gay organization meets these criteria and secures recognition from the Internal Revenue Service, a donor to such an organization may also deduct his contribution from his federal taxable income.[30] Here again, legal advice should be obtained before an organization claims tax-deductible status. While several gay organizations have been successful in obtaining tax-exempt status, exemption has been denied to others, and those denials are presently being litigated.

What types of tax-deductible gay organizations presently exist?

At this time there are tax-deductible gay organizations for religious purposes,[31] for charitable and educational purposes,[32] and for scientific and educational purposes.[33] Some of the purposes of these groups are to protect the legal rights of homosexuals; to provide educational and scientific information about homosexuality; and to provide counseling services.

May gay organizations receive government funds to conduct programs and projects?

Yes. Various federal, state, and local governmental agencies and departments have funds available that they may grant to private organizations for specific programs or projects authorized by law. Such programs include, for example, providing halfway houses for prisoners and conducting training programs for counselors in drug programs. Several gay organizations have received grants from federal and local governmental bodies to conduct such programs. One such program, for example, trains drug-program personnel to deal with problems of gay drug users.

Do gay organizations have the right to provide legal services to their members to assist them in the assertion of their legal rights?

Yes. The Supreme Court has held that for minority groups seeking equal treatment under the law, association for litigation may be the most effective and sometimes the sole practicable form of political association and may not be abridged by governmental action.[34] "[C]ollective activity undertaken to obtain meaningful access to the courts is a fundamental right within the protection of the First Amendment."[35] The principle has been specifically found applicable to an organization formed for the purpose of protecting the legal rights of homosexuals.[36]

Do gays have a right to speak out publicly in support of their right to be gay and in support of changing laws that discriminate against them?

Yes. The right to freedom of speech is one of the fundamental guarantees under the United States Constitution and under most state constitutions. The right includes advocacy of ideas and beliefs that may be unpopular with the majority. The only limitations are on words that amount to imminent incitement to lawless action,[37] "fighting words," that is, words that by their very utterance inflict injury and are thus libelous,[38] and obscenity.[39]

Do gays have a right to assemble peacefully and to demonstrate in support of equal legal rights for homosexuals?

Yes. The First and Fourteenth Amendments to the Constitution guarantee the rights to assemble peacefully and to petition for the redress of grievances, and these rights have been held to include peaceful picketing and demonstrating.[40] Local officials who have attempted to abridge the right of gay organizations to demonstrate peacefully have been enjoined from doing so by the courts.[41]

Does the right of free speech include the right to distribute literature concerning gay issues?

Yes. The right to distribute circulars, handbills, or other literature advocating ideas and beliefs is guaranteed as a corollary to freedom of speech and the press under the First and Fourteenth Amendments to the Constitution.[42] While the right may be regulated by laws prohibiting littering, the basic right to distribute such material may not be abridged.

May the right to demonstrate peacefully and to picket in support of gay issues be regulated at all?

Yes. While such activity may not be prohibited, it may be regulated in a nondiscriminatory way designed to promote public convenience.[43] The police may, for example, reasonably regulate the number of pickets in a given area.[44]

Does the right of free speech protect gay students and teachers in public schools and colleges from disciplinary action for wearing gay-movement badges or buttons?

Yes. The wearing of various items such as armbands, buttons, etc., that have a symbolic meaning, is a form of free speech called "symbolic speech." Symbolic speech is an act that, although not necessarily exclusively speech, is nonetheless a public expression of belief or opinion, and it comes within the protection of the free-speech clause of the First Amendment.[45] Such symbolic acts are generally protected by the Constitution from governmental interference, including interference by school officials. In upholding the right of high-school students to wear armbands protesting the Vietnam war,[46] for example, the Supreme Court stated that "[i]t can hardly be argued that neither students nor teachers shed their constitutional rights to freedom of speech or expression at the schoolhouse gate. . . ." The right of students to wear "freedom buttons" has also been specifically upheld where the students wearing the buttons were not engaged in any disruptive activities.[47] The principles of these cases would appear to apply equally to the wearing of symbols of the gay movement. Mere fear on the part of school officials that to permit the wearing of such items would lead other students to cause a disturbance is not sufficient justification for prohibiting such free expression or for disciplining it. "[I]n our system, undifferentiated fear or apprehension of disturbance is not enough to overcome the right to freedom of expression. . . . [O]ur Constitution says we must take this risk."[48]

In practice, it should be noted, *teachers* may have a difficult time enforcing their rights to wear symbols of the gay movement in school.

May a gay public-school teacher be dismissed or transferred to nonteaching duties for exercising freedom of speech on gay issues outside the classroom?

No. It has been held that school officials' transfer of a gay teacher to nonteaching duties could not be sustained on the grounds that he appeared on television and made other public statements in support of his right to teach.[49] The Supreme Court had previously held that while a teacher's right to freedom of speech may be balanced against the importance the state properly attaches to the uninterrupted education of its youth, a teacher's comments on public issues that are neither knowingly false nor made in reckless disregard of the truth afford no ground for dismissal when they do not impair the teacher's performance of his or her duties or interfere with the operation of the schools.[50]

Have the courts uniformly upheld those who speak out on gay rights to be free from governmental reprisals?

Not always. The law concerning gay rights is still very much in a developing stage. A federal court of appeals has thus upheld the refusal of a state university to employ a gay person, otherwise completely qualified, as head of the university library's cataloging division.[51] The grounds for the refusal were that the applicant's "personal conduct, as represented in the public and University news media, is not consistent with the best interest of the University."[52] James McConnell, the applicant, a gay man, had applied for a marriage license to marry another gay man, and the event received much publicity. The university's refusal to employ McConnell was challenged on the grounds that it was based on his desire to profess publicly his earnest belief that homosexuals are entitled to privileges equal to those afforded heterosexuals. A lower federal court agreed

with this position and enjoined the university from re-
fusing to hire McConnell "solely because . . . he is a homosexual and that thereby 'his personal conduct, as
presented in the public and University news media, is not
consistent with the best interest of the University.' "[53] The
court of appeals agreed with the university, however, and
reversed the lower court.[54] The court of appeals' decision
clearly indicates that the refusal to hire was not sustained
merely on the basis of McConnell's homosexuality, but
flowed directly from his outspoken public posture and activism on behalf of gay rights. McConnell was thus penalized for exercising freedom of speech and association on
behalf of gay rights. The result is in conflict with other
federal-court holdings to the effect that a gay person cannot be penalized for exercising his First Amendment
rights to freedom of speech and association.[55] Hopefully,
other courts will ultimately adopt the latter position.

NOTES

1. *See generally* D. Teal, *The Gay Militants* (1971); D. Altman, *Homosexual Oppression and Liberation*, Chapter 4 (1971); J. Lauristen & D. Thorstad, *The Homosexual Rights Movement* [1864–1935] *(1973)*.
2. *Gay Students Organization of University of New Hampshire* v. *Bonner*, 367 F. Suppl. 1088 (D.N.H. 1974) *aff'd* 509 F.2d 652 (1st Cir.) *Owles* v. *Lomenzo*, 38 A.D. 2d 981, 329 N.Y.S. 2d 181 (3d Dep't 1972), *aff'd* 31 N.Y. 2d 965, 341 N.Y.S. 2d 108 (1973).
3. *Gay Activists Alliance* v. *Lomenzo*, 31 N.Y. 2d 965, 341 N.Y.S. 2d 108 (1973).
4. *Id.*
5. *Owles* v. *Lomenzo*, *supra* note 2, 329 N.Y.S. 2d at 183.
6. *Id.* at 182.
7. *Id.* at 183.
8. *Id.* at 183.
9. *Healy* v. *James*, 408 U.S. 169 (1971): *Gay Students Organization of University of New Hampshire* v. *Bonner*, *supra* note 2.
10. Gay Students Organization, id.
11. *Healy* v. *James*, *supra* note 9.
12. *Gay Students Organization of University of New Hampshire* v. *Bonner*, *supra* note 2. *Wood* v. *Davison*, 351 F. Supp. 543 (N.D. Ga. 1972).
13. *Healy* v. *James*, *supra* note 9.
14. *Gay Students Organization of University of New Hampshire*, *supra* note 2.
15. *Scoville* v. *Board of Education of Joliet Township*, 425 F.2d 10 (7th Cir. 1970).
16. *NAACP* v. *Alabama*, 357 U.S. 449 (1958).
17. *Bates* v. *Little Rock*, 361 U.S. 516 (1960).
18. *Id.* at 527.
19. *Gibson* v. *Florida Legislative Investigation Committee*, 372 U.S. 539 (1963).
20. *Id.*; *Uphaus* v. *Wyman*, 360 U.S. 72 (1959).
21. *Communist Party of the United States* v. *Subversive Activities Control Board*, 367 U.S. 1 (1961).
22. *Barenblatt* v. *United States*, 360 U.S. 109 (1959).
23. *Id.*; *Wilkinson* v. *United States*, 365 U.S. 399 (1961); *Braden* v. *United States*, 365 U.S. 431 (1961).
24. *Belian* v. *Board of Education*, 357 U.S. 399 (1958).
25. *Id.*
26. *Shelton* v. *Tucker*, 364 U.S. 479 (1960). *See also De-Gregory* v. *Attorney General of New Hampshire*, 383 U.S. 825 (1966).
27. *Acanfora* v. *Board of Education of Montgomery County*, 491 F.2d 498 (4th Cir., 1974), cert. denied—U.S.—(1974).

28. Internal Revenue Code of 1954, §170; IRS Regulations, 26 CFR §1.170.
29. *Id.*
30. Internal Revenue Code of 1954, §501 (c) (3); IRS Regulations, 26 CFR §1.501 (c) (3)-1.
31. Metropolitan Community Church.
32. Whitman-Radclyffe Foundation; Lambda Legal Defense & Education Fund, Inc.
33. Erickson Foundation; Institute for Human Identity.
34. *United Transportation Union* v. *Michigan Bar*, 401 U.S. 576, 585 (1971). *See also Brotherhood of Railroad Trainmen* v. *Virginia State Bar*, 377 U.S. 1 (1964); *United Mine Workers* v. *Illinois State Bar Association*, 389 U.S. 217 (1967).
35. *Brandenburg* v. *Ohio*, 395 U.S. 444 (1969).
36. Application of Thom, 33 N.Y. 2d 609, 347 N.Y.S. 2d 571, 575 (1973) (Burke, J., concurring).
37. *Beauharnais* v. *Illinois*, 343 U.S. 250 (1952).
38. *Chaplinsky* v. *New Hampshire*, 315 U.S. 568 (1942).
39. *Miller* v. *California*, 413 U.S. 15 (1973).
40. *Thornhill* v. *Alabama*, 310 U.S. 88 (1940); *Schneider* v. *Irvington*, 308 U.S. 174 (1939).
41. *Gay Activists Alliance* v. *Murphy*, Unreported mem. decision, No. —, (S.D.N.Y. 1972).
42. *Schneider* v. *Irvington*, 308 U.S. 147 (1939).
43. *Cox* v. *Louisiana*, 379 U.S. 536 (1964).
44. *Id.*
45. *West Virginia* v. *Barnette*, 319 U.S. 624 (1943).
46. *Tinker* v. *Des Moines Independent Community School District*, 393 U.S. 503, 504 (1969).
47. *Burnside* v. *Byars*, 363 F.2d 744 (5th Cir. 1966).
48. *Tinker* v. *Des Moines Independent Community School District*, *supra* note 46.
49. *Acanfora* v. *Board of Education of Montgomery County*, 491 F.2d 498, (4th Cir. 1974).
50. *Pickering* v. *Board of Education*, 391 U.S. 563 (1968).
51. *McConnell* v. *Anderson*, 451 F2d 193 (8th Cir. 1971), *cert. denied*, 405 U.S. 1046 (1972).
52. *Id.* at 194.
53. *McConnell* v. *Anderson*, 316 F. Supp. 809 (D. Minn. 1971), *rev'd* 451 F.2d 193 (8th Cir. 1971).
54. 451 F.2d at 196.
55. *Acanfora* v. *Board of Education of Montgomery County*, 491 F.2d 498, (4th Cir. 1974).

II
The Right to Equal Employment Opportunities

The law long ago abandoned the notion that employment is a matter that should be left exclusively to agreements between workers and employers. Legislators and judges now generally recognize that many aspects of the employment relationship must be regulated for the protection of the worker. In particular, it is now widely acknowledged that society should undertake to assure all citizens fair-employment opportunities consistent with their training and abilities. A series of federal and state statutes now provides varying degrees of protection against employment discrimination on the basis of race, sex, or age. As described below, however, the law offers substantially less protection against discrimination on the basis of sexual preferences. As a general matter, such protection is given only in two situations: where government itself is the employer, and where a local government has forbidden discrimination by private employers on the basis of sexual preferences. The protection is partial and inadequate, but more effective controls are likely to be obtained only by legislation.

May private employers lawfully discriminate against employees because of the employees' sexual preferences?

In most situations, yes. There is no existing state or federal legislation that has been construed to prohibit discrimination by private employers on the basis of sexual preference. There are, however, local ordinances and regulations in several cities that provide varying degrees of protection against such discrimination, and similar ordinances are now under consideration in other cities. San Francisco, the District of Columbia, East Lansing, Ann Arbor, Seattle,

21

Detroit, Toronto, Minneapolis, St. Paul, Minn.; Madison, Wisconsin; Palo Alto, Calif.; Ithaca, New York; and Portland, Oregon are among the cities that have adopted one form or another of such legislation. After a long and difficult controversy, the New York City Council recently rejected such an ordinance.

The situation is, however, changing rapidly, and it is important to consult qualified counsel to determine accurately the situation in your own community. If you believe that you have been treated unfairly by a private employer because of your sexual preferences or behavior, you should contact a local gay organization, the local chapter of the ACLU, or a legal-aid office to determine whether applicable local laws may offer a remedy.

Absent such local legislation, only two possible avenues of relief against a private employer are available. First, it is possible, although unlikely, that such discrimination may be forbidden by an applicable employment contract. The possibility should be explored with a qualified legal adviser or, if you are a union member, with your union representative. Second, it is possible to initiate litigation to establish that the employer's conduct violated a right guaranteed by the Constitution. The current likelihood of success of such litigation is, however, small. First, it would be necessary to establish that the employer's conduct was sufficiently supported by or identified with governmental activities to bring it within the constitutional restrictions placed on such activities. Second, if that could be done, it would also be necessary to show that the employer's discriminatory conduct was arbitrary and capricious. As a matter of principle, no reason exists why in appropriate situations such cases might not prove successful, but they certainly do not now represent a form of quick or certain relief.

May governmental employers discriminate against employees on the basis of sexual orientation?

As a general rule, no. Governmental employers—whether local, state, or federal—are subject to constitutional requirements that they act fairly and evenhandedly to all citizens. As explained elsewhere in this book, those requirements do not demand that governmental agencies act identically with respect to all citizens. It is generally sufficient if any differences in treatment have some rational relationship to the purposes of the governmental program involved. With respect to matters of employment, this generally means that any differences in treatment must bear some rational relationship to the efficiency or effectiveness with which government work may be performed.

The principles applicable here have been developed chiefly in connection with federal employment. Section 3301 of Title 5 of the United States Code provides the basic standard for regulating federal employment. The section states that the president may prescribe such regulations for the admission of individuals into the Civil Service as "will best promote the efficiency of that service. . . ." The section also provides that the president may ascertain the fitness of applicants "as to age, health, character, knowledge, and ability for the employment sought. . . ." Pursuant to this statutory authorization, the Civil Service Commission has issued regulations that require federal employees and applicants for employment to provide certain information, and that create various mandatory standards of conduct for employees. Among other things, the regulations forbid "criminal, infamous, dishonest, immoral, or notoriously disgraceful conduct." Under those regulations, the Civil Service Commission has sought to exclude from federal employment those who have engaged in homosexual conduct. The commission's regulations are not technically applicable to all federal employees, but similar attitudes have often been adopted by other parts of the federal government. As described below, the regulations are now being revised by the Commission.

What reasons have been given for the commission's policies regarding homosexual conduct?

The ultimate bases for the commission's policies are the hostility and fear that have for so long characterized society's attitudes toward homosexuality. Until 1950, however, there was little discussion of the employment of

homosexuals in government. The issues were treated with
a mixture of indifference and embarrassment. In 1950, a
special Senate subcommittee conducted an inquiry into the
question and issued a report that demanded the complete
exclusion of gay persons from federal employment. The
subcommittee argued that homosexuality among federal
employees should not be tolerated because it is "immoral"
and "scandalous." It complained that gay persons lack
emotional stability, have a "corrosive" influence on other
employees, and are dangerous security risks. More recently,
it has frequently been argued that the employment of gay
persons may bring "discredit" upon the government. The
same reasons, sometimes expressed with greater subtlety,
have since been the principal justifications for the commission's policies.

Are there signs of change in the commission's attitudes?

Very slow and modest changes. The commission repeatedly announced over a period of almost two years
that it was considering revised regulations regarding the
employment of gay persons. In December 1973, however,
the commission issued proposed regulations that provided a new series of factors to be considered under its
previous standards in connection with its decisions whether
to dismiss or exclude employees. The factors include
whether the individual's conduct would interfere with effective performance of the individual's job, the kind of job
involved, the recency of the conduct, and any efforts
toward rehabilitation. The factors proposed by the commission at least appear to recognize that the suitability of
employees must be determined individually and not on the
basis of the supposed characteristics of an entire class of
persons. Nonetheless, much will depend on the attitudes
with which the factors are considered, and it must be assumed that efforts will continue to be made to discriminate against federal employees on the basis of their sexual
preferences.

May dismissal occur only because of recent conduct?

Not necessarily, although the commission's new rules include the recency of conduct among the factors to be considered by it in connection with dismissals and exclusions. In one early case, however, a federal employee was dismissed because of conduct that had occurred eight years before, at the age of 18, despite evidence that it was unlikely to recur.[1]

What should federal employees do if they are accused of having engaged in homosexual conduct?

It is almost always best to refuse to answer questions or to provide information until you have consulted with an attorney or other qualified adviser. A federal employee is, however, required by regulations of the Civil Service Commission to provide information reasonably related to the employee's fitness for federal employment, and it is important to avoid an absolute refusal to provide such information. The commission's rights of inquiry are matters of continuing dispute, and decisions whether to give or to refuse to give it information should be made carefully and only after qualified advice has been obtained.[2] Do not provide false or misleading information, but do not let yourself be forced into admissions of guilt. The investigators are likely to press very hard to obtain a confession of homosexuality, and any information should be given to them only with considerable care.

How does the commission learn of homosexual conduct involving federal employees?

Much of its information appears to come from police records, military records, statements obtained from other applicants or employees, and prior employers. Any of the various forms that applicants and employees are required to fill out may disclose information that leads to evidence of homosexual conduct. The likelihood of discovery is increased if the federal position requires a security clearance since an investigation into the employee's background will be conducted. The investigation will not necessarily be thorough, but it is likely at least to involve a review of governmental records and inquiries to previous employers.

The special problems created by security clearances are discussed elsewhere in this book.

Should the employee simply deny all charges and threaten to pursue every available remedy?

Silence is often appropriate, but no response is prudent in all situations. The only advice that is invariably correct is that no admissions should be made and no information provided until a competent adviser has been consulted.

Do federal employees have rights of administrative appeal from dismissals because of homosexual conduct?

Yes. There are several levels of administrative review, all of which generally must be exhausted before an employee may take his grievances to the courts. The procedures used for administrative review are, when compared to court proceedings, simple and free of technicalities, but it is nonetheless highly desirable to obtain the assistance of an attorney or other competent adviser. Help may be available from local gay groups or the ACLU.

Have the courts imposed restrictions on efforts to discriminate against federal employees on the basis of sexual preferences?

Yes. Efforts to challenge the commission's policies in court have been difficult and slow, but important progress has been made. The courts have traditionally deferred to an agency's decision on the reasonableness of grounds for dismissal,[3] and have accordingly been reluctant to interfere with dismissals for homosexual conduct. Until relatively recently, the courts merely satisfied themselves that the agency adhered to the procedures required by statute and regulations. In 1950, the Court of Claims held that an employee should be permitted to show that, apart from any procedural deficiencies, the dismissal was arbitrary and capricious.[4] Successful review of a dismissal remains difficult, but the way is at least now open for the assertion of more than procedural claims.

Over the last decade, the courts have gradually imposed a series of important restrictions on efforts to discriminate

against federal employees on the basis of sexual preferences. In 1969, the United States Court of Appeals for the
District of Columbia held that although the Civil Service
Commission has wide discretion with respect to dismissals,
it may act only for such causes as will promote the efficiency of the civil service.[5] More important, the court emphasized that it would inquire closely into the adequacy of
the nexus between the alleged misconduct and the efficiency of the agency. It rejected the notion that merely
because conduct may be styled "immoral," there is an adequate cause for removal. The court strongly denied that
the federal bureaucracy may impose its code of conven-
tional conduct on the private lives of its employees.

The decisions in such cases represent important steps
forward. The courts have rejected the most blatant forms
of discrimination and have provided a framework within
which more progress may be achieved. Nonetheless, many
judges and administrators do not share the views expressed
in those cases, and it is clear that much more litigation
will be necessary. Future litigation will, however, turn on
the specific facts of each employee's situation rather than
broad issues of the commission's authority. It should be
anticipated that the commission may seek evidence of collateral forms of instability or misconduct to justify the dismissal of gay employees. Gay employees may find that
any emotional or other difficulties, however common or
trivial they may seem, may be used to support dismissal.

Two recent cases have placed still another restriction on
the commission's policies. The commission has in the last
several years taken the position that among the reasons
why gay persons should be excluded from federal employment is that public knowledge of such employment might
bring the government into public contempt. The commission has regarded an arrest or other official record,
whether or not it is properly available to the public, as evidence of such public knowledge. Two federal district
courts have recently made clear that any such fear of
"public contempt" cannot justify the dismissal of a federal
employee.[6] Both courts made clear that the commission

must decide the fitness of employees individually, on the basis of specific evidence, rather than on the supposed characteristics of groups.

Even apart from these decisions, there are at least three principal deficiencies of the commission's claim. First, it is clear that public attitudes toward homosexuality do not remain as hostile as the commission alleges. There have been many important signs of change in recent years. Second, whatever the attitudes of the general public, constitutional rights to fair treatment and a lack of arbitrariness cannot be made to depend on a popularity vote. Many Americans may be outraged by the employment of blacks or other citizens, but such hostility certainly does not justify discriminatory employment opportunities. Third, it is not sufficient merely to allege the existence of public hostility. There must be a clear showing that the hostility has a significant impact on the efficiency of the agency's activities.

Do these same principles also apply to employment with state and local governments?

Many of the cases involving federal employment have turned on the specific provisions of federal statutes and regulations. State and local governments have separate statutes and regulations, and certain of the issues may as a result be different. Nonetheless, the underlying constitutional principles remain largely the same, and state and local governmental employees should also be protected against arbitrary dismissals and exclusions. As a practical matter, however, litigation regarding state and local employees has not yet been extensive, and the applicable principles have been less fully developed in that context.

There are, however, municipalities in which local legislation has been adopted that has placed significant restrictions on discrimination against local governmental employees on the basis of sexual preferences. San Francisco and the District of Columbia have adopted such legislation, as have several other towns and cities. The New York City Council has recently rejected broad protective legislation, but such discrimination is nonetheless prohibited by an executive order issued by the former mayor John Lindsay. State and local government employees should consult their local ACLU chapter or gay organizations to determine the precise legal situation in their own localities.

Are teaching and other positions in the public schools also governed by these same principles?

As a general matter, the same principles should be applicable, but many courts have proved particularly hostile to the employment of gays as teachers and other school employees. There can be little doubt that many judges and others are still strongly influenced by a fear of "contagion." Any evidence or suggestion that students may be influenced by a teacher's sexual preferences may be regarded by such judges as enough to sustain a dismissal. On the other hand, the boards of education of the District of Columbia and New York City, among other places, have abandoned or modified their efforts to exclude gay teachers and other school employees. As this suggests, progress may in some cities be made more easily through quiet and informal understandings with local authorities than through the courts or legislation.

The basic rules applicable here were concisely stated by the Supreme Court of California in 1969 in a case in which the court overturned the dismissal of a public-school teacher because of homosexual conduct.[7] The court held that "immoral conduct" permits the dismissal of a teacher only if an unfitness to teach is shown. In determining fitness, the court held that the state board of education may take into account such matters as adverse consequences on students or other teachers, the degree of such adversity, the recency of the conduct, motive, the likelihood of recurrence, and the extent to which disciplinary action may have an adverse impact on the exercise of constitutional rights. In the court's view, the law neither prohibits the employment of all gay persons nor forbids educational authorities to consider the possible implications of homosexuality in order to determine a teacher's fitness.

The strength of feeling against the employment of gay persons in educational positions is shown by a recent case

in a federal court of appeals. The court upheld the refusal
of the University of Minnesota to employ a widely known
gay activist in the university library.[8] It reversed the decision of a federal district court[9] that had held that the university had acted arbitrarily. The court of appeals emphasized that the university's board of regents has broad
discretion with respect to such matters, and that its discretion should not be disturbed in the absence of a "clear and
affirmative" showing of arbitrariness. The court thought it
quite reasonable to reject the applicant because he sought
actively to "implement" his sexual preferences, and his
employment by the university would place its "tacit approval" on the "socially repugnant concept" that the applicant
represented. The court appeared to be disturbed not only
by the applicant's sexual preferences, but also by his un-
willingness to hide them.

**What if the teacher lies about his or her sexual prefer-
ences?**

The fact of the lie or deliberate omission may itself permit the teacher's dismissal. For example, a federal court
of appeals recently upheld the dismissal of a public-school
teacher for such an omission.[10] The court rejected the
claim, which had been adopted by the district court, that
the teacher should be denied reinstatement because of
public statements he had made after his removal. Nonetheless, the court emphasized that the teacher had deliber-
ately failed to provide information regarding his sexual
preferences and associations at the time of his original employment and held that his intentional withholding of facts
prevented him from challenging the school system's refusal
to employ gays as teachers.

NOTES

1. *Dew* v. *Halaby*, 317 F.2d 582 (D.C. Cir. 1963), *cert. granted*, 376 U.S. 904, *cert. dismissed*, 379 U.S. 951 (1964).
2. *Richardson* v. *Hampton*, 345 F. Supp. 600 (D.D.C. 1972).
3. *Bailey* v. *Richardson*, 182 F.2d 46 (D.C. Cir. 1950)
4. *Gadsden* v. *United States*, 78 F. Supp. 126 (Ct. Cl. 1948), *cert. denied*, 342 U.S. 856 (1951).
5. *Norton* v. *Macy*, 417 F. 2d 1161 (D.C. Cir. 1969) *See also Scott* v. *Macy*, 349 F.2d 182 (D.C. Cir. 1965); 402 F.2d 644 (1968). *See generally* Note, *Government-Created Employment Disabilities of the Homosexual*, 82 Harv. L. Rev. 1738 (1969); Comment, *Homosexuals in Government Employment*, 3 Seton Hall L. Rev. 87 (1971).
6. *Society for Individual Rights* v. *Hampton*, (S.D. Calif. 1973); *Baker* v. *Hampton*, No. 2525-71 (D.D.C. 1973).
7. *Morrison* v. *State Board of Education*, 82 Cal. Rptr. 175, 461 P.2d 376 (1969).
8. *McConnell* v. *Anderson*, 451 F.2d 193 (8th Cir. 1971).
9. *McConnell* v. *Anderson*, 316 F. Supp. 809 (D. Minn. 1970).
10. *Acanfora* v. *Board of Education of Montgomery County*, F.2d (4th Cir. 1974).

III

Occupational Licenses

In our discussion of employment restrictions confronting gays, we have been primarily concerned thus far with restrictions imposed directly by the federal government. The role of the federal government in this area is well known, has been much-criticized, and increasingly has been subjected to challenge both in the courts and in other forums. We have also touched on the practices pursued by state and other local governmental entities in their role as public employers, about which much less is known but which have been thought generally to parallel the practices of the federal government.

Perhaps the closest analogue of the control exercised by the federal government through its industrial security-clearance program over employment in the private sector[1] stems from the conceded authority of state governments, and, derivatively, of lesser governmental entities such as counties and municipalities, to require people in certain occupations to be licensed. Occupational licensing laws and administrative agencies to enforce those laws exist in every state. The result is a network of restrictions covering a broad range of extremely diverse occupations.

Occupational licensing laws are often administered in such a way as further to restrict the employment opportunities of gays. While the purported justification of such laws lies in the public's asserted interest in ensuring that people in certain occupations are duly qualified, in practice such laws have often been used as vehicles for enforcing majoritarian social and political views.[2]

33

What is an occupational license?

An occupational license generally takes the form of a certificate awarded by a state, county, or municipality attesting that the holder has satisfactorily met all official prerequisites for engaging in a particular occupation. Often such certificates or licenses are awarded only if the applicant has completed a prescribed course of study or a prescribed apprenticeship and has passed a written test administered by the licensing agency or board.

Since licensing agencies and boards ultimately derive their authority from a particular state, the licenses awarded by them may permit the holder to practice the occupation for which he had been awarded a license only in that state. Reciprocity agreements are now in effect for many occupations, however, permitting people who have been licensed in one jurisdiction to move to another jurisdiction without having to reapply for an occupational license.

Many occupational licenses are good for the life of the holder—that is, so long as the licensee conducts himself in accordance with the conditions set out by the licensing authority, he may continue to practice the occupation throughout his life. Other occupational licenses are good only for a stated period of time and require periodic updating or reapplication by the holder. Licenses are generally considered to be personal to the holder; rarely may they be transferred from one person to another without the approval of the licensing authority.

How many occupations are subject to licensing restrictions?

At last count, over 300 different occupations were covered by licensing restrictions in one or more states.[3] Some occupations—such as law—are uniformly subject to licensing restrictions throughout the United States. Many other occupations are subject to licensing restrictions in only one or a few states. It has been estimated that some 7 million people in the United States are presently working in licensed occupations.

What is the source of the authority of a state or other local governmental entity to require a license as a prerequisite to engaging in certain occupations?

In *Dent* v. *West Virginia*, the Supreme Court held that "the power of the State to provide for the general welfare of its people authorizes it to prescribe all such regulations as, in its judgment, will secure or tend to secure them against the consequences of ignorance and incapacity as well as of deception and fraud."[4] Inherent in such a statement is the implication that the authority of states in the area of occupational licenses is not entirely without limit; in fact, however, until comparatively recently, courts have rarely been willing to strike down specific licensing restrictions as being outside of the powers reserved to the states by the Constitution.

Local governmental entities created by the several states—such as counties and municipalities—have the authority to impose licensing restrictions within their jurisdictions only insofar as that authority has been delegated to them, either expressly or by implication, by the state of which they are a part.

How are occupational licensing restrictions generally enforced?

Virtually every jurisdiction that has enacted occupational licensing restrictions has also created one or more licensing boards or agencies whose job it is to enforce those requirements. Depending upon the restrictions to be enforced and the resources committed to the job of enforcement, the licensing board or agency may be either quite passive in nature (amounting to little more than an information clearinghouse) or very active and intrusive.

Many licensing statutes and ordinances expressly provide that carrying on an occupation subject to licensing restrictions without a valid license is a criminal offense. Depending upon the terms of the particular enactment, persons engaging in such prohibited conduct may be subject to penalties such as fines or imprisonment.

What forms do occupational licensing restrictions normally take?

The licensing restrictions that have been enacted by most state and other local governmental entities may be usefully characterized for present purposes as taking the form of either minimum "standards" or "prohibitions." The occupational standards that have been enacted normally require individuals to be of a certain age before engaging in a particular occupation and to satisfy certain education, skill, or experience requirements. The technical competence of individuals to engage in particular occupations is often measured by a written examination.

The prohibitions that have been enacted restricting initial or continued access to certain occupations have generally taken one of four related and often overlapping forms:

1. Provisions referring specifically to conviction or commission of a criminal offense (a misdemeanor or, more often, a felony);

2. Provisions referring specifically to conviction or commission of a criminal offense involving "moral turpitude";

3. Provisions giving licensing boards or agencies wide discretion to deny occupational licenses to and to suspend the licenses of those found not to possess "good moral character"; and

4. Provisions relating to other indicia of unprofessional or negligent conduct.*

What special problems do gays confront in securing and retaining occupational licenses?

The unique problems that gays face in securing and retaining occupational licenses are related to what we have characterized above as licensing "prohibitions." Gays have been excluded from a variety of occupations on the grounds that their sexual orientation or activities are evidence of bad moral character. Conviction of one of the offenses often applied to homosexual activity has also been used to deny or revoke an occupational license on the grounds that such offenses involve moral turpitude.

* See Appendix 2 for a state-by-state listing of licensing restrictions analyzed according to "prohibitions" 1–3.

The vagueness of the phrases "good moral character" and "moral turpitude" virtually ensures the uneven and inconsistent application of licensing restrictions to gays and to other persons possessing any number of personal characteristics not possessed, or not admitted to, by most members of society. The experiences of gays in applying for occupational licenses or in attempting to retain such licenses after the fact of their sexual orientation has been communicated to the relevant licensing agency or board have varied widely.

It is difficult to quantify the experience of gays before licensing boards or agencies or to discern any illustrative patterns because the decisions made in individual cases are seldom published, and the criteria employed by such boards or agencies in reaching their decisions, if written at all, are not widely circulated. Despite such problems, however, a few generalizations are possible:

1. The access of gays to sensitive or "public interest" occupations such as teaching or law has traditionally been more restricted than has access to other occupations. Particularly in those cases in which the occupation involves contact with young people, licensing boards and agencies have often rationalized withholding licenses to gays on the ground that the public has a significant interest in minimizing such contact because of the vulnerability of young people to "immoral influences."

2. Almost without regard to the occupation for which the license has been sought, the difficulties that have confronted gays have increased significantly whenever the applicant has a criminal conviction. Conviction of violating a statute or ordinance directed at homosexual activity has often posed particular difficulties because of the tendency of many licensing boards or agencies to equate such convictions with bad moral character or to regard them as conclusive proof of moral turpitude.

3. Some licensing boards or agencies have been willing to disregard homosexual conduct to the extent that the applicant has been able to demonstrate that the conduct was aberrational or that it took place under ameliorating circumstances. Factors such as the age of the applicant at

the time the homosexual conduct took place, whether the
applicant had been drinking at the time, whether the activity was private and consensual (that is, did not involve
force or fraud on the applicant's part), and whether the
conduct was isolated or an integral part of the applicant's
life style or general sexual orientation, have all been regarded by licensing boards or agencies at various times as
relevant to the fitness of the particular applicant to engage
in a given occupation.

**If in the process of applying for an occupational license
or while holding a license my sexual orientation or activities becomes an issue, what should I do?**

The first thing you should do is attempt to retain an attorney qualified to advise and assist you. Most licensing
boards or agencies are required by statute or ordinance to
afford applicants and license holders certain procedural
rights while considering whether to award, suspend, or
revoke a particular occupational license. At least in those
cases in which all of what we have characterized above as
licensing "standards" have been met, due process would
generally require the licensing board or agency to hold a
hearing before denying or revoking an occupational license on the ground that your conduct or activities ran
afoul of one of the "prohibitions" listed above.

One important service a lawyer can render at this point
is to ensure that you have taken advantage of all of the
procedural rights available to you. Counsel can also make
sure that your application or case is placed before the
board or agency in the most favorable possible manner. If
there are ameliorating or exceptional circumstances, those
circumstances should be presented to the board or agency.
A lawyer can help to ensure that that is done and that
your right to personal privacy is not unduly invaded in the
process. Finally, a lawyer can advise you of your right of
review in the event the licensing board or agency decides
adversely to you. In all cases, the right of review will include judicial review, either in the state or federal courts.
It is important to keep the possibility of judicial review in
mind during the proceedings before the licensing board or

agency since in the event of such review the record that you have made before the board or agency will form the core of your case on review.

How have appeals from the denial or revocation of occupational licenses fared in the courts?

Courts have traditionally been reluctant to substitute their judgment of fitness to engage in a particular occupation for the judgment of a state legislature or a licensing board or agency created by a state legislature or some other lesser governmental entity.[5] Such reluctance appears to be eroding somewhat, however, and there are now a number of reported cases in which courts have found the actions of a licensing agency in denying or revoking an occupational license to have been arbitrary and unreasonable, in contravention of the individual's constitutional rights.

Perhaps the leading case in this area is *Schware* v. *Board of Bar Examiners*,[6] a case involving the refusal of the New Mexico Board of Bar Examiners to permit an applicant to take the New Mexico bar examination on the ground that the applicant had not demonstrated "good moral character." In making the determination, the Board of Bar Examiners had relied on the fact that the applicant had used several aliases some twenty years prior to his application, had been arrested but not convicted some seventeen years before, and had been a member of the Communist Party. In reversing the Board's decision, the Supreme Court stated:

A state cannot exclude a person from the practice of law or from any other occupation in a manner or for reasons that contravene the Due Process or Equal Protection clause of the Fourteenth Amendment.

A state can require high standards or qualifications, such as good moral character or proficiency in its laws, before it admits an applicant to the bar, *but any qualification must have a rational connection with the applicant's fitness or capacity* to practice.... (Emphasis added.)[7]

More recently, in *Morrison* v. *State Board of Education*,[8] a case involving revocation of a teaching license be-

cause of an isolated incident of homosexual conduct, the
California Supreme Court held that the terms "unprofessional," "moral turpitude" and "immoral" were not void
for vagueness insofar as they were construed to encompass
only fitness to perform the particular licensed occupation.
But in reaching this conclusion, the court noted:

> Terms such as "immoral or unprofessional conduct" or
> "moral turpitude" stretch over so wide a range that they
> embrace an unlimited area of conduct. In using them the
> Legislature surely did not mean to endow the employing
> agency with the power to dismiss any employee whose per-
> sonal, private conduct incurred its disapproval. Hence the
> courts have consistently related the terms to the issue of
> whether, when applied to the performance of the employee
> on the job, the employee has disqualified himself.[9]

The court in *Morrison* then went on to state that
" '[t]he right to practice one's profession is sufficiently
precious to surround it with a panoply of legal
protection . . . .' "[9] Since the Board had failed to conduct
the sort of particularized inquiry into the petitioner's fitness to teach that the court had found was required by the
relevant statute and by the Due Process Clause of the
Constitution, it reversed the decision of the Board of Education in revoking petitioner's teaching certificate.

The decision of the California Supreme Court in the
Morrison case and decisions in other recent cases such as
Acanfora v. *Board of Education*[11] and *Application of
Kimball*,[12] will hopefully stimulate other courts to look
more carefully than they have in the past at decisions
made by licensing agencies in cases involving homosexuality or homosexual conduct. In addition to the progress
that has been made in the courts in recent years, it should
also be noted that several state legislatures and municipal
governing bodies have recently enacted statutes or ordinances easing all occupational licensing restrictions
formerly applicable to gays within their respective jurisdictions.

One of the most significant recent developments in the
area of occupational licensing restrictions and private sex-

ual activities between consenting adults was the resolution
recently passed by the Law Student Division and the Section on Individual Rights and Responsibilities of the
American Bar Association (ABA), but not yet formally
adopted by the ABA's House of Delegates. That resolution
provides as follows:

WHEREAS: The practice of law is a personal privilege
which has been limited to persons of good moral character.
Although a state may require high standards of qualification such as good moral character before it admits an applicant to the bar, any qualification must have a rational
connection with the applicant's fitness or capacity to practice law.

The test of "GOOD MORAL CHARACTER" is a vague qualification which can become a dangerous instrument for arbitrary and discriminatory denial of the right to practice law.

While a Bar composed of lawyers of good character is a
worthy objective, it should not be necessary to sacrifice vi-
tal freedoms in order to obtain that goal. Sexual orientation and private sexual behavior between consenting adults
are matters having no rational connection with an applicant's fitness or capacity to practice law. Furthermore, official inquiry into a person's private sexual habits does violence to his constitutionally protected area of privacy.

RESOLVED: That the sexual orientation or sexual conduct of an applicant for admission to the Bar or of a member of the Bar should not be a proper subject for investigation, denial of admission, or any disciplinary action by the
Bars of the several states or of any state or federal court,
provided that such sexual conduct occurs in private with
other consenting persons of the age of legal consent. Sexual
orientation, as used in this resolution, includes heterosex-
uality, homosexuality, and ambisexuality.

While actions taken by the ABA are not binding on local bar associations or on those directly responsible for
setting standards for admission to the bar, if the resolution
set out above is formally adopted by the House of Delegates of the ABA, that action is likely to cause a re-exam-
ination and easing of licensing restrictions both in the legal
profession and in other occupations.

NOTES

1. See discussion, Chapter V.
2. Licensing restrictions imposed as revenue or taxing devices are outside the scope of this chapter.
3. A list of occupations subject to licensing restrictions, compiled by the National Clearinghouse on Offender Employment Restrictions, is reproduced in the Appendix.
4. 129 U.S. 114, 122 (1899); *accord, Olsen* v. *Nebraska,* 313 U.S. 236, 246 (1941); *Great Atlantic & Pac. Tea Co.* v. *Grosjean,* 301 U.S. 412, 417 (1937).
5. 363 U.S. 232 (1957).
6. Ironically, the courts have been somewhat less reluctant to strike down licensing restrictions relating to minimum "standards," particularly when the restriction has specified that the requisite level of skill to engage in the occupation may be obtained only in a particular manner (*e.g., Blumenthal* v. *Board of Medical Examiners,* 195 Adv. Cal. App. 100, 15 Cal. Rep. 724 [2d Dist. 1961]) than they have been to strike down restrictions relating to the "prohibitions" referred to above (*i.e.,* minimum character requirements, etc.). Note, "Entrance and Disciplinary Requirements for Occupational Licenses in California," 14 *Stan. L. Rev.* 533, 539-40 (1962).
7. *Id.* at 241.
8. 1 Cal.3d 214, 461 P.2d 375, 82 Cal. Rptr. 175 (1969). Cf. *Purtifoy* v. *State Bd. of Education* (No. 1 Civ. 30, 109, Sup. Ct. of Calif. March 30, 1973).
9. 461 P.2d at 382.
10. 461 P.2d at 394, *citing Yakov* v. *Board of Medical Examiners,* 68 Cal.2d. 67, 75, 435 P.2d 553, 559, 64 Cal. Rptr. 785, 791 (1968).
11. 359 F.Supp. 843 (D. Md. 1973).
12. 33 N.Y.2d 586, 347 N.Y.S.2d (1973).

IV

The Armed Services

It is important to recognize at the outset of any discussion of gays and the armed services that vast numbers of gays have served honorably in the armed services in times of peace and war and that many gays are still in uniform. This central fact stands in stark contrast to official military pronouncements on the subject and serves to make the exclusionary policies that are so vigorously pursued by the armed services all the more distressing.

Because of the complexities of the subject, it is impossible to do more here than to indicate the thrust of official military policy with respect to gays and to provide a brief outline of applicable military procedures. Our hope is that the discussion that follows will afford some insight into several of the major pitfalls faced by gays in the military. Probably the most important lesson to be learned here is that gays need not sacrifice the basic constitutional rights enjoyed by all Americans during the period of their military service and that the assistance of a lawyer or of some other qualified person can help to ensure that those rights are respected in the event your sexual orientation becomes an issue while you are serving in the military.[1]

What is the official military policy regarding military service by gays?

The official military line regarding homosexual activity is typified by Secretary of the Navy Instruction 1900.9A (amended, July 31, 1972) as follows:

Members involved in homosexuality are military liabilities who cannot be tolerated in a military organization. In developing and documenting cases involving homosexual conduct, commanding officers should be keenly aware that members involved in homosexual acts are security and reliability risks who discredit themselves and the naval service by their homosexual conduct. Their prompt separation is essential.[2]

Are degrees of homosexual involvement or orientation recognized in the military?

To some extent, yes. On the one hand, it is the official policy of all branches of the military to bar from enlistment and to discharge not only those who have actually engaged in homosexual activity of some sort but also those about whom there is evidence of homosexual "desires, tendencies or proclivities." Associating with known homosexuals or frequenting establishments at which homosexuals are known to gather are specific grounds for discharge.

On the other hand, the type of discharge given is generally dependent upon the degree of homosexual involvement or orientation for which there is evidence. For the latter purpose, three rather amorphous and overlapping classifications are commonly used:

Class I. Includes persons who have engaged in one or more homosexual acts accompanied by force, fraud, or intimidation or involving a child under the age of 16 whether the child cooperated or not.

Class II. Includes persons who have engaged in one or more homosexual acts while in the military or have proposed or attempted to do so under "aggravated" circumstances, but not involving force, fraud, intimidation, or a child under the age of 16.

Class III. Includes persons who "exhibit, profess, or admit homosexual tendencies," have proposed or attempted to engage in a homosexual act in the absence of "aggravated" circumstances, or "habitually" associate with persons known to the person to be homosexuals.

In addition to these three classifications, the navy has recently made specific provision for a fourth classification:

Class IV. Includes persons who failed at the time of their most recent enlistment or appointment to reveal the fact that they had prior to that time engaged in one or more homosexual acts, thereby perpetrating a so-called "fraudulent entry" into the military.

A strong factor in the Navy's decision to make specific provision for those servicemen and women who failed to disclose the fact of their involvement in homosexual activity prior to their most recent appointment or enlistment was the upsurge in the late 1960s in the number of people claiming prior homosexual activity in an attempt to gain an early out from the military. While the Navy is still the only branch of the military to have specifically classified such people in terms of their homosexual involvement, the Army, Air Force, and Coast Guard also deal severely with cases of so-called fraudulent entry or enlistment. (See discussion below.)

What disposition is generally made of persons found to fall within the four classifications noted above?

The imprecision of the four classifications means that military authorities are left with substantial discretion in deciding how to proceed with most cases involving charges of homosexuality. Once the decision regarding classification of the "offense" has been made, however, the following dispositions generally follow conviction, an adverse finding, or acquiescence by the individual to separation:

Class I. Persons whose activity fits within Class I are generally referred for trial by court-martial, although the relevant regulations do not preclude a less formal administrative disposition.[3] Persons convicted of Class I homosexual conduct are subject to the same penalties as are others convicted of engaging in criminal conduct while in the military, including reduction in rank, fines, forfeiture, confinement, and a punitive discharge (either bad conduct or dishonorable).[4] In addition, such persons lose veterans benefits, as discussed below.

Class II. Most Class II cases are processed administratively, with most individuals involved being given an undesirable discharge on grounds of unfitness.[5] On a few occasions, however, Class II cases have been referred for trial, and either a bad conduct or a dishonorable discharge has been given. An equally small but growing number of Class

II cases have resulted in a general[6] or honorable discharge.[7] The majority of cases processed during the last ten years involving homosexuality have been Class II cases and have resulted in undesirable discharges.

Class III. All Class III cases are processed administratively. The individuals involved may receive either an honorable or a general discharge. In a few cases, Class III homosexuals have been administratively discharged for unsuitability based on medical reasons rather than for homosexuality per se, again with either an honorable or a general discharge.[8]

Class IV. All Class IV cases are processed administratively, the individuals involved generally receiving the same discharges as Class II homosexuals—that is, most are given an undesirable discharge, although a few have received either a general or honorable discharge.

Officers who have been charged with conduct that falls within Classes II through IV above are generally given the option of resigning "for the good of the service." Resignations "for the good of the service" generally result in "other than honorable" discharges (the officer's equivalent of an undesirable discharge).

How many people are separated from the military each year on grounds of homosexuality?

While reliable data are not easily obtained, it has been estimated that during the past ten years or so an average of at least 2,000 people were separated from the military each year on less than fully honorable terms for reasons relating to homosexuality.[9] These figures represent less than 1 per cent of the total number of persons discharged from the military during each of those years and probably something less than 2 per cent of the total number of predominantly homosexual males serving in the military during that period. At a minimum, it can be said that in dealing with its "homosexual problem" the military has not been remarkably successful. That fact provides scant solace, however, to the officer or enlisted man or woman who is actually caught up in the web the military has created to deal with those involved in, suspected of, associated with, or inclined toward homosexuals or homosexuality.

What events or circumstances generally trigger an investigation of a serviceman or woman for homosexual involvement?

Most commonly, an investigation of a particular individual's sexual orientation or associations is initiated because of a report from some source indicating that the individual has participated in or attempted to participate in a homosexual act or that he or she has been observed fraternizing with known or suspected homosexuals. Such a report may come from civil authorities, particularly if the individual has been arrested on any of the several grounds often used to deal with gays (*e.g.,* vagrancy). Military psychiatrists have also been known to submit such a report, while military chaplains are more likely to suggest that the individual tell his or her story to someone having administrative authority over such matters. Quite often the individual's name surfaces in connection with another case: in conducting their investigation of a serviceman or woman already suspected of homosexual involvement, military investigators invariably make a concerted effort to gain as much information as possible about the homosexual involvement of others from the individual ostensibly under investigation. Sometimes servicemen and woman volunteer information regarding their homosexual involvement or tendencies to military authorities. Finally, there are occasions, although they are rare, in which the process begins because the serviceman or woman has been observed engaging in sexual relations with a person of the same sex.

At what point is the serviceman or woman suspected of homosexual involvement of some sort informed that an investigation is being conducted or about to be initiated?

At the time a formal investigation is begun, the individual suspected of homosexual involvement may be summoned to appear before his or her commanding officer or, more often, before the investigative agent involved in the case.[10] The individual is informed at this point that a thorough investigation is being conducted and is given an often exaggerated indication of the nature of the adverse evidence already obtained. Sometimes the individual is first informed in writing that an investigation is underway.

If you have a security clearance, it will probably be suspended at this point. You will also probably be removed from any job that requires a security clearance and be assigned to nonsensitive work.

If I am called before my commanding officer and/or an investigative agent, what rights do I have?

During every stage of the process, beginning with the time you are initially questioned and thereafter, you have certain basic rights, which include the following:

1. To be informed of the specific "offenses" of which you are suspected;
2. To remain silent;
3. To be informed that anything you say may be used against you;
4. To have the advice and assistance of a lawyer or other qualified counsel, either an appointed military lawyer or one selected by you (which includes the right to retain civilian counsel);
5. To consult with a lawyer or other qualified person prior to responding to the charges made against you.[11]

If after being informed of these rights I decide to waive one or more of them, am I then foreclosed from insisting that they be recognized at a later point.

Absolutely not! But the best advice is not to waive them in the first place, particularly the right to consult with an attorney before doing anything else. In most circumstances, two heads are better than one—and seldom is this more true than when you are informed that an investigation has been initiated by military authorities involving charges of homosexual activity. *Immediately upon being informed that you are under investigation you should refuse to answer questions of any sort and you should contact a lawyer or other qualified counsel!*

If for some reason you do waive one or more of your rights at the outset of the investigation, you may nevertheless assert those rights later.

How are charges involving homosexuality generally investigated?

The most significant part of the investigative process, from the military's as well as from the accused serviceman's or servicewoman's point of view, is the personal interrogation conducted by the services' investigative agents. The interrogation may last several hours, stretching over several days. As recommended above, if you have not seen a lawyer to this point, you should not submit to the interrogation at all. The investigative agents will attempt to convince you that they are your friends; that you really do not need to see a lawyer prior to speaking with them; that they are hopeful that the charges can be disposed of quickly on a basis favorable to you if only you will cooperate; that everything will be fine once you cooperate and are released from the service; that they will help to get you medical assistance; that they have really all the information about you that they need but would like to have you clarify a couple of "details"; that no one need know of the military's action if you cooperate; that once you are released, you stand a good chance of having your discharge reviewed and upgraded; and that if you don't "cooperate" by confessing, the maximum penalty is likely to be imposed (that is, you will be referred for trial by court-martial and be given a punitive discharge). Often, there will be two investigative agents present at the interrogation. One will try to gain your confidence as a good guy, and the other will play the role of the bad guy. They may try to get you to take a lie-detector test. *You should refuse*.

In short, while the investigative agents are obligated to inform you of certain of your rights, they will do their level best to convince you that you have no option other than confessing to the charges and otherwise cooperating with them. In fact, you do have other options. You should not "cooperate," but should insist on seeing a lawyer instead.

Charges are often brought against individuals in the military on the scantiest of evidence. The personal interrogation by investigative agents is, as a consequence, often the crucial factor in the entire process. The facts disclosed by you at that point may well be of pivotal importance in determining whether the charges against you are subsequently dismissed or pursued.

In addition to the personal interrogation, the investigative agents may also—even without your permission—search your personal belongings for evidence tending to support the charges that have been made (looking for incriminating magazines, letters, advertisements, pictures, address books, etc.). You should not consent to such a search—even if the investigative agents produce a warrant—but should insist on seeing a lawyer instead. As a general rule, you should also take care to see that your personal belongings stored on base do not contain anything that could incriminate you or other persons.

Once you have confessed, there may be little a lawyer or other qualified person can do to help you. If your confession was obtained without your first having been informed of your rights, however, an attorney can help to ensure that it is not used against you if your case proceeds to trial by court-martial. Whether a confession secured without informing you of your rights can be used against you in an administrative proceeding leading to discharge under other than honorable conditions has not yet been definitively resolved. You should nevertheless contact a lawyer even if you have signed a confession.

If I am referred to a psychiatrist, will any statements I make to him be kept confidential?

No. Military law does not recognize the principle of confidentiality in relationships between military doctors and patients. Referral of an individual suspected of homosexual involvement to a psychiatrist (or to a medical officer if no psychiatrist is available) for a professional evaluation is an important step in the *investigative* process.

It is not intended to "help" you. Any statements you make to the psychiatrist (or medical officer) that tend to support the conclusion that you are an overt homosexual or possess homosexual tendencies will find their way into the psychiatrist's report. The psychiatrist or medical officer may also conclude that you need medical attention and may recommend separation under medical regulations. Depending on the type of information contained in the report, you may or may not be given a copy. A copy definitely will be forwarded to those in charge of the investigation, however, and a copy will be included in your permanent record.

What happens once the investigation has been completed?

Once the investigation has been completed, you will be either (1) informed that the evidence did not support the charges that had been made, and that the charges were consequently dropped, (2) referred for trial by general or special court-martial,[12] or (3) informed that an administrative discharge appears to be warranted, and that you have a right to appear before a board of officers but that you may waive that step and agree to accept an administrative discharge. Generally, if you agree to waive your right to appear before a board of officers and to accept an administrative discharge, you will be given an undesirable discharge.

If you are in the Navy, however, the situation may be slightly different. At the conclusion of the investigation, enlisted people in the Navy are sometimes offered in writing a general discharge if they will agree to waive their right to appear before a board of officers. If you are in the Navy and are presented with the alternative, you should not make a decision until you have discussed fully the facts of your case with a lawyer or with some other qualified person. Specifically, you should not agree to accept a general discharge if your service record merits your receiving an honorable discharge, but you should not attempt to make that determination unassisted.

If the charges against me are being handled administratively, and I am threatened with an undesirable discharge, should I exercise my right to an appearance before a board of officers?

The answer is almost always "yes," although, again, on this and other points you should consult a lawyer or other qualified person.[13] The available statistics appear to indicate that individuals charged with homosexual involvement who insist on appearing before a board fare better than those who do not.[14] If you are an enlisted person, are well represented before the board, and your service record is otherwise creditable or impressive, the board may recommend that you be given an honorable discharge if you are classified as a Class III homosexual, a general or possibly even honorable discharge if you have been classified as a Class II or IV homosexual. It is even conceivable, although not very likely, that the board would recommend that you be retained in the service, particularly if your "offense" occurred as the result of intoxication, curiosity, or like circumstances and your service record is exceptional.

What rights do I have before the board of officers?

Before the board of officers you may testify on your own behalf (although you can not be compelled to do so), question the witnesses appearing against you, call witnesses on your own behalf, and introduce other evidence in your favor. Again, you have the right to be represented by an attorney during your appearance before the board of officers, and you should exercise that right in the event the process gets to that point.[15]

What procedure is followed if the board of officers recommends that I be discharged from the military or if I agree to discharge?

You will be returned to your unit, and the record of the administrative proceedings will be turned over to a designated officer—the "Discharge Authority"—for review. The Discharge Authority has several options at that point. He may accede to the recommended discharge, direct that

the recommended type of discharge be entered on your
permanent record, and have your discharge papers signed.
If the Discharge Authority concludes that the recommended action is too severe, he may upgrade the discharge
recommended by the board of officers. The Discharge Authority may not, however, give you a less favorable type
of discharge than that recommended by the board of officers. Finally, the Discharge Authority may initiate a further review of your case if he concludes there are grounds
for doing so, or he may order your conditional retention,
giving you an opportunity to "demonstrate successful rehabilitation." Those who are serving in the Army will be reduced to the lowest rank before discharge if they are to be
given an undesirable discharge.[16]

**What are the consequences of receiving a discharge un-
der other than completely honorable conditions?**

Because more than 90 per cent of those servicemen and
women who leave the military every year receive honorable discharges, a certain stigma attaches to all other types
of discharges. Discharge papers often contain a reference
to the regulation under which the discharge was effected.
For the most discriminating employers, this reference may
be sufficient to permit them to determine the general reason or reasons for your discharge. At a minimum, separation from the military because of homosexual involvement
of some sort may bar you from holding many federal and
state jobs, particularly those that are regarded to be sensitive or for which receipt of a government-issued security
clearance is a prerequisite. You may also be barred from
holding any jobs in private industry that involve access to
classified information. (See discussion in Chapter V).

In addition to these employment disabilities, recipients
of undesirable discharges forfeit their rights to pay for accrued leave and to burial in a national cemetery. Numerous other service-related benefits accrued during your current term of service—such as educational benefit, pensions
for disabilities, vocational rehabilitation, loans, special
housing, hospitalization, out-patient medical or dental
treatment, compensation for service-connected injuries or

disabilities, etc.—will be available to the recipient of an undesirable discharge only if extension of the benefit is approved by the administering agency, usually the Veterans' Administration (VA). Many recipients of undesirable discharge have been denied the benefits listed above.[17]

Recipients of honorable and general discharges are eligible for all of the benefits listed above. Recipients of bad conduct and dishonorable discharges are generally not permitted to receive any of them.[18]

Once I have been administratively separated from the military on the basis of homosexual involvement of some sort, is there any chance that I will be able to get my discharge upgraded?

A chance, but not a very good one. The prospect of a post separation upgrading of your discharge is often held out by military authorities (particularly investigative agents) as a reason why you should cooperate fully and freely in the investigative process and why you should agree to accept a discharge under other than fully honorable conditions. In fact, in the usual case, the prospects of getting an administrative discharge upgraded are slim. If an investigative agent suggests that you would be able to get your administrative discharge upgraded after separation, you should report that fact to your lawyer. That suggestion may provide sufficient grounds for successfully attacking your discharge. Before applying for review of your discharge, you should seek the assistance of a lawyer or some other qualified person.

What procedures are available for post separation review of an administrative discharge?

Two relatively distinct administrative bodies have been created to review administrative discharges. The Discharge Review Board (DRB) of the service involved has the authority to review administrative discharges on its own motion, although they almost never do so; cases are almost always brought before the DRBs on the request of the individual who has been discharged.[19] The DRBs may review and upgrade a discharge or issue a new discharge at any time within fifteen years following discharge. The DRBs do not have the authority to revoke a discharge, order reinstatement, or grant back pay. If the former serviceman or woman requests a hearing, the DRBs are obligated to grant that request. In the Navy, any decision made by the DRB to upgrade a discharge is subject to review by the Secretary.

Each branch of the military has also set up a Board for the Correction of Military Records (BCMR), staffed by civilians, to handle "appeals" from decisions made by the DRBs and to deal with demands for reinstatement and back pay.[20] In the past, the BCMRs have very rarely acted favorably on demands for reinstatement or back pay. Hearings before the BCMRs are discretionary. Full relief may be granted without a hearing. If a hearing is granted, however, the procedure utilized by the BCMRs closely resemble those utilized by the DRBs. Unfortunately, all of the DRBs and BCMRs are located in Washington, D.C., and no expenses are paid servicemen or women wishing to have their cases reviewed. You may get forms from any VA office.

Is there any appeal from a conviction after trial by court-martial or from an adverse decision by a DRB or a BCMR?

Yes. Every general or special court-martial resulting in a punitive (bad conduct or dishonorable) discharge is automatically referred to a Court of Military Review. Appeals from adverse decisions made by one of the DRBs or the BCMRs may be filed in the federal courts. On the completion of military appellate review, many court-martial convictions may also be challenged collaterally in the federal courts.[21]

Administrative discharges are reviewable in the federal courts[22] on any of three grounds: (1) failure of the particular service to follow its own procedural regulations, (2) absence of statutory authority to discharge, and (3) failure to accord constitutional due process protections. Most successful challenges to administrative discharges have been based on the failure of the particular service to observe its own procedural regulations.[23]

Perhaps the primary thing that you must guard against while serving in the military is being a party to your own undoing: the sad fact is that most servicemen and women charged with homosexual involvement convict themselves by succumbing to the inducements and threats that confront them at every stage of the process leading to their discharge. If charges are lodged against you during the period of your military service, you should very carefully consider the following:

1. *You should never attempt to go it alone.* Secure the assistance of a lawyer, either retained or appointed, or of some other qualified person as soon after being informed that charges have been made against you as possible. If you cannot afford to hire a lawyer on your own, ask that a lawyer be appointed to represent you. Do not make any statements or cooperate in any way until you have had an opportunity to consult counsel.

2. *Remember that you do not sacrifice your fundamental constitutional rights while serving in the military.* Those rights were designed to protect you. Exercise them. You should not waive any of your rights before having consulted counsel. Insist that you be given a written list of all charges against you, and demand access to all relevant evidence.

3. *Do not accept the advice of military authorities regarding the consequences of any of the options available to you.* From the very beginning of the administrative process leading to discharge, you will be pressured into "cooperating." The pressure will take many forms. You will be told, for example, that you will be dealt with more leniently if you confess and accept an undesirable discharge. You may also be told that once you have again become a civilian, you will stand a good chance of getting your discharge upgraded. These and like assertions are simply not true. Get counsel first. Then try to identify your options and determine how to proceed.

4. *Do not accept an undesirable discharge as the best*

option available to you. If you are charged with homosexual conduct that falls within Classes II through IV, you should insist on being given the discharge warranted by your service record as a whole. If you have an impressive service record, insist that you be given an honorable discharge. Otherwise, insist on a general discharge. Most individuals charged with homosexual involvement are given undesirable discharges because they do not exercise their rights and because they do not press for the discharge to which they are entitled.

NOTES

1. One of the forthcoming ACLU handbooks in this series will focus on veterans' rights and the upgrading of administrative discharges. A previously published ACLU handbook dealing with the rights of servicemen and women is R. Rivkin, *The Rights of Servicemen* (1972).

2. *See also,* Army Regulation 635-89, Air Force Regulation 35-66, Air Force Manual 39-12, Coast Guard Regulation 12-B-10, and Marine Corps Separation and Retirement Manual Sections 6016, 6017 and 6018.

3. Persons referred for trial by court-martial are generally prosecuted for sodomy (Article 125, U.C.M.J.), lewd acts (Article 134, U.C.M.J.), or attempts to commit such acts (Article 80, U.C.M.J.).

4. Discharges from the military may be characterized as either "punitive" or "administrative." Punitive discharges may be given only by sentence of a court-martial and are termed either "bad conduct" or "dishonorable." Any other discharge is administrative in nature. The three types of administrative discharge presently used by all branches of the military are the "honorable discharge," the "general discharge," and the "undesirable discharge." For a comparison of these various types of discharge, see Dougherty & Lynch, "The Administrative Discharge: Military Justice," 33 Geo. Wash. L. Rev. 498 *et seq.* (1964).

5. Undesirable discharges are reserved for three broad categories of "offenses": some cases involving desertion, fraudulent enlistment, unfitness, and misconduct. Gays who receive undesirable discharges are found either to be unfit or to have enlisted under fraudulent circumstances (*see* discussion *infra*).

6. For a discussion of the specific grounds on which a general discharge may be given, see Lunding, "Judicial Review of Military Administrative Discharges," 83 *Yale L.J.* 33 (1973).

7. In 1969, available figures reveal that 1,096 servicemen and women were discharged from the military for homosexuality. Of these, more than one-half received undesirable discharges. In 1973, the number of discharges for homosexuality had dropped to 550—only about one-sixth of whom were given an undesirable discharge. Over one-half of the servicemen and women discharged for homosexuality in 1973 received general discharges.

8. The service regulations relating to unsuitability and unfitness may be found at Air Force Manual 39-12, Ch. 2, §§ A, B; Army Regulations 635-212; Coast Guard Personnel Manual §§ 12-B-10, 12-B-12; Marine Corps Separation

and Retirement Manual ¶¶ 6016, 6017; and Bureau of Naval Personnel Manual §§ C-10310, C-10311. For a general discussion of these classifications, see Note, "Due Process in Undesirable Discharge Proceedings," 41 *U. Chi. L. Rev.* 164, 166-67 (1973).

9. There is some evidence, however, that the number of individuals so discharged has been declining during the past 3 or 4 years. C. Williams & M. Weinberg, "Homosexuals and the Military," 38-53 (1971).

10. Depending on the service, the investigative agent would be from the Criminal Investigation Division (C.I.D.) of the Army, the Naval Investigative Service (N.I.S.) of the Navy, or the Office of Special Investigations (O.S.I.) of the Air Force.

11. *See, e.g.,* Article 31, U.C.M.J.; and *United States* v. *Tempia,* 16 U.S.C.M.A. 629, 37 C.M.R. 249 (1967)

12 For the jurisdictional bases of general and special court-martial, see 10 U.S.C. § § 818, 819 (1970).

13. Under Department of Defense Directive No. 1332.14, 32 C.F.R. Pt. 41 (1972), recipients of general discharges do not have the right to a hearing before a board of officers except in those cases in which the basis of the discharge is unsuitability and the individual has eight or more years of continuous active military service. The navy and marine corps adhere strictly to this directive. The army and air force grants hearings in certain circumstances in addition to those specified in the directive.

14. *E.q.,* Williams & Weinberg, "The Military: Its Processing of Accused Homosexuals," *American Behavioral Scientist* 212-15 (No. 1970).

15. For a general discussion of your rights before the board of officers, see Lunding, "Judicial Review of Military Administrative Discharges," 83 *Yale L.J.* 33, 38-40 (1973).

16. For further details, see Lunding, "Judicial Review of Military Administrative Discharges," 83 *Yale L.J.* 33, 40-41 (1973); and Lynch, "The Administrative Discharge: Changes Needed?" 22 *Main L. Rev.* 141, 150-58 (1970).

17. For a discussion of the discretion exercised by the Veterans' Administration in this regard, see *Joint Hearing on Drug Addiction and Abuse Among Military Veterans Before the Subcomm. on Health and Hospitals of the Senate Comm. on Veterans Affairs and the Subcomm. on Alcoholism and Narcotics of the Senate Comm. on Labor and Public Welfare,* 92d Cong., 1st Sess., pt. 1, at 143-46 (1971).

18. *See generally* 38 U.S.C. §§ 101 (2) (1970), and 38 C.F.R. §§ 3.12(a) (1972). It should be noted, however, that the recipient of a bad-conduct discharge awarded by a special

court-martial may be eligible for certain veterans' benefits if the discharge did not stem from one of the reasons listed in 38 U.S.C. §§ 3103 (1970) or 38 C.F.R. §§ 3.12(c) (2) (1972).

19. Use DoD Form 293 for this purpose. Such forms are available at any Veterans Administration Office.

20. Use DoD Form 149.

21. *See generally* H. Moyer, *Justice and the Military,* Ch. 6 (1973).

22. This includes the Court of Claims, which has recently been empowered to order both reinstatement and back pay and which in several recent cases has shown some willingness to correct abuses by the military in this area. *See generally* Glosser & Rosenberg, "Military Correction Boards: Administrative Process and Review by the United Court of Claims, 23 *Am. U.L. Rev.* 391 (1973).

23. See, for example, discussion and authorities cited in Lunding, "Judicial Review of Administrative Discharges," 83 *Yale L.J.* 33 (1973).

V

Security Clearances

The problems that confront gays in their efforts to secure and maintain suitable employment increase significantly whenever the particular job at stake has been deemed for one reason or another to be unusually sensitive. The jobs from which professed gays have been most uniformly excluded—and with respect to which administrative and judicial challenges to exclusionary policies based on sexual orientation have been least successful—have been those involving access to governmentally classified information.

The federal government's present policy of requiring holders of a wide range of jobs to possess security clearances and of uniformly denying clearances to known or suspected homosexuals has many of its roots in the immediate post-World War II period. Prior to that time, neither the federal government (except the military branches of the federal government) nor private employers routinely inquried into the sexual orientation of their employees. As a consequence, the freedom of at least those gays who were scrupulously discreet about their private sexual lives to pursue any given nonmilitary occupation appears to have been relatively unencumbered.

With the increasing anxiety of Americans in the late 1940s and 1950s about the threat of international communism, the situation changed dramatically. Buoyed by a shared perception of the dictates of national security, those in positions of authority embarked during the Cold War period on a concerted campaign to exclude gays from all positions bearing any conceivable relation to our national security. The campaign continues largely unabated to the present day.

Are all employees of the federal government required to have a government-issued security clearance?

Strictly speaking, only those federal employees who occupy "sensitive" positions must possess a security clearance. A "sensitive" position is defined in Executive Order 10450, as amended, to encompass "any position ... the occupant of which could bring about, by virtue of the nature of the position, a material adverse effect on the national security . . . ."[1] The heads of all federal departments and agencies are required to designate as "sensitive" any position within their respective jurisdictions that meets the definition and have the responsibility of ensuring that all permanent occupants of those positions possess a security clearance.

How is the security-clearance program for federal employees administered?

Several federal departments and agencies—such as the Department of Defense, the State Department, and the Federal Bureau of Investigation—have their own security-clearance programs. Most federal departments and agencies, however, rely on the Civil Service Commission to conduct security investigations, or to cause such investigations to be conducted, and to issue security clearances to those of their employees occupying "sensitive" positions.

Have gays been able to secure and retain the security clearances required of federal employees occupying sensitive positions?

As one would expect, gays are employed at all levels of the federal bureaucracy and in positions classified as "sensitive" as well as "nonsensitive." Thousands of gays undoubtedly hold federal security clearances, many have held them for many years. The key to the initial and continued employment of such persons, however, is discretion. Mere suspicion that an applicant for or a holder of a security clearance is gay, or has in the past engaged in homosexual activity, is often enough to pose problems so far as access to classified material is concerned. Actual proof of homosexuality or homosexual activity commonly results in the denial of applications for security clearances as well as the revocation of clearances already held.

What reasons are generally given for withholding security clearances from gays and from others who have engaged in isolated incidents of homosexual conduct?

Federal departments and agencies are directed by the terms of Executive Order No. 10450, which governs access to classified material by federal employees, to deny applications for security clearances unless it can be determined that employment of the particular individual being investigated "is clearly consistent with the interests of the national security." In reaching this conclusion, administrators of the various federal employee security programs are instructed by Executive Order No. 10450 to gather information relating, among other things, to the following:

(i) Any behavior, activities, or associations which tend to show that the individual is not reliable or trustworthy.

(ii) Any deliberate misrepresentations, falsifications, or omissions of material facts.

(iii) Any criminal, infamous, dishonest, immoral, or notoriously disgraceful conduct, habitual use of intoxicants to excess, drug addiction, sexual perversion, or financial irresponsibility.

(iv) Any illness, including any mental condition, of a nature which in the opinion of competent medical authority may cause significant defect in the judgment or reliability of the employee, with due regard to the transient or continuing effect of the illness and the medical findings in such case.[2]

While practices vary from agency to agency and department to department, evidence of homosexual conduct brought out in the course of a security investigation is sometimes used not to deny or revoke a security clearance but as a basis for finding that the applicant or employee is "unsuitable" for federal employment of any sort. (See discussion, Chapter II.) When the security investigation does culminate in an adverse decision regarding the application for a security clearance, however, one or more of the considerations noted above are generally pointed to in purported justification of the decision.

How does evidence of homosexual conduct normally come to the attention of security investigators?

Applicants for federal jobs requiring security clearances are required to fill out forms calling for detailed information about their activities. In the case of federal civil service jobs, applicants are required to fill out Standard Form 171 and Standard Form 78. Question 23C of Standard Form 171 asks whether the applicant has ever been discharged from the military under other than honorable conditions. Question 29 asks whether the applicant has ever been convicted of breaking a law, has ever forfeited collateral, or is presently subject to a criminal proceeding. Standard Form 78, which is concerned primarily with the applicant's medical condition, inquires among other things into whether the applicant has ever been hospitalized or treated for a mental illness. The applicant's answers to any of these or similar questions could of course provide a predicate for a more direct and detailed inquiry into whether the applicant has ever engaged in anything that could be construed as homosexual conduct.

In addition, the Civil Service Commission and others charged with monitoring the access of federal employees to classified information almost always check arrest and court records and the files of other state and federal agencies—including those maintained by the FBI. The record checks are supplemented by personal interviews with the applicant and with acquaintances of the applicant. Particularly if the applicant has answered one or more of the questions appearing on a form in a manner that gives rise to a suspicion of homosexual conduct, the applicant and acquaintances of the applicant may be asked directly whether the applicant has ever engaged in homosexual conduct.

Evidence of homosexual conduct relating to employees already possessing a security clearance often arises in connection with an updating or upgrading of that clearance. The type of investigation conducted in those circumstances closely resembles the investigation conducted when an initial application is filed. A security investigation may also be initiated on the basis of a report that the holder of a security clearance has been arrested or has been observed frequenting places known also to be frequented by gays.

Is receipt of a government-issued security clearance a prerequisite only to certain jobs with the federal government?

No, in fact the earliest formal program requiring security clearances as a prerequisite to employment was designed to prevent the unauthorized disclosure of government-classified material by the employees of private companies performing government work. The decision to create a coordinated mechanism to control access to classified material by those in the private sector was made jointly by the Department of Defense and the Secretaries of the Army, Navy, and Air Force in the late 1940s.[3] The Supreme Court ultimately held in *Greene* v. *McElroy* that this program had not been sufficiently authorized.[4]

President Eisenhower responded to the court's decision in *Greene* v. *McElroy* by issuing an executive order specifically authorizing the Department of Defense to create a program restricting the release of classified information in the private sector to those who had applied for and received a security clearance.[5] In its present form, the program covers various industries engaged in defense-related research and manufacturing activities. Approximately 2.2 million workers in private industry are presently subject to industrial security-clearance procedures.

How is the present industrial security program administered?

The initial processing of security-clearance requests and requests for an upgrading or updating of a current clearance is done by the Defense Industrial Security Clearance Office (DISCO) in Columbus, Ohio.[6] If DISCO approves the application, the employer and employee are notified, and the matter ends. If DISCO recommends that the application be denied, however, the matter is referred automatically to the Industrial Security Clearance Review Office (ISCRO) in Washington, D.C., for a final decision.

Have gays been able to secure and retain industrial security clearances?

Again, the answer is yes, but again, under present circumstances, discretion is essential. The administrators of the industrial security-clearance program—like those responsible for administering the various security programs governing federal employees—pay lip service to the notion that each application for a security clearance is considered independently, with relevant individual circumstances being taken into account. In fact, the opposite appears to be true in those cases in which there is evidence that the applicant or employee is gay or has engaged in isolated incidents of homosexual activity. The director of the industrial security-clearance program has stated, for example, that while it is "conceivable" that a professed gay would be permitted to hold a security clearance, he has "never seen the case."

How is the policy justified by those responsible for administering the industrial security-clearance program?

The justifications advanced in support of the policy denying access to classified material by those in the private sector closely resemble those employed in support of the policy of denying security clearances to federal employees about whom there is evidence of homosexual conduct. While the precise formulations sometimes differ, what generally happens in the industrial security program—as in other federal security clearance programs—is that evidence of homosexual conduct invokes a sort of irrefutable presumption that the individual (1) is subject to blackmail, (2) is generally unreliable because of certain character traits that in the minds of the administrators are associated with homosexual activity, and/or (3) has committed criminal or immoral acts and therefore should not be allowed to fill a "sensitive" position.

What if a person is a professed homosexual and resides in a state in which private consensual homosexual conduct is not proscribed?

Regardless of the security program, the answer is essentially the same; that is, it makes little difference, at least so far as those who administer such programs are concerned.[7] Under the circumstances described in the question, the applicant or employee would be greeted with the argument that security clearances are granted on a nationwide basis, and that if the security clearance holder moved to most other states, he or she would be subject to blackmail and possible criminal prosecution for engaging in homosexual conduct. It is important to recognize here that an important subsidiary purpose of all federal security-clearance programs is the maintenance of public confidence in government and government-related activities. Unfortunately, those responsible for administering the various federal security programs appear to have concluded that public confidence would be shaken by the involvement of gays in such activities.

What are the significant steps in the processing of a security clearance?

We have already discussed how security investigations are generally initiated. The procedures followed from that point in the various programs differ rather substantially, although the procedures employed in processing industrial security clearances are not atypical.

The security forms filled out at an early stage of the industrial security-clearance process are sent to DISCO in Columbus, Ohio, for initial review. If because of an adverse recommendation by DISCO the application is referred to ISCRO in Washington, the matter is generally either assigned to the ISCRO Screening Board or returned to DISCO for further consideration.

If assigned to the Screening Board, a further investigation by one of the security divisions of the three branches of the military is sometimes conducted. The investigation sometimes takes the form of written questions being sent to the applicant with a request for a written reply and/or personal interviews with the applicant and with acquaintances of the applicant. A decision is then made by the Screening Board, and a Statement of Reasons is issued if that decision is unfavorable to the applicant.

The applicant is then afforded an opportunity to file a written reply to the charges made in the statement of reasons, and he may request a hearing before a hearing examiner. The applicant may be accompanied by counsel before the hearing examiner, and he may introduce evidence and present witnesses on his own behalf as well as confront and cross-examine all witnesses against him.

If the examiner rules against the applicant, the decision may be appealed to the Appeal Board. The Appeal Board decision is based exclusively upon the written record as transmitted to it by the hearing examiner. If the Appeal Board sustains the prior decisions to revoke or deny a security clearance, the applicant's only remaining recourse is to the courts.

It is not unusual for several years to lapse between the filing of the initial application and the issuance of a final decision.[8]

Will I be permitted access to classified information during that time?

If you do not have an outstanding security clearance, the answer is almost invariably no—rarely, if ever, are "temporary" clearances granted during the pendency of the review process. Particularly if your employer performs little but government-related contract work, this may mean that you will not be able to continue or begin to work for that employer until and unless your application for a security clearance is granted. If you already have a security clearance, you will generally be permitted to continue to hold that clearance during the review process. That will depend, however, on the seriousness of the reservations motivating DISCO to recommend against granting the application or continuing the clearance and on the extent of your willingness to "cooperate" with those conducting the security investigation.

How have challenges to the denial of security clearances to gays and others who have engaged in isolated instances of homosexual conduct fared in court?

The decisions that have been rendered thus far have

generally favored the government. In *Adams* v. *Laird*,[9] for example, the United States Court of Appeals for the District of Columbia affirmed a lower court decision in favor of the government without any real evidence that the applicant was a security risk—other than evidence tending to show that the applicant had at times engaged in homosexual activity. The applicant had held a *Secret* security clearance for approximately eight years without at any time misusing the classified material to which he had had access. The investigation that ultimately led to revocation of the applicant's *Secret* clearance began when he applied for a *Top Secret* clearance. Despite the absence of any evidence that the applicant had misused classified information, the court upheld revocation of his security clearance.

A point that may well have weighed rather heavily against the applicant in *Adams* v. *Laird* was that he had apparently admitted during the course of an interrogation conducted by security investigators that he had engaged in homosexual activity in the past. Before the hearing examiner and subsequently, however, he refused to admit that such conduct had occurred and argued that the circumstances attending the interrogation had been so coercive as to render any admissions made by him at that time unreliable. The court rejected the argument that the interrogation had been unfairly coercive and noted as well that the applicant's subsequent denials "hardly cast[ ] him in the role of the avowed but aggrieved homosexual who insists that his qualifications to maintain security are no less than those of anyone else."

In three subsequent cases involving the revocation of industrial security clearances (*Gayer* v. *Schlesinger, Ulrich* v. *Schlesinger,* and *Wentworth* v. *Schlesinger*),[10] decided on November 15, 1973, the United States Court of Appeals for the District of Columbia again resolved many of the basic issues that had been raised against the applicants—even though all three applicants were avowed gays and even though again there was no evidence that any of the applicants had abused the classified information to which they had had access.

If I plan to apply for a position requiring a security clearance or a question is raised regarding my current clearance on grounds of homosexual conduct, what should I do?

If you plan to apply for a security clearance, the first thing you should do is to contact a lawyer or a group with expertise in such matters. Another good starting point would be to contact a gay organization if one exists in your area.* Unfortunately, it is not possible to do more here than to sketch the outlines of the various security-clearance processes. Decisions concerning the handling of individual cases are best made with knowledge of the specific facts of those cases: Ultimately, this means that you should secure legal assistance.

If you already hold a security clearance and a question is raised concerning your sexual orientation, you should not respond to any inquiry—no matter how innocuous or innocent it may appear—prior to consulting with counsel. The importance of your getting the advice of an attorney, or of some other qualified person, before answering questions of any sort arising in connection with your security clearance cannot be overemphasized. Get counsel first; then, after consultation, decide how to proceed.

Wouldn't that be a largely futile exercise given the apparently impenetrable barriers to security clearances for gays?

Not necessarily, for several reasons. First, and probably most importantly, the policy of denying gays access to classified information on a class basis—and thereby restricting their employment opportunities—is an unwise and, we think, unlawful policy. While neither the administrators of the various programs nor the courts have thus far conceded this, there is some reason to hope that the day may not be far off when the rights of gays to security clearances are recognized and when sexual orientation is viewed as almost purely a personal matter. The advent of this day can only be hastened by good-faith efforts to con-

* A list of such organizations is included in Appendix 7.

vince administrators and courts of the inequity of present policies.[11]

Second, while much of the present law governing the access of gays and others who have engaged in isolated instances of homosexual activity is hardly favorable, that does not mean that you do not have a number of rights that must be observed by those who process your application for a security clearance. One of the most important of these rights is your constitutional right to privacy. The Court of Appeals did not in the *Gayer* trilogy attempt precisely to determine the constitutionally permissible scope of an inquiry into the details of the applicants' private sexual activities, holding instead that the relevant executive order did not permit the administrators of the industrial security-clearance program to require answers to some of the questions that had been asked. Specifically, the court held that while it is generally permissible for administrators of the programs to go beyond the applicant's admission that he or she is gay or has engaged in homosexual activity, they may not insist on the identity of sex partners unless in the particular case some special reason exists to justify eliciting that sort of information. The court in the *Gayer* case summed up its holding on the privacy issue by stating that whatever information requested of the particular applicant's sexual life "must be only that which is reasonably necessary to make a determination with respect to any criteria being invoked. . . ."[12]

The imprecision of the latter formulation again points to the wisdom of consulting a lawyer prior to submitting to questioning. This is particularly so since your refusal to answer questions later held to be proper can itself be a sufficient reason to justify denying an application for a security clearance and revoking any clearance already held.

If the issue is ever raised, should I attempt to hide the fact of my sexual orientation or lie about my sexual activities?

Unless the issue of your sexual conduct or orientation is raised by someone else, you probably should not volunteer that information. On the other hand, you should try never to answer inaccurately a question put to you in the course of a security investigation. Your choice in such circumstances is not between answering a question truthfully or falsely, but between answering it truthfully or not answering it at all.

NOTES

1. 18 Fed. Reg. 2489 (1953), *as amended*, 3 C.F.R. 55 (1973).
2. The grounds that are sometimes used to deny gays industrial security clearances, see discussion *infra*, are set forth in Department of Defense Directive No. 5220. 6, VI. N., P., Q., S. (1966).
3. The express functions of this early program were "to deny clearance for employment on aeronautical or classified contract work when such consent was required, and to suspend individuals, whose continued employment was considered inimical to the security interests of the United States, from employment on classified work." Comm'n on Government Security, S. Doc. No. 64, 85th Cong., 1st Sess. 239 (1957).
4. 360 U.S. 474 (1959).
5. Exec. Order No. 10,865, 25 Fed. Reg. 1583 (1960), *as amended*, 3 C.F.R. 512 (1968). Such a program was actually set up by Department of Defense Directive No. 5220.6, VII B., E., F., H. (1966).
6. The procedures for updating and upgrading clearances is essentially the same as those for originally obtaining a clearance.
7. Such facts, however, might make a difference in court, as would the recency, incidence, and type of homosexual conduct involved. Note, "Security Clearance for Homosexuals," 25 *Stan L. Rev.* 403, 412-13 (1973); Note, "Government-Created Employment Disabilities of the Homosexual," 82 *Harv. L. Rev.* 1783, 1750-51 (1969).
8. For a more detailed explanation of present industrial security clearance procedures, see Note, "Security Clearance for Homosexuals," 25 *Stan. L. Rev.* 403, 406 *et seq.* (1973).
9. 136 U.S. App. D.C. 388, 420 F.2d 230 (1969), *cert. denied*, 397 U.S. 1039 (1970).
10. 490 F.2d 740 (1973), *as amended*, 494 F.2d 1135 (1974).
11. An excellent discussion of the legal theories that might be used to challenge present administrative practices denying gays access to classified information appears in Note, "Security Clearance for Homosexuals," 25 *Stan. L. Rev.* 403, 416-29 (1973).
12. 490 F.2d at 751. *See also Scott* v. *Macy*, 131 U.S. App. D.C. 93, 97, 402 F.2d 644, 648 (1968) ("Where disclosure is required of circumstances of an intensely private and personal nature, the discloser is arguably entitled to know the standards by which his revelations will be assessed.").

VI

Immigration and Naturalization

May aliens be excluded from the United States because they have engaged in homosexual conduct?

Yes, at least in some situations. Section 1182 of Title 8 of the United States Code provides that various categories of aliens, including those "afflicted with psychopathic personality, or sexual deviation, or a mental defect," are ineligible to receive a visa or to enter the United States. Other categories of aliens treated in the same fashion include the insane, professional beggars, polygamists, and those afflicted with dangerous contagious diseases. The phrases "psychopathic personality" and "sexual deviation" have complex histories, and various arguments could be drawn from those histories to prevent their application to many persons who have engaged in homosexual conduct. The controlling fact is, however, that the Supreme Court held in 1967, in *Boutilier v. Immigration and Naturalization Service*,[1] that an alien may be excludable as having a "psychopathic personality" if he or she is, at the time of attempted entry into the United States, a "homosexual."

Did the Court define a "homosexual"?

No. Nor is there any clear definition of the statutory terms "psychopathic personality" and "sexual deviation." A very important problem here is the imprecision with which such terms are used and the frequency with which very different people are unthinkingly treated in the same way. Some guidance as to what the court intended in *Boutilier* may, however, be obtained from the facts presented in that case. The alien there had engaged regularly in homosexual conduct over a period of several years, both before and after his last entry into the United States. He had also engaged on "three or four occasions" in heterosexual conduct. The court described the alien's activities as involving a "continued course" of homosexual conduct. Although the courts might not regard isolated and unrepeated homosexual conduct as proof of a "psychopathic personality" or "sexual deviation," it should be assumed that any pattern of homosexual activity continuing up to the time of attempted entry into the United States may permit the exclusion of an alien.

These rules may seem vague and imprecise—and they are. The alien in *Boutilier* argued that it was unfair to punish him by deportation when he had not been given a fair warning of the applicable rules when he entered the United States. The claim was, however, rejected by the court. On the other hand, a lower federal court held on an earlier occasion that these rules were impermissibly vague.[2] Perhaps the Supreme Court will one day agree.

What about aliens who have already entered the United States?

In most situations, immigration officers are unaware of an alien's sexual preferences or activities at the time of entry. The question of excludability frequently arises after the alien has entered the United States, usually in the context of a deportation proceeding. Under Section 1251 of Title 8 of the United States Code, an alien is subject to deportation from the United States for a variety of grounds. The rules are complex, but there is no doubt that homosexual conduct may, in some situations, permit deportation.

The first ground for deportation under Section 1251 includes situations in which an alien was excludable at the time of his last entry into the United States. The idea here is that an alien who could have been excluded should not be permitted to remain here merely because that fact escaped notice at the time of entry. The effect of this provision is to make all aliens who were excludable at the time of their last entry on the basis of a "psychopathic personality" or "sexual deviation" permanently subject to deportation. In *Boutilier*, the Supreme Court case referred to above, for example, the alien first entered the United States in 1955 and re-entered in 1959. He applied for citizenship in 1963 and ultimately acknowledged in the course of the naturalization process that he had from time to time prior to 1959 engaged in homosexual conduct. The Supreme Court held in 1967, twelve years after his first entry and eight years after his latest entry, that he was deportable because he had been excludable in 1959.

The first ground for deportation is concerned exclusively with the alien's situation at the time of his latest entry into the United States. This does not necessarily mean, however, that conduct that occurs within the United States may not be relevant. It is possible that evidence of post-entry homosexual conduct may be used in combination with evidence of pre-entry conduct to establish the existence of a "psychopathic personality" or "sexual deviation" at the time of entry. More important, homosexual conduct within the United States may permit exclusion or deportation of an alien if, after the conduct has occurred, he leaves the United States and then returns. The Supreme Court's decision in *Boutilier* illustrates the dangers of such departures and re-entries. The alien in that case left and later re-entered the United States in 1959 and by so doing made his homosexual conduct within the United States between 1955 and 1959 grounds for his deportation. The critical date for determining excludability, and hence for deportability under the first ground, is the alien's last entry. Any conduct before that date, wherever it occurs, will be relevant to determine whether the alien may be excluded.

Does this mean that I should never leave the United States even temporarily?

It is not quite that simple. The Supreme Court held in 1963, in *Rosenberg* v. *Fleuti*.[3] that an "entry" after only a very brief departure from the United States—in that case, an afternoon's visit to Mexico—will not always be counted for this purpose. The rules here are not exact, but it may be assumed that courts will take into account the duration of the absence from the United States, the purpose of the

visit, what travel documents and other formalities were involved, and any other facts pertinent to measure the significance of the departure. Uncertainty is increased by the
fact that the court was divided in *Rosenberg*, and it is by
no means clear that it would reach the same result today.
The best advice here is caution. It is wise to assume that
any departure, however brief, involves a measure of possible danger. Unnecessary departures should be avoided.
When you balance the relative advantages of a week in
Florida and a week in Nassau, take full account of the added risks of a new entry into the United States.

**Does it matter that I have been convicted of a criminal
offense based on homosexual conduct?**

Yes. Another important ground for deportation under
Section 1251 is conviction of certain criminal offenses.
Two alternative formulae will permit deportation. An
alien may be deported if he or she is convicted of a crime
"involving moral turpitude" within five years after entry
into the United States, and he or she is either sentenced to
confinement or confined in a prison or corrective institution for a year or more. A sentence to confinement, even
if it is not served, will suffice. Although the conviction
must occur within five years after entry, each new entry
into the United States will have the effect of extending the
application of the statute. The requirement of a sentence
to confinement may raise important technical questions.
One federal court has held that a person convicted of
"open lewdness" and given a suspended sentence under the
New Jersey Sex Offenders Act was not sentenced to confinement within the meaning of the deportation laws.[4] The
court emphasized that the New Jersey Act had humani-
tarian, not punitive, goals and that the sentence was only a
technical means of assuring treatment for the convicted
person.

Alternatively, deportation may be ordered even without
confinement or a sentence to confinement if an alien is
convicted of two crimes "involving moral turpitude,"
provided that they do not arise out of a "single scheme"
of criminal misconduct. Two convictions will satisfy this

second standard even if they are the result of a single trial. It is important that no time limitation has been placed on this rule. Two such convictions will permit deportation, no matter how long they occur after entry.

The central question under both formulae obviously is whether a crime involves "moral turpitude." Although considerable attention has been given to that question by the courts and the Immigration Service, no clear rules have been developed. It is said that the governing issue is the "inherent nature" of the crime, as defined by statute or interpreted by the courts. Some examples may help to clarify the confusing positions that have been adopted on this matter. It has been held that indecent exposure, without evidence of motive or circumstances, does not involve "moral turpitude"; that solicitation in a public restroom to commit a homosexual act does involve "moral turpitude"; that consensual sodomy does involve "moral turpitude"; and that an undefined offense of "gross indecency" under Canadian law does involve "moral turpitude."[5] These and other similar results give us little meaningful guidance regarding the nature of the offenses that will be held to involve "moral turpitude," but it is wise to assume that any criminal conviction based on homosexual conduct may be held to satisfy the requirements of Section 1251.

The severity of the deportation requirement makes clear that any alien who is charged with a criminal offense should obtain careful advice before he or she responds to the charge. Be certain to emphasize to your attorney that you are an alien and subject to the dangers of deportation under Section 1251. Aliens have sometimes bargained with prosecuting attorneys and pleaded guilty to a lesser offense, only to find that they had become subject to deportation.[6] No alien should permit a plea of guilty to be entered on his or her behalf with respect to any criminal charge until the risks of deportation have been carefully weighed.

I entered the United States on a nonimmigrant visa and now wish to have my status adjusted to permit me to re-

main in the United States permanently. Are there dangers
to such a request?

Yes. An adjustment of status permits a new examination to determine if an alien should be excluded from the
United States.[7] Let us assume, for example, that an alien
has lawfully entered the United States as a student, and
that his sexual and other conduct at the time of his entry
was such that he could not have been excluded for a "psychopathic personality," "sexual deviation," or other reason.
If the alien has, since his entry into the United States, engaged in conduct that would support a finding that he has
now developed a "psychopathic personality" or "sexual
deviation," an adjustment of status creates new risks of
exclusion from the United States. It may well be, of
course, that the terms of an alien's entry will require his
or her departure from the United States unless an adjustment of status is obtained, thus leaving little realistic alternative. No effort to obtain adjustment should, however, be
undertaken unnecessarily or without careful consideration
of the possible dangers.

**I wish to become a naturalized American citizen. Will
homosexual conduct disqualify me?**

It may, although the law remains unsettled. Section
1427 of Title 8 of the United States Code provides that, in
addition to various requirements regarding residence in the
United States, a petitioner for naturalization must be, and
have been for the previous five years, "a person of good
moral character, attached to the principles of the Constitution of the United States, and well disposed to the good
order and happiness of the United States." For purposes
of determining "moral character," the statute permits the
courts to take into account a petitioner's "conduct and
acts at any time prior" to the statutory five-year period.
The term "good moral character" is partially defined by
Section 1101 (f) to exclude various categories of persons,
none of which directly involves homosexual conduct. Section 1101 (f) does, however, contain two significant exclusions: It provides that a person lacks "good moral character" if he or she has given false testimony for the purpose

of obtaining immigration or naturalization benefits, or if he or she has been confined to a penal institution during the previous five years for an aggregate period of 180 days or more.

It appears to be clearly settled that the burden of proving "good moral character" is on the petitioner.[8] Any doubts may be resolved against the petitioner.[9] A lower New York court took the position in 1968 in *Matter of Schmidt* that one who admits homosexual acts during the five years prior to the filing of a petition for naturalization should be denied naturalization for want of "good moral character."[10] The court acknowledged that the petitioner had not violated any criminal statute and that all of her activities were conducted in private between consenting adults, but averred that the "ordinary man or woman" would find petitioner's habits inconsistent with "good moral character."

In contrast, a federal district court held in 1971, in *In re Labady,* that a petitioner's private homosexual conduct did not prevent his naturalization.[11] The court emphasized that a judge's individual beliefs or preferences should not be controlling, and the important standard should instead be "the ethical standards current at the time." It held that private conduct and habits may not be inquired into or made the basis for the denial of naturalization. It noted that there has in recent years been a gradual relaxation of the severe penalties heretofore imposed on homosexual conduct and a slow change in public attitudes regarding homosexuality. It observed that adultery and private heterosexual conduct between unmarried adults have been held not to prevent naturalization.

The opinions in *Schmidt* and *Labady* mark the two competing approaches that the courts have adopted with regard to the naturalization of those who have engaged in homosexual conduct. It may be hoped that, as the penalties on homosexuality continue to fall gradually away, more courts will accept the enlightened view shown by *Labady*. For the moment, however, it must be assumed that evidence of homosexual conduct may cause a court to deny naturalization.

Why are inquiries into sexual habits and preferences not invasions of privacy?

They often are, but the law governing matters of privacy still remains largely undeveloped. The protection given to individual privacy is partial and inadequate. Here, as elsewhere, the law's movement toward more nearly adequate protection is slow and uneven. If you become involved in an immigration or naturalization proceeding based on allegations of homosexual conduct, you will undoubtedly receive demands for detailed personal information. The questions will certainly be irritating and will probably be embarrassing. They may go beyond any information to which the Immigration Service has been held to be entitled. The court in *Labady* distinguished for purposes of naturalization between public and private sexual behavior, and restricted the Service to questions involving "public" behavior.[12] This does not necessarily mean that questions involving private behavior will not in fact be asked. It does mean that you may be held to have a right not to answer them.

What should I do if I receive demands for information?

Consult an attorney or other competent adviser. You should indicate simply that you will neither answer nor refuse to answer until you have had a reasonable opportunity to obtain advice. You must avoid making damaging admissions and also not refuse to give information to which the Service is entitled under the law.

Should I lie?

No. Lying exposes you to additional penalties, including the loss of whatever status you hope to be granted.[13] Section 1101 of Title 8 of the United States Code specifically provides that lying to obtain immigration or naturalization benefits is inconsistent with "good moral character." Moreover, deportation is permitted when a visa has been procured by fraud or by willful misrepresentation of a material fact.[14]

What should I do if I am uncertain as to how the rules

described above apply to me or if I am considering a change in my status?

You should consult an attorney. This book is designed to give you general guidance and information, not to act as a substitute for expert advice regarding any specific situation. If you have any doubts as to your situation, or are considering any step that might trigger an important change in that situation, it would be wise to get such advice. If you are uncertain as to whom to consult, contact local gay-activist groups, the nearest ACLU chapter, or your local legal-assistance office. If they cannot offer help, ask them to refer you to an appropriate attorney. You should remember that you are a member of two groups that have long been treated by the courts and others with special harshness: aliens and those who have engaged in homosexual conduct. In this situation, it is always better to go forward carefully, after all of the possible dangers have been thoroughly explored and evaluated. Various administrative and judicial remedies may be available to you, but the proper course to follow in each case should be carefully discussed with a qualified adviser.

Are there other materials that I can read for additional information?

Yes. A good survey of the applicable law, which provides a more detailed discussion of the questions referred to above, is Gordon and Rosenfield, *Immigration Law and Procedure* (1973). It suggests numerous other cases and materials that may be relevant to your specific questions.

NOTES

1. 387 U.S. 118 (1967).
2. *Fleuti* v. *Rosenberg,* 302 F.2d 652 (9th Cir. 1962), *vacated and remanded on other grounds,* 374 U.S. 449 (1963).
3. 374 U.S. 449 (1963).
4. *Holzapfel* v. *Wyrsch,* 250 F.2d 890 (3d Cir. 1958).
5. *See generally, Velez-Lozano* v. *Immigration & Naturalization Service,* 463 F.2d 1305 (D.C. Cir. 1972); *Hudson* v. *Esperdy,* 290 F.2d 879 (2d Cir. 1961); *Marinelli* v. *Ryan,* 285 F.2d 474 (2d Cir. 1961).
6. *E.G., Velez-Lozano* v. *Immigration & Naturalization Service, supra.*
7. *Campos* v. *United States Immigration & Naturalization Service,* 402 F.2d 758 (9th Cir. 1968).
8. *Berenyi* v. *District Director,* 385 U.S. 630 (1967).
9. *United States* v. *Macintosh,* 283 U.S. 605 (1930).
10. *Matter of Schmidt,* 56 Misc. 2d 456 (Sup. Ct. 1968).
11. *In re Labady,* 326 F. Supp. 924 (S.D.N.Y. 1971).
12. *Id.*
13. *E.g., Kovacs* v. *United States,* 476 F2d 843 (2d Cir. 1973).
14. *E.g., Granduxe y Marino* v. *Murff,* 183 F. Supp. 565 (S.D.N.Y 1959)

VII

Housing and Public Accommodations

Housing

Although housing, like food and clothing, is one of the basic essentials for human life, gays are now afforded little protection by the law against discrimination in housing. Recent developments, which will be discussed in this chapter, may augur a day when gays will enjoy greater protections under the law. Since there is little law specifically concerned with the housing rights of gays, this chapter chiefly treats related matters that may affect such rights. Those matters suggest various means by which the housing rights of gays may be broadened.

The Constitution of the United States guarantees that government shall not deny to any person "the equal protection of the laws."[1] This clause has not yet been interpreted to protect gays against discrimination in housing. The federal government has enacted numerous laws proscribing discrimination in housing, but none of them protects gays as such. The Civil Rights Act of 1866[2] assures equal property rights to nonwhites; this pertains to private as well as governmental conduct.[3] The Civil Rights Act of 1870[4] assures equal rights under the law to nonwhites, including the right to make and enforce contracts. Title VI of the Civil Rights Act of 1964[5] prohibits discrimination on the ground of race, color, or national origin under any program or activity receiving federal financial assistance. Title VII of the Civil Rights Act of 1968[6] generally prohibits private and governmental discrimination in the sale, rental, financing, and provision of housing on the basis of race, color, religion, or national origin.[7]

Many states have also enacted fair housing and human rights laws, but, at the time of this publication, none have

dealt with discrimination on the basis of sexual preference.[8] Such bills have, however, been introduced in the
Colorado, Connecticut, Massachusetts and New York
legislatures. The state antidiscrimination laws generally
shadow the protections afforded by the federal statutes.
Some municipal governments have, however, adopted broad
fair housing or human rights laws that prohibit discrimination on the basis of such criteria as sex, marital status, and
sexual preference. As this book goes to press, those cities
that have passed antidiscrimination bills that specifically
protect gays include San Francisco, Palo Alto, San Jose,
and Berkeley, Calif., Seattle, the District of Columbia,
Columbus, Ohio, and Detroit, East Lansing and Ann Arbor, Michigan, Minneapolis and St. Paul, Minnesota,
Alfred and Ithaca, New York, and Urbana, Illinois. Similar
bills are pending in various other cities.

As discussed in Chapter IV, the employment rights of
gays depend in part on the existence and type of governmental involvement. Similarly, the availability of housing
to gays is affected by whether the housing is private or
governmental, and, if governmental, the nature of the governmental involvement. With respect to private housing,
the only protections gays have against discrimination, except in the small number of municipalities listed above,
are those accorded all citizens against discrimination only
on the basis of race, creed, color, or national origin. The
bill introduced by Congressperson Bella Abzug in March,
1975, H.R. 166, to extend the Civil Rights Act to gays
includes protection against private and government housing
discrimination.

The housing programs of the federal government may
be divided into two broad categories: public housing and
federally subsidized housing. Public housing is built or
managed by an arm of government. Federally subsidized
housing is built (or rehabilitated) and managed by private
persons or organizations. The federal public-housing program is administered by the Housing Assistance Administration (HAA) of the Department of Housing and Urban
Development (HUD). HAA neither produces nor man-
ages public housing itself; its role is assisting local commu-

nities in providing safe and decent housing for low-income families, pursuant to the Housing Act of 1937, as amended.[9] Public-housing programs are administered locally by local housing authorities (LHAs), which are quasi-autonomous bodies established by local governments pursuant to state enabling legislation.[10] Federally subsidized housing programs are administered by another agency within HUD, the Federal Housing Administration (FHA). The federally subsidized housing programs include mortgage insurance for long-term mortgages at FHA-set below-market interest rates[11] and for market-rate mortgages.[12] In certain programs, rent-supplement payments may be made by the FHA in order to make rental housing available to low-income tenants.[13]

Some state and local governments also maintain housing programs, but their details are beyond the scope of this discussion. For information on the programs in a particular jurisdiction, contact the housing agency of the state or local government.

May gays be excluded from private housing?

Generally yes. Private housing is any housing that is owned and managed by private persons, organizations, or corporations. Generally, gays may be barred from private housing without legal recourse.

An important barrier to housing for gays is the differential treatment often accorded unmarried persons. There are numerous "groupie" ordinances by which local communities do not allow occupancy by persons unrelated by blood or marriage. Conversely, there are jurisdictions that prohibit discrimination in housing on the basis of marital status, but not on the basis of sexual preference.[14] Persons denied housing on the basis of marital status or sexual preference should determine whether state or local laws prohibit such discrimination. Additional information may generally be obtained by contacting the local or state human rights commission, its equivalent, or a local gay organization.

May gays be excluded from public and federally subsidized housing?

Under present laws, gays do not have specific protection against discrimination in housing except in the few municipalities listed above. However, where there is governmental involvement in a housing program, there may be some protection, which will be discussed below.

Federal public housing is available solely for "families of low-income."[15] A family is commonly defined by statute as two or more persons related by blood, marriage, or operation of law, who occupy the same dwelling or unit. Some single people may be treated as a family for eligibility purposes; these include certain elderly, handicapped, disabled, or displaced persons and the remaining sole member of a family who has been a tenant.[16] Most gay couples and individual gays do not qualify for public housing under these statutory eligibility requirements. A gay person with children or a gay person living with relatives may, however, qualify.

In addition to the statutory eligibility criteria, LHAs have authority to consider other factors in determining whether you are eligible. Under HUD regulations,[17] LHAs may exclude otherwise eligible people whom they consider "nondesirable."[18] Applicants can be considered undesirable only where there exists "conduct of [the applicant] ... [which] does or would be likely to interfere with other tenants in such a manner as to materially diminish their enjoyment of the premises." Such interference must "relate to the actual or threatened conduct of the tenant and not be based solely on such matters as marital status of the family, the legitimacy of the children in the family, police records, etc."[19]

Standards frequently used by LHAs include confirmed drug addiction, a pattern of violent behavior, criminal history of a member of the family who lives with the family,[20] unsanitary housekeeping practices, dangerous behavior, and convictions or rape, indecent exposure, sodomy, or carnal abuse.

Does the mere status of being a homosexual make you ineligible?

It is not yet settled whether LHAs may bar gays on the grounds that their behavior or presence may be offensive to other tenants. The "family" eligibility provision generally renders that determination unnecessary. However, as discussed below, an exclusion based on the sole stated ground that the applicant is a homosexual might be held unconstitutional, absent a showing that the particular applicant threatens to interfere with the enjoyment of the premises by other tenants. LHAs are empowered to investigate applicants only to the extent that verification of eligibility is necessary. You should not be questioned about your private sexual acts since they should not provide a reason for exclusion. Investigators may be able to ask you questions about any public display of sexual acts, but if you are questioned about public displays of affection such as holding hands, which would be suitable for heterosexuals to do in public, contact the local gay group or ACLU for help.

What due-process rights do you have regarding your application for public housing?

Applicants to public housing are entitled to certain due-process rights; that is, the LHA is constitutionally required to do or not to do certain things in dealing with applications. The LHA must establish fixed procedures and standards for processing applications.[21] The LHA must publish the "nondesirability" criteria that it uses, which includes posting those criteria at the LHA office.[22] The LHA must, within a reasonable time, inform the applicant of the disposition of his or her application and the reasons for that disposition.[23] Moreover, the LHA may not automatically exclude all persons who are members of a particular class, such as unwed mothers,[24] welfare recipients,[25] or, presumably, homosexuals. Instead, each applicant must be evaluated as an individual.[26]

An additional complication arises in Section 23 public-housing programs.[27] Such programs empower the LHA to lease dwelling units from private owners and to sublet these units to eligible low income families. In such programs, the owner of the dwelling units has the authority to select the tenants who will occupy his premises. Thus, as in the case of purely private housing, it may be held that gays may be excluded at the discretion of the owner-landlord.

Applicants for federally subsidized housing generally must constitute a family, as defined earlier. There are, however, certain programs[28] under which up to 10 per cent of the dwelling units may be rented to single persons less than 62 years of age. Persons 62 or older are considered to be a "family." Since government funds are involved in such programs, it may be argued that the sponsor must afford due process and other constitutional rights to applicants for tenancy. The sponsor may not automatically exclude a class of persons such as welfare recipients[29] and, presumably, homosexuals. There has, however, not yet been litigation concerning the exclusion of gays from such programs.

Many state and local governments have their own housing programs. The eligibility requirements for those programs vary, and a complete survey of each jurisdiction is beyond the scope of this chapter. Those interested should contact the housing agency in their area.

What can you do if you are unfairly denied public or federally-subsidized housing?

If you believe that impermissible standards were applied to your application for housing or that you were denied due-process rights by a government agency, you should determine whether there are administrative appeal rights. If there are not, the only recourse may be to challenge the governmental action in court. Contact your local gay organization or the ACLU for assistance.

What are some legal arguments that may be used to support the rights of gays to government housing?

In addition to the due-process protections described above, recent developments provide some support for an argument that the housing rights of gays are protected against discrimination by the Fourteenth Amendment to the Constitution. In *United States* v. *Moreno*,[30] the court considered the rules used to determine eligibility for participation in the federal food-stamp program. Eligibility was based on households rather than individuals, and the term "household" was defined to include only those groups whose members were all related to each other.[31] The United States Supreme Court held that this was an irrational classification in violation of the due-process clause of the Fifth Amendment to the United States Constitution. The court concluded that the discrimination against unrelated persons was not rationally related to any legitimate governmental objective, and hence was invalid.

A similar result was reached by the United States Court of Appeals for the Second Circuit in *Boraas* v. *Belle Terre*.[32] The town of Belle Terre had enacted a zoning ordinance that restricted occupancy in each dwelling unit to a single "family." The ordinance essentially defined a "family" as consisting of related persons or up to two unrelated persons living and cooking together as a single housekeeping unit. The Court of Appeals examined the objectives that the town asserted were promoted by the ordinance, found that the exclusion of nonfamilies was not rationally related to those objectives, and held that it was a violation of the equal-protection clause of the Fourteenth Amendment.

The judgment of the Court of Appeals has, however, now been reversed by the Supreme Court. The court upheld the ordinance, emphasizing that state and local authorities have broad authority to regulate the use of property to achieve economic and social goals. The implications of the decision are not yet clear, but it may represent a significant barrier to the achievement of wider housing rights for gays.

May a person be evicted from private housing for being a homosexual?

Generally, yes. As pointed out above, gays have little protection against discrimination in private housing. Legal protection exists only in those few jurisdictions that prohibit discrimination on the basis of sexual preference. Tenants, however, may have other rights which do not arise from fair housing and human-rights laws.

The most obvious source of tenant rights is a lease, if one exists. A lease commonly provides that the tenant may remain for a fixed term, during which period he or she may not be evicted except for stipulated conduct, such as nonpayment of rent. It is very important, especially in a household unit of unrelated persons, that each tenant sign the lease. Otherwise, on the death or departure of the lease signator, the others will be subject to eviction at the discretion of the landlord.

In some jurisdictions tenants are protected by rent-control laws. Such laws generally control both rent levels and eviction. The gay tenant is entitled to the same protections under such laws as any other tenant and may not be evicted except in accordance with the applicable law. In the absence of rent-control laws or a lease, the tenant may be protected from eviction by certain judicial doctrines. For example, a landlord may not evict a tenant in retaliation for conduct which the tenant had a lawful right to engage in, such as reporting housing-code violations or organizing a tenants' association.[33] If the tenant can establish that the eviction is a retaliatory one, a court will usually refuse to aid the landlord.

In any case, whether or not the housing is rent-controlled or is covered by a lease or not, a tenant may be evicted only pursuant to a court order arising out of a formal eviction proceeding in the appropriate local court. The tenant is entitled to prior notice of such a proceeding. If a landlord threatens eviction or actually commences an eviction proceeding, the tenant should immediately contact an attorney. If you cannot afford a private attorney, contact the legal-aid or legal-services office in your area.

May a person be evicted from public and federally subsidized housing for being a homosexual?

Probably not. As discussed above, gays are seldom eligible for participation in government housing programs. If, however, a person meets the eligibility requirements and is a tenant, he or she probably may not be evicted solely on the basis of homosexuality.

A tenant may be evicted from federal public housing only for "overincome"[34] or for "actual or threatened conduct ... [which] does or would be likely to interfere with other tenants in such a manner as to materially diminish their enjoyment of the premises."[35] Such determinations must be made on the basis of individual, not class, considerations.[36] Merely being gay probably would not justify eviction, without consideration of individual conduct and threatened conduct. Absent a conviction for a sexual crime or antisocial behavior that would "interfere with other tenants," the gay tenant probably is protected from eviction on the basis of "nondesirability" criteria. It should be noted that a conviction for consensual sodomy may constitute grounds for eviction.

As noted earlier, the question of whether a LHA may discriminate against homosexuals has not yet been addressed by the courts. However, as in the admissions process, the tenant clearly has certain due-process rights. The leading case dealing with the due-process rights of a public-housing tenant threatened with eviction is *Escalera* v. *New York City Housing Authority*.[37] Although HUD regulations require that LHAs give tenants the reasons for eviction,[38] the court held in *Escalera* that due process also demands that tenants be given access to LHA files that relate to them and an opportunity to confront and cross-examine those who provide information adverse to them.

After *Escalera*, HUD issued regulations that established minimum requirements for public-housing leases[39] and for grievance procedures.[40] HUD also issued a model lease and model-grievance procedures, both of which incorporated the minimum requirements. The regulations offer protection for tenants against eviction from public housing.

The due-process protections for tenants in federally subsidized housing and state or local housing programs should be comparable to those applicable to public housing.

May gays obtain mortgages?

Decisions whether to approve a mortgage application are made by the particular lending institution involved. The principal sources of mortgage funds for single-family housing are savings banks, savings and loan associations (building and loan associations), and commercial banks. Such institutions are typically concerned chiefly with the "creditworthiness" of the potential borrower. The personal life of the applicant should be irrelevant so long as it does not affect the lender's risks. However, many lending institutions evidently consider both marital status and homosexuality in determining "creditworthiness." Unmarried persons and gays are considered to be unstable and therefore less desirable lending risks than married persons. Unless specific local legislation exists that forbids such lending practices, the aggrieved person has no legal remedy. H.R. 166, if passed, would protect against such discrimination.

What is the best guidance for gays on housing rights?

1. *Learn about housing rights in general.* All tenants have certain statutory and judicial rights, especially under rent-control laws, building codes, and local ordinances. There are also judicially created doctrines that protect tenants in certain situations, including certain warranties. The following books are useful resources: Striker & Shapiro, *Super Tenant* (1973); Steven Burghardt, *Tenants and the Urban Housing Crisis* (1972); Emily Jane Goodman, *The Tenant Survival Book* (1972). Tenants' councils and organizations are good sources for information in many areas.

2. *Use tenant organizations.* Such organizations are not only sources of information, but they can also be used to produce legislative change and to protect individual rights.

3. *Get a lease, read it carefully, and have each member of household sign it.*

4. *Where applicable, challenge discriminatory conduct on the basis of a traditionally protected class such as discrimination based on race, creed, color, and national origin.* If such discrimination exists, contact your local attorney general, the state or local housing administrator,

the local human-rights commission, or, where public or federally subsidized housing is involved, the local HUD or FHA office or the Assistant Secretary for Equal Opportunity, HUD, Washington, D.C.

5. *Where there is a state or local fair-housing ordinance that specifically prohibits discrimination on the basis of sexual preference, contact the local authority indicated in the ordinance.*

6. *Seek legal representation,* particularly if you are threatened with eviction. Go to legal aid or community legal services if you qualify. You also may contact gay organizations—which are listed in the appendix—for legal referrals. For major cases of discrimination, contact the local ACLU chapter. The addresses are listed in the appendix.

7. *Legislation.* Work for local, state, and national fair-housing laws that prohibit discrimination on basis of sexual orientation.

8. *Have a will.* Since under present laws marriages between gays are not recognized as legally valid, it is especially important to execute a will to provide for disposition of property upon death. Otherwise, the state law of intestate succession will determine who will receive the property in the estate. Those whom you wish to benefit may be excluded, even if you shared equally in the purchase of property and, implicitly or explicitly, have agreed that if one of you die, the other will own all the property. (See Chapter VIII, the gay family, for a more detailed discussion of wills.)

Public Accommodations

Discrimination against gay people in employment, licensing, and housing and available remedies against it are discussed in other chapters in this book. Another area in which gays sometimes suffer discriminatory treatment is public accommodations, which includes bars, restaurants, discotheques, etc. Sometimes the discrimination is embodied in the law itself. Until 1971, for example, regulations

of the New York City Department of Consumer Affairs
prohibited homosexuals from congregating in cabarets and
dancing clubs, and prohibited the employment of homosexuals in cabarets in any capacity. Puerto Rico currently
has similar provisions in its statute. Any such laws
or regulations still on the books in any cities now would
undoubtedly fall under constitutional attack. That such
prohibitions could exist, however, is indicative of an attitude toward gay people that has only recently begun to
change.

**Has Congress passed any laws prohibiting discrimination
against gay people in places of public accommodation?**
Not yet. Presently, federal legislation extends only to
such categories as race, religion, and national origin. Legislation has been introduced in Congress, however, which
would amend the Civil Rights laws to prohibit discrimination in public accommodations based on sexual or "affectional preference."[41]

**Do any states have legislation that would prohibit
discrimination against gay people in public accommodations?**
Not at this time, although such legislation has been introduced in some states and has been supported by bar associations.[42]

**Do any cities or municipalities in the United States have
local laws prohibiting discrimination in public accommodations based on sexual orientation or preference?**
Yes. Local laws have been adopted in Alfred, New
York; Ann Arbor,[43] East Lansing,[44] and Detroit,[45] Michigan; Columbus, Ohio,[46] and Washington, D.C.[47] prohibiting
discrimination in public accommodations based on sexual
orientation. Seattle and San Francisco have ordinances
prohibiting various types of employment discrimination
against gay people, but their ordinances do not extend
to public accommodations. Similarly, the Columbus ordinance, while covering public accommodations, does not

cover employment discrimination. Comprehensive local laws prohibiting discrimination based on sexual orientation are pending but not enacted in Chicago, New York City, and Philadelphia.

What should a gay person do who is discriminated against in public accommodations in one of the cities with a local ordinance prohibiting such discrimination?

Most of these ordinances are administered by a city commission or department of human rights, and procedures are established for filing complaints with these agencies. It is advisable to secure the assistance of a lawyer in filing a complaint and preparing for a hearing on it. If you do not have a lawyer, you should contact a local gay organization or the local ACLU affiliate for assistance in obtaining one.

Is there any protection against discrimination based on sexual orientation in public accommodations in places that do not have laws specifically prohibiting it?

Only if the discrimination can be brought within the scope of some other legally proscribed discrimination. For example, both local and state laws in some places make discrimination based on sex or marital status illegal. If a couple in which both partners are of the same sex is refused service or made to leave a club because they were, for example, dancing together, it can be argued that the discrimination was because they were both of the same sex; the management would have no way of knowing whether the people dancing together were gay or straight unless the couple volunteered the information. Thus, a complaint could be filed against the establishment involved for discrimination based on sex.

Absent this type of situation, however, where privately-owned public accommodations are involved, there is presently no legal recourse against discrimination based on sexual orientation in the absence of specific legislation.

If the public accommodation is government operated, such as a park, beach, swimming pool, camp ground, etc., discrimination can be challenged in court as a denial of equal protection of the laws. Whether such challenges would succeed or not has yet to be determined, however.

Is it legal for gay people to dance together in public places?

It is not illegal, per se, but gays in some localities can still expect to be harassed and possibly arrested on charges such as disorderly conduct for dancing together in nongay establishments. These charges should be contested on the grounds that the conduct is not disorderly or a violation of any law. One New York court has been held that indulgence in the inference that men in a grill were "from their dress and makeup, homosexuals, does not support the additional inference that they would create disorder. It is reasonable to think that even though he dresses strangely a homosexual may be orderly . . . ,"[48] and that "there is no sound reason to distinguish between the actions of homosexuals and that of heterosexuals with respect to the dancing of slow dances. . . ."[49]

NOTES

1. Fourteenth Amendment, Section 1.
2. 42 U.S.C. 1982.
3. *Jones* v. *Alfred H. Mayer Co.* 392 U.S. 409 (1968) (A private individual could not discriminate against a black who wanted to buy property.)
4. 42 U.S.C. 1981.
5. 42 U.S.C. 2000d *et. seq.*
6. 42 U.S.C. 3600 *et seq.*
7. U.S.C. 3603 (B).
8. *See Equal Opportunity in Housing* (Prentice-Hall Publishers), which is a looseleaf service that contains all the various state fair housing and human rights laws pertaining to housing.
9. 42 U.S.C. 1401 *et. seq.*
10. A detailed description of the various types of public-housing programs is beyond the scope of this chapter. An excellent source for such information is the *Handbook on Housing Law*, National Institute for Education in Law and Poverty, Northwestern University School of Law, Chicago, 1969.
11. The principal programs of this type are §221 (d) (3) (12 U.S.C. 1715 L. (d)), which has not been funded since 1968, and §221 (h) (12 U.S.C. 1715 L. (h)).
12. These programs were created under the HUD Act of 1968. The principal programs of this type are §235 (12 U.S.C. 1715), which provides for purchase of housing low-income families, and §236 (12 U.S.C. 1715 Z-1), which provides for *rental* housing for low-income families. It should be noted that housing law is in a great state of flux and there are many bills pending before Congress now.
13. See, 12 U.S.C. 1701 S.
14. In New York City, for example, marital status and sex are impermissible criteria, while sexual preference is not. The City Commission on Human Rights, which is charged with investigating charges of improper discrimination, has declined to apply the "marital status" protection to gays as an interpretation of the legislative intent. This interpretation is supported in New York City by the fact that the City Council has repeatedly refused to pass a bill adding sexual preference to the list of impermissible criteria.
15. 42 U.S.C. 1402 (1).
16. 42 U.S.C. 1402 (2).
17. HUD has issued a Low-Rent Management Manual pursuant to statutory authority—Department of Housing and Urban Development Act, 79 Stat. 669, 42 U.S.C. 3534 (a). Changes in the manual are promulgated as circulars, which have the same effect as the manual and are binding

on the LHA. See, *e.g. Hud Low-Rent Housing Manual,* §100.2 at 2 (Sept. 1963): *Thorpe* v. *Housing Authority of Durham,* 393 U.S. 268 (1969), (the case held a HUD circular dealing with the eviction rights of tenants was binding on LHA): *Housing Authority of the City of Omaha, Nebraska* v. *United States Housing Authority,* 468 F. 2d 1 (8th Cir. 1972), (HUD grievance procedure circulars were ruled to be binding on the LHA).

18. See the Dec. 17, 1968 HUD *Circular,* which was incorporated into the *Low-Rent Management Manual.*

19. *Id.*

20. *Tyson* v. *New York Housing Authority,* 369 F. Supp. 513 (S.D.N.Y., 1974).

21. *Holmes* v. *New York City Housing Authority,* 398 F. 2d. 262 2nd Cir. (1968) (Due process requires that selections among applicants for public housing be made by LHAs in accordance with fixed procedures and ascertainable standards.)

22. See, *Colon* v. *Thompkins Square Neighbors, Inc.,* 294 F. Supp. 134 (S.D.N.Y. 1968) (Applicants for federally subsidized housing—§221 (d) (3)—could not be excluded solely because they were welfare recipients).

23. Id.

24. *Thomas* v. *The Housing Authority of the City of Little Rock,* 282 F. Supp. 575 (E.D. Ark. 1967) (LHA could not *automatically* exclude unwed mothers from public housing).

25. *Op. cit.* at 26.

26. December 17, 1968 HUD *Circular.*

27. 42 U.S.C. 1421 (6).

28. See footnote 16; the 10 per cent provision is found at 12 U.S.C. 1715 z. See Footnote 15; the 10 per cent provision is found at 12 U.S.C. 1715 L (f).

29. *Colon, op. cit.* at 26.

30. 413 US 528. 37 L Ed 2d 782, 92 S. Ct. 2821 (1973).

31. §3 (e) of the Food Stamp Act, 7 U.S.C.S. 2012 (e).

32. 476 F. 2d 806 (2d Cir. 1973), *rev'd.* 416 U.S. 11 (1974).

33. See, *Edwards* v. *Habib,* 397 F. 2d 687 (D.C. Cir 1968): *Hosey* v. *Club Van Cortlandt,* 299 F. Supp. 501 (S.D.N.Y. 1969).

34. 42 U.S.C. 1410 (8) (3).

35. See footnote 18.

36. See footnotes 24–26.

37. 425 F. 2d 853 (2d. Cir.), *cert. den.* 400 U.S. 853 (1970).

38. February 7, 1967 HUD *Circular.*

39. Lease Circular, RHM 7465.8.

40. Grievance Procedure Circular, RHM 7465.9.

41. H. R. 166, 94th Cong., 1st sess. (1974) (Abzug).

42. See, *e.g.*, N.Y.S.B. 4198A (Goodman) and N.Y.A.B. 4180 (Passannante), introduced in 1973, supported by the Association of the Bar of the City of New York, State Legislation Rept No. 147 (May 21, 1973).

43. Title IX, Ch. 112, §§9:151–9:155, Code of the City of Ann Arbor.

44. Title I, Ch. 4, §§1.214, 1.126, 1.127, Code of the City of East Lansing.

45. Art. 7, Ch. 10, §7-1004, Charter for the City of Detroit.

46. Title 23, Ch. 2325, Columbus City Codes.

47. Title 34, District of Columbia Human Rights Law.

48. *Kerma Restaurant Corp.* v. *New York State Liquor Authority*, 21 N.Y.2d 111, 115–116, 286 N.Y.S.2d 822, 824–25 (1967).

49. *Becker* v. *New York State Liquor Authority*, 21 N.Y.2d 289, 291–92, 287 N.Y.S.2d 400, 401 (1967).

VIII
The Gay Family

Many gay people now live together as "families" and seek to obtain the benefits that society and government confer on married couples. There is no reason in principle why two gays should be prevented from entering into a relationship that is deemed for all purposes to be a lawful "marriage." Nonetheless, the law, which first developed in an agrarian society that required procreation to produce a sufficient labor force, has consistently refused to recognize gay marriages. Today, we live in a society that regards it as desirable to limit population growth. Such a society should encourage people to remain single and to refrain from producing children. Such a policy is, however, not yet reflected in the law.

The law clearly discriminates in favor of monogamous, heterosexual marital relationships. An elaborate body of law has developed with respect to the benefits, rights, and privileges of persons who commit themselves to such relationships. Marital partners have advantages in income, gift, and estate-tax rates. They may inherit from one another without a will; they may own property in tenancy by the entirety; they may run businesses at lower cost in taxes; each may recover for the wrongful death of the other; they may adopt children more easily than singles; and they may lawfully have sexual relations. All of these and other benefits are denied to those who elect not to marry or who are not permitted to marry. Private organizations such as airlines, insurance companies, and banks also offer their goods and services on terms that discriminate in favor of married persons.

This chapter describes the legal barriers to gay marriages and the financial disabilities that result for gays because they cannot lawfully marry. It explores alternative means for obtaining the financial benefits that are based on marriage. Finally, it discusses the problems of gay people who have natural children of their own or who seek to adopt or care for children.

Gay Marriages

Does every state have a law forbidding marriage licenses for same-sex marriages?

No. Every state has marriage laws that define what requirements must be met before two people may obtain a marriage license or enter into a marriage. Such requirements usually specify that the applicants must be of a certain age, not closely related by blood, single, and free from certain types of venereal disease. There are no state laws that specifically require that the couple must be of opposite sexes. There are, however, in the language of the marriage laws of a number of states references to "husband and wife" or "man and woman."

Are gay marriages now recognized by any state?

No.

What are the consequences of the states' refusal to recognize gay marriages?

When a state refuses to recognize a marriage, the couple may not represent that they are married for purposes of gaining legal benefits that are conditional upon marriage. Those benefits are described more fully below. It also means that the couple may not enforce the marriage contract against each other for benefits, such as support and alimony, that most states provide by law for married couples.

What are the risks of obtaining a marriage license from the state without the state being aware that you intend to enter a same-sex marriage?

You may be accused of fraud.

There are various ways in which gays may obtain licenses to marry without detection by the state.[1] Not all states require that both parties be present to apply for the license.[2] In such states, if one of the applicants has a name typical of a member of the opposite sex, and if the application form does not require specification of gender, the form may be accepted without detection. The health tests required by nearly every state for venereal disease are seriological and do not involve inspection of genitalia. In addition, several states provide that statutory requirements for obtaining a marriage license before solemnization may be waived for certain religious groups such as the Quakers, B'Hai, Muslims, and Hindus.[3]

Finally, in California any couple, not minors, who have been living together may be married by any member of the clergy without having to obtain a marriage license or a health certificate. The marriage may then be reported by the clergyman to the clerk for official recording in the state records.[4] The law was intended to encourage couples living in common-law marriages to legitimize their marriages and their children. The county clerks are, however, now beginning to return reports of marriages when they recognize the names of clergy who regularly perform same-sex marriages, and they are careful to check for same-sex names.

Even if the state fails to detect a same-sex marriage, it is important to remember that such a marriage would probably not be considered valid. In addition, there is some possibility that the participants may be accused of fraud. Moreover, if a couple "married" in such a situation were to attempt to represent themselves as married for pecuniary gain—so as, for example, to collect government benefits that are available only to married persons or to file a joint tax return available only to married couples—they may be subject to still other charges of criminal fraud.

Are gay marriages that are performed in churches and synagogues valid?

They are not recognized as legally valid marriages by

the state. A gay marriage, also known as a holy union, is a marriage ceremony or rite performed by clergy in the church or temple between members of the same sex, and the marriage may be recorded in the annals of the gay church or synagogue. The holy unions are performed in gay churches of the three major religions across the country. The Metropolitan Community Church, which has numerous member churches, is the principal gay church for members of the Protestant faith. It is now seeking approval from the National Council of Churches as a recognized sect. "Dignity" is the name of the gay church for Catholics, and the Gay Synagogue is one of the synagogues for members of the Jewish religion.

Is it unlawful to perform or to participate in gay church marriages?

No. The actual performance of the religious marriage ceremonies are not banned in any state, as are, for example, polygamous marriages.

Is the fact that the states do not recognize such religious ceremonies a violation of freedom of religion?

The United States Supreme Court has held with respect to polygamous marriages that the state may criminally punish the performance and entry into a marriage that is contrary to public policy even if that marriage is entered into because of religious belief.[5] No couple has yet sought to obtain legal recognition of a gay church marriage in the courts under the doctrine of religious liberty.

Have the courts ever upheld the rights of gays to obtain marriage licenses?

No. Gays in Minnesota,[6] Kentucky,[7] and Washington[8] have unsuccessfully challenged the denial of marriage licenses in state courts. In each case the courts held that the couples did not have a right to obtain licenses because the draftsmen of the applicable legislation contemplated heterosexual marriages only. The United States Supreme Court has not, however, ruled on this question.

Although no gay couple has attempted to obtain legal

recognition in this country for a foreign marriage, it is unlikely that such an effort would be successful.[9]

**What are the legal arguments that may be used to chal-
lenge the refusal of the states to sanction gay marriages?**

The constitutional arguments most commonly used are
that the refusal is a violation of the First Amendment
right to freedom of association, an invasion of privacy as
protected by the Fourth, Ninth, and Fourteenth Amendments, and a denial of due process and equal protection of
the laws as guaranteed by the Fifth and Fourteenth
Amendments.[10]

The First Amendment generally protects the rights of
individuals to associate with one another. No right to
marry or to engage in sexual relations has, however, yet
been recognized by the Supreme Court to be protected
specifically by the First Amendment.[11]

The right of privacy has been more clearly defined by
the Supreme Court to guarantee freedom from unwarranted government interference in what has been styled as the
individual's zone of privacy. Matters so personal and intimate as decisions whether to use contraceptives or not,[12]
or whether to have an abortion or not,[13] have been held to
be protected. Similarly, the decision of two people to
marry and to choose with whom they wish to have consensual sex and an intimate relationship should be protected against needless government interference.[14]

The Supreme Court has recognized that the right to
marry is a fundamental right in the context of miscegena-
tion.[15] The denial of such a right to one group while allowing it to others may be said to deny equal protection of
the laws unless a substantial reason may be shown for the
difference in treatment.

A plurality of the Supreme Court has used three standards to determine whether statutes impermissibly deny
equal protection of the laws. The most stringent standard is
reserved for situations in which specific groups that are
commonly victimized are discriminated against and the
rights taken from them are fundamental. In such situations,
the state must establish a compelling reason for the discrim-

ination. Gays have not yet been considered by the Supreme Court to be such a "suspect" group. Another and less stringent standard requires a balancing of the interests of the individuals involved against the interests of the state. This test is reserved for other groups who are being deprived of their fundamental rights. The least stringent standard is that a statute must be upheld if it is shown to be reasonably designed to achieve any lawful purpose. This test is usually reserved for challenges to laws involving economic regulation and not fundamental rights. The middle standard probably would now be used to determine the validity of statutes denying the validity of gay marriages.[16]

The Supreme Court has held that discrimination on the basis of sex may violate the equal-protection clause.[17] Since refusal of a marriage license because the partners are of the same gender may be argued to be a distinction on the basis of sex, and because the right to marry is a fundamental right, the court must examine the social interests assertedly served by such a refusal and determine whether those interests outweigh individual interests.

The reasons commonly advanced to justify the refusals to sanction gay marriages are (1) that the government should try to cure homosexuals and not encourage homosexuality by tolerating and legalizing it; (2) that issuing a marriage license would place states in the anomalous position of officially sanctioning a relationship that may encourage the commission of illegal acts such as sodomy; (3) that most Americans view marriage as a untion between a man and a woman who can consummate a marriage by heterosexual intercourse, and almost the same number believe homosexuality to be morally reprehensible.

Many responses are possible. First, the American Psychiatric Association has concluded that homosexuals are not "sick" and need not be "cured."[18] In any event, prevailing medical opinion has long been that it is almost impossible to change sexual orientation.[19] Second, the laws that prohibit consensual sexual acts in private between adults are arguably unconstitutional. Further, in all states except Kansas, New York, and Pennsylvania, many sexual acts are prohibited even if they are committed by married heterosexuals. Moreover, there are various sexual acts that may be performed by gays in private that are not proscribed by statute.[20]

Finally, the Bill of Rights was intended in part to protect minorities against discriminatory treatment imposed by reason of a majority's deeply felt beliefs. Many Americans believed that interracial marriages were immoral, but the courts have nonetheless held unequivocally that such marriages may not be prohibited.[21] Society's moral preferences, whether based in religion or not, should not permit the denial of a fundamental right.

Financial Benefits and Disabilities

May two gays enter into the equivalent of a marriage contract, enforceable in court, by executing an agreement to define their mutual rights and domestic obligations?

Many persons entering into marriage have in recent years executed contracts defining their domestic rights and obligations toward each other. Such contracts may include provisions regarding such matters as dishwashing, cooking, cleaning, and child care. We doubt that such agreements are intended to be, or could be, enforceable in the courts. Instead, they are presumably intended merely to set forth, for the private guidance of the parties, the outlines of their mutual obligations. Gays, if they wish to do so, could lawfully create similar guidelines for themselves.

May gays intending to live together enter into a contract setting forth their financial obligations toward each other? Will such an agreement be enforceable?

Middle-aged or elderly persons about to marry, particularly those with children by a prior marriage, frequently enter into what is termed a "prenuptial" or "antenuptial" agreement with each other. The agreement customarily recites that in consideration of each marrying the other, the parties wish to set forth their financial obligations toward each other. Such an agreement commonly sets forth financial obligations that one will owe the other while they are married as well as financial obligations either will owe the other upon the death of one of them.[22] Such agreements cannot limit or define the terms of support of the wife in the event of divorce because such an agreement is unlawful.[23]

You will notice that such an agreement is made in "consideration" of the marriage. Under the law, with certain exceptions not material here, a contract must have "consideration" in order to be enforceable. In simple terms, "consideration" is something that one party gives to the other in return for the other party entering into the contract (a *quid pro quo*) or a detriment that one party incurs by entering into the contract, such as doing something that he would not otherwise have to do or refraining from doing something that he would otherwise have a right to do. Entering into a marriage contract is considered to be such a detriment and therefore constitutes consideration for the contract.[24] Since gays cannot lawfully marry, it might be questioned whether a prenuptial agreement between two gays would be enforceable.

The requirement for consideration may, however, be satisfied by a great variety of mutual promises. If two gays enter into an agreement to provide for their mutual living costs whereby each promises to make financial payments to the other or on behalf of the other at certain times or upon the death of either party, the contract would probably be held to be enforceable.

May two gays enter into joint financial obligations to third parties?

Yes. Many unmarried persons living together sign leases obligating both of them to pay the rent and to assume the other obligations of the lease. Many unmarried persons, whether living together or not, sign notes at banks obligating both of them to pay the amounts due under the loans. Such obligations are termed "joint and several," which means that the creditor may, at his election, sue either or both of the parties and collect the full amount from either of them.[25] It does not necessarily mean that if the creditor sues one party and collects the whole amount, the other

debtor will escape all liability. Depending on the understanding between them, the debtor who has been required
to pay the creditor may have a right to obtain contribution from the other debtor of a portion of the amount involved.

**If two gays are living together, will one be liable for the
debts of the other?**

Not unless the one who did not incur the debt has undertaken to be responsible for its payment. When married
couples are concerned, a wife has a right to purchase
"necessaries" (food, clothing, etc.) for which the husband
will be liable.[26] In addition, when a wife customarily buys
items from a particular store and the husband customarily
pays the bills, the store may be justified in assuming that
the wife acts as agent for the husband and that her purchases are made on the credit of the husband. In such situations, the husband may be liable to the store for anything that the wife purchases.[27] However, when single people are involved, unless one has expressly or impliedly indicated to a third party that the other acts as agent, the
person who did not incur the debt should not be liable.

May two gays own property together?

Certainly. Many persons not married to each other are
co-owners of property. There are essentially three forms
of co-ownership of property: (1) tenancy in common;
(2) joint tenancy with right of survivorship, and (3)
tenancy by the entirety. A tenancy in common means that
two or more persons own undivided interests in the same
property. If one of the co-owners dies, his estate receives
his share of the property, and it is passed to his heirs or
legatees.[28] A joint tenancy with right of survivorship means
that two or more persons own undivided interests in the
same property and that upon the death of one of the owners, his or her share passes to the surviving owners.[29] The
most common illustration is the joint bank account, which
customarily is registered in the form "A or B, payable to
either or survivor." If the parties intend a true joint account, each party is entitled to one-half of the account

while both are living, and upon the death of either the survivor is entitled to the entire account.

The last form of co-ownership, tenancy by the entirety, is available only to married couples.[30] It is, however, so similar to joint tenancy with right of survivorship that it cannot be said that unmarried persons suffer any disability. In fact, the most substantial difference may be an advantage for unmarried persons. If one of two or more tenants in common or joint tenancy with right of survivorship is unhappy with the situation and wishes to terminate the tenancy, he may bring an action in court to "partition" the property. The court will direct the property to be sold and the proceeds divided among the tenants in accordance with their respective interests. Tenants by the entirety, however, may not bring such an action of partition, and if one party is dissatisfied, he is without remedy until the marriage is dissolved, at which time the tenancy by the entirety is automatically transformed into a tenancy in common, or until one of the parties dies, at which time the survivor takes full rights of ownership.

What is community property, and may two gays hold property as community property?

Community property is a system of ownership of property derived from Spanish law and now used in eight states: Texas, California, Washington, Arizona, Louisiana, Nevada, New Mexico, and Idaho.[31] Under the law of community property, income earned by either married party during the marriage is deemed to be held in "community" and owned one-half by each party. Property earned prior to marriage and property acquired during marriage by gift, bequest, devise, or inheritance is not part of the "community" and is the "separate" property of the spouse earning or receiving it. Since community property applies only to married couples, two gays living together will not be affected by it.

If two gays are living together, is there any legal obligation to support each other?

No. Obligations of support apply only to married or

formerly married persons, and there are no laws requiring unmarried persons living together to support each other.

Do two gays living together have rights of inheritance from each other?

No. If a person dies without a will, his or her property is distributed in accordance with the intestate statutes of the state in which he or she was domiciled (permanently resident) at the time of death. Such statutes commonly provide that the decedent's estate will be distributed to his or her surviving spouse or descendants in varying shares. If there is no surviving spouse or descendants, the estate is usually distributed to the parents of the deceased; or, if they are not living, to the brothers and sisters of the deceased; or, if none are living, to nephews and nieces of the deceased, and so on to more distant relatives.[32]

May gay persons living together name each other as beneficiaries in their wills?

Certainly.

Would the will be subject to challenge by blood relations?

Every will is subject to challenge by persons interested in the estate. In general, wills are subject to challenge on any one of the following grounds: (1) improper execution;[33] (2) lack of mental competency of the testator;[34] (3) undue influence[35]; and (4) fraud.[36]

The probable ground for contesting such a will would be that the testator had been unduly influenced in the preparation and execution of the will. Undue influence has been defined as influence so potent as to take away and overcome the power of the decedent to act freely and upon his own volition, to deprive the decedent of the free exercise of his will or his intellectual powers, or to overpower the will and subject it to the will and control of another.[37] Undue influence does not exist merely because there is a relationship of affection or friendship between the parties.[38] To the contrary, such a relationship is a circumstance favorable to sustaining a will.[39] A person is entitled to bequeath his property to whomever he desires,

and nothing is more natural than to bequeath one's property to one for whom one has an emotional fondness.
Moreover, that a person is said to have ingratiated himself
with another in order to encourage a bequest is not cause
for upsetting a will.[40]

Nonetheless, despite these general rules, undue influence
is ultimately a question of fact to be decided by a judge or
jury. It is possible that a judge or jury might consider an
affectionate relationship between gays so improper as to
constitute undue influence.[41]

**What may be done to avoid any possible challenge to
such a will?**

Every possible step should be taken to provide evidence
that the will is the independent choice of the testator. The
testator should, for example, take care to consult an attorney with no business or other relationship with the proposed beneficiary. The testator should explain the matter
fully to the attorney. At a minimum, he should acquaint
the lawyer with the extent of his assets and the identity of
the relatives whom he is excluding from the will. The reason for this is that one of the prerequisites for establishing
competence to make a will is that the testator knew the
extent of his estate and the identity of the natural objects
of his bounty. The testator should ask his attorney to
make a memorandum of such information to provide evidence that it was considered by the testator at the time
that the will was made.

If a gay relationship is of long standing, the parties
might consider doing a new will periodically without de-
stroying the prior versions. The repetition will itself
provide evidence of the testator's seriousness of purpose,
and those interested in contesting the will may be deterred
by the fact that even if they are successful in contesting
the last will, they will also have to contest each of the
earlier versions.

**If a gay person fails to provide for another by will,
would the survivor have any recourse against the deceased's estate?**

No, unless such a right had been created by contract.

May an unmarried person recover damages for the wrongful death of another unmarried person?

No. Almost every state has provided by statute that a surviving spouse or other family member may recover damages from those responsible for the accidental death of a husband, wife, or child. No such right has been given to unmarried people.

May a gay person purchase life insurance and name anyone he or she prefers as beneficiary?

Yes. There are no legal restrictions on a gay person's purchasing life insurance and none on the persons whom she or he may designate as beneficiary. It has, however, been suggested that insurance companies may hesitate to issue policies to those who wish to name as beneficiaries those with whom the insureds have "meretricious" relationships. One solution that has been used is to purchase a policy naming the insured's estate as beneficiary, reserve the right to change the beneficiary, and thereafter change the beneficiary.

May gay persons purchase life insurance on each other?

In order to purchase life insurance, the applicant must have an "insurable interest" in the life of the person to be insured.[42] The rule is obviously intended to avoid inducements for homicide and to prevent unlawful wagering contracts. In New York, for example, the term "insurable interest" means (a) in the case of persons related closely by blood or law, a substantial interest engendered by love and affection and (b) in the case of other persons, a lawful and substantial economic interest in having the life, health, or bodily safety of the insured continue.[43] The statutes of other states are generally comparable.

Any question of insurable interest may be avoided by having the insured purchase the insurance on his own life, designating the other as beneficiary. If the insured wants to be certain that the insurance will not be taxed for estate-tax purposes upon death, he or she may assign ownership of the policy to the beneficiary. In this way, although the beneficiary may be forbidden to purchase the policy, he or she may ultimately obtain ownership. If the relationship between the insured and the beneficiary continues, the arrangement may be convenient for both.

Will the next of kin of the insured person have a right to contest the beneficiary designation in the same manner as they could contest a will?

No. Insurance policies are governed by the law of contracts and not by the laws pertaining to wills. An insurance policy is a contract between the insured and the company, whereby the company agrees to pay a third party the proceeds of the policy upon the death of the insured.

Are automobile insurance rates and homeowner's insurance rates higher for unmarried people?

Yes. Automobile insurers and home insurers use marital status as a premium-rating criterion. Single people generally are looked upon as poor risks by insurers, employers, landlords, and those who extend credit because they view single people as relatively unstable, pleasure-oriented, and rootless. Married people, on the other hand, are viewed as relatively stable, job-oriented, and nonmobile.

A survey of insurers was done by the Law Student Division of the ABA to ascertain the differences in rates for married and unmarried people.[44] It was found that automobile insurance may cost between 25 per cent more (for singles over 25) to 40 per cent more (for singles under 25) than for married people.[45] Many insurers refuse to sell homeowners' or tenants' insurance to singles living alone or together. If they do, the rates for singles are higher than for marrieds.[46]

What may be done about such unequal rates?

Very little now. Automobile insurers and homeowner insurers are private companies and, absent statute or administrative regulation, cannot be forced by the courts to treat all citizens evenhandedly. An effort is, however, now being made to compel the New York Commissioner of

Insurance to stop discriminatory practices by private insurers in the sale of insurance and extension of credit to women,[47] and comparable efforts could be made for unmarried persons.

May one gay person name another as a beneficiary of pension proceeds that are payable upon death?

Generally, yes. Pension plans are essentially insurance agreements for the payment of money upon retirement or death. The terms of pension plans vary widely. They are tailored to the needs of the group participating in the plan. It is not common for such plans to limit the persons who may be named as beneficiaries, although plans for state employees occasionally limit beneficiaries to family members.

Are unmarried people living together eligible for family rates in nongovernmental medical insurance plans such as Blue Cross and Blue Shield?

Generally, no. "Families" are usually defined as married people and their children.

What is the difference in federal-income-tax treatment between married persons and unmarried people living together and sharing expenses?

There are numerous differences in the ways in which married people and unmarried people are treated for purposes of federal taxation.[48] A bill is pending in Congress to eliminate those differences.[49] Under the Internal Revenue Code there are four separate tax schedules: married persons filing joint returns; heads of household; single persons; and married persons filing separate returns.[50] We have designated them in their order of desirability. Assuming the same taxable income, married persons filing joint returns will pay the least; heads of household will pay a little more; single persons will pay still more; and married persons filing separate returns will pay the most.

The schedules may, however, produce unexpected results. For example, if a husband has a taxable income of

$20,000, and his wife has no income, their income tax on a joint return would be $4,380. If, on the other hand, two gay persons live together, one of whom has earned $20,-000 and the other nothing, their income tax would be $5,-230. If, however, a husband and wife both work, and each has a taxable income of $10,000, for a combined income of $20,000, their total income tax on a joint return would be $4,380. If two gay persons each show taxable income of $10,000, their total income tax would be 4,180, or $200 less than the married couple.

Nonetheless, even if the tax rates are not necessarily unfair to unmarried persons, other provisions of the Internal Revenue Code are discriminatory. The inability of unmarried persons to file a joint return denies them the benefits of various other provisions of the Code. For example, if one person has capital gains, and the other person has capital losses, the two may be offset on a joint return, but not on two separate returns.

May a gay person file an income-tax return as a head of household?

Stated generally, a head of household is an individual who is not married at the close of the year and who maintains as his home a household that is also the residence of any person who is a dependent of the taxpayer.[51] There are many circumstances in which a gay person may properly file an income-tax return as a head of household, but your specific situation should be discussed with a qualified tax adviser.

Do unmarried persons suffer any disadvantages under the federal estate tax?

Yes. Up to one-half of a decedent's "adjusted gross estate"—the gross estate, less debts and expenses—passing to a surviving spouse is not subject to tax.[52] This is referred to as the "marital deduction." It is not available to single people. Additionally, a spouse may exclude up to $1,000 in interest income he or she receives from life-insurance proceeds.

Do unmarried persons suffer any disadvantages under the federal gift tax?

Yes. Any person may make a gift of $3,000 to any one person in any one year without gift taxes.[53] The Internal Revenue Code provides, however, that a spouse may consent that one-half of any gift made by the other spouse will be deemed to be made by the consenting spouse.[54] Thus, a husband may give $6,000 and if the wife consents, each will be deemed to have made a gift of $3,000, and neither will have to pay a gift tax. In addition, each person is entitled to a lifetime exemption of $30,000 for all gifts made over the annual $3,000 exemption.[55] Again, one spouse may consent that all gifts made by the other should be deemed to have been made one-half by him or her. As a result, a married person may, with the consent of his or her spouse, have a lifetime exemption of $60,000.

How may estate taxes be minimized when two unmarried persons live together and one wishes to leave property to the other upon death?

Various methods may be used, but you should consult a qualified tax adviser.

Are there any tax disadvantages under state law for unmarried persons?

The law of each state is different, but most states have provisions similar to the federal rules described above. The results of such provisions will generally also be similar to those described above.

Government

Are there government benefits that are available to married people but are denied to single people who are living together and sharing expenses?

Yes. Some federal and state government benefits such as health and medical insurance for the aged and unemployment insurance may only be collected by the person who qualifies for the benefit. There are, however, other programs such as Social Security, veterans' benefits, and some disability insurance in which benefits may be paid to certain family members after the insured's death. The law specifically excludes all others and even limits the instances in which family members may receive such benefits.[56]

May married persons living together who qualify financially participate in the Food Stamp Program?

Yes. The Food Stamp Program provides that any "household" that satisfies the financial criteria may qualify to receive food stamps to buy food at a fraction of the retail price.[57] The pertinent statute originally provided that a household could qualify only if all members of the household were related by blood or marriage. The limitation was evidently intended to discourage communes. The Supreme Court of the United States held in *United States* v. *Moreno*[58] that the limitation is impermissible because it is unrelated to the purpose for which the law was adopted—to provide food at relatively low cost for needy persons. Marital status is not necessarily related to need. The court found that unrelated persons may elect to live together and to pool their resources. It did not, however, hold that all discrimination on the basis of marital status is unconstitutional.

May a person be denied welfare on the basis of homosexuality?

No. For a full description of rights to receive welfare and food stamps, see the ACLU Handbook *The Rights of the Poor* in this series of books.

May a gay parent receive welfare?

A gay parent who has custody of his or her child may receive assistance from the state in which he or she resides under the Aid to Dependent Children (ADC) program.[59]

May the state deprive a gay parent of welfare for homosexual conduct?

No.[60]

Must the income of other adults in a household be taken into account in determining a family's financial need?

No. In determining need for ADC the state may not assume that a person who is not legally bound to support a child is in fact doing so. Accordingly, the income of other adults in a household may be disregarded in determining a family's need.[61]

May other adults in a household be eligible to receive welfare as part of a needy family?

Yes. If the adult is not self-supporting, and the parent of the children asserts that he or she is an "essential person" who contributes to the raising of the children, he or she may be eligible for welfare assistance.[62] If the adult later becomes self-supporting, the additional sums will stop. The welfare agency may not assume that the adult has become self-supporting; it must be proved.[63] If you are deprived of any of the rights described above, you are entitled to a hearing.[64] You should contact the local OEO, Community Legal Services, Legal Aid, or welfare lawyers group for help.

Should gay persons adopt one another? What are the financial benefits? What are the disadvantages?

Any person may adopt another with the consent of the person to be adopted, if he or she is an adult, and the consent of the natural living parents of the person to be adopted. Adoption should, however, be undertaken with caution, particularly if it is intended chiefly to take advantage of financial benefits that are available to families, but not to single persons living together. Such financial benefits may be relatively insignificant in amount. Some such benefits are available only to families in which the children are below the age of 18.[65] Thus, unless the adopted person is less than 18, no financial benefits at all may be obtained from the adoption. A parent's right to obtain government benefits in connection with an adopted child upon the child's death may also be limited by the courts. In *Craig* v. *Gardner*,[66] the court held that a person may not collect benefits pertaining to an adopted child if the adoption was made for the purpose of pecuniary gain.

The tax benefits of adoption may also be insignificant. The tax exemption of $750 for a child is available only if the "child" has earned less than $600.[67] Moreover, a parent and child may not file a joint return. A person who has adopted a child is, however, eligible to file a return as a head of household.

In addition, there may be substantial disadvantages to an adopting parent. An adopting parent is responsible for the financial support of the adopted person he or she adopts and may be guilty of incest in some states if he or she has sexual relations with the adopted child.[68]

May a gay couple benefit by entering into a partnership agreement?

It has been suggested that unmarried persons who live together and who work in related fields (such as a writer and an editor) might usefully enter into business-partnership agreements under which they could share expenses and obtain various tax deductions. Such agreements may, however, also create obligations that one or both of the parties may eventually find onerous, and before entering into any such agreement, you should consult an attorney.

Custody and Visitation Rights

The children produced of prior heterosexual relationships is presenting a thorny and frightening problem to more and more gay people as they decide to live openly as homosexuals. Given the homophobia in this society, the parents and grandparents of the children, the courts, and child-welfare agencies are all beginning to challenge the rights of gay people to maintain custody and visitation rights of their natural children because of the fear that a parent's homosexuality is detrimental to the children.

The problem faced by gay parents in maintaining their parental rights is obviously a new one because until recently very few parents admitted openly that they were gay. That is one reason why the legal precedent concerning these problems is very limited.

The right to child custody is simply the right of one parent or both parents to have their child or children live with them and be raised by them substantially all of the time. A parent's right to have custody of a child may only be terminated by an order from the judge of a family court.

The right to visitation is essentially the right of the parent who does not have custody to see the child for brief periods of time, most usually for weekends, two weeks' vacation, and holidays. The visitation rights of a parent are set down by family court order as well.

The discussion that follows will sketch out exactly when and how the challenge to gay parental rights may occur, what should be done if those rights are challenged, what the legal rights of gay parents are, and what they should be.

When may challenges to child custody arise?

Custody questions are most likely to arise at the time of divorce. Every divorce must be officially granted by order of a court. Customarily, when couples separate and divorce, the family court that entertains the divorce decides which parent will have custody of the children and what the visitation rights of the other parent will be.

A parent may confront challenges to custody even after custody has been awarded pursuant to court order. If one parent discovers that the other is gay only after the divorce and custody are granted, he or she may go back to the family court and seek custody of the children on the basis of the other's homosexuality.

No custody order is truly final. Juvenile and family courts are given very wide discretion to protect the children brought before them, and they have continuing authority until the children leave the jurisdiction or reach majority. If the court believes that it would be best to remove custody from the parent, it may do so at any time. Moreover, custody questions may be reopened in any state in which the children reside. If, for example, the original custody order was issued in New York, and the mother thereafter moves to Arizona, any suit by interested persons wishing to challenge custody on the basis of "changed circumstances" may do so in the Arizona courts. The Arizona court is not bound by the New York order, but it is unlikely to alter the order if it can be shown that there are no new circumstances that were unknown to the New York court at the time the order was issued.

What should a parent do if custody rights are challenged?

Obtain the help of a lawyer. You are entitled to a hearing to determine whether you should have custody of your children. Some courts insist that you must be represented by a lawyer at such hearings and will appoint a lawyer if you cannot afford one. If the court does not appoint a lawyer, you are still entitled to have one at the hearing. If you cannot afford a lawyer, consult a local legal-aid society, community legal-services office, or other law groups that provide free legal services. Be certain that the lawyer is sympathetic to the rights of gay parents to have custody of their children. You can contact a local gay organization, listed in Appendix 6, for the names of lawyers who have handled such cases before or are sympathetic to the issue. It is important to be open with your lawyer about the fact that you are gay so that you may explore the lawyer's feelings about your right to custody and also so that the lawyer will be prepared to defend your rights. If the lawyer has never defended such a case before, you should encourage him or her to contact the ACLU Sexual Privacy Project or a local gay organization for advice as to how best to handle such cases. Unfortunately, neither the ACLU Sexual Privacy Project nor the local ACLU affiliates can represent every gay parent in every custody and visitation case. The ACLU can take only a limited number of test cases to help establish legal authorities for those rights.

Have the courts upheld the rights of gays to have custody of their children?

Some have, and some have not. Many cases are settled

prior to trial. Only a small number of cases have actually gone to trial, and even fewer have been officially reported. Moreover, every family court has the option of sealing records and decisions concerning juveniles in order to protect the children, and the records in many cases may as a result not be available. If you have been involved in a custody case that has been decided but not reported, you should contact the ACLU Sexual Privacy Project to make it available for use in subsequent cases.

What have been the decisions in the adjudicated cases?

There are four cases in which custody was removed from lesbian mothers.[69] Two were in California, one in Oregon, and one in Georgia. In one of the cases, *Nadler* v. *Superior Court of California,* the California court of appeals reversed a decision of a family court that found against the mother. The appellate court returned the case to the family court, holding that a mother is not unfit simply because she is gay. It must be proved that the mother's homosexuality is detrimental to the best interests of the child. Nonetheless, custody was ultimately lost by the mother.

In a Georgia case, the court gave custody of a child to grandparents because the child was exposed to the mother who was having sexual relations with members of her own sex. There was testimony by a psychiatrist that the child was well adjusted, properly cared for, and exposed to much love and affection. A dissenting opinion argued that the decision displayed narrow-minded morality and ignored the rights of natural parents to raise children in the manner they see fit as long as the child is not in danger of physical abuse and mistreatment. In an Oregon case, a father was given custody rights, and the lesbian mother was given visitation rights. A harsh result was reached in another California case; the children were put in foster homes. A gay father who is a political activist had his visitation limited in New Jersey in *In the Matter of S.S. and C.* The case is being appealed.

There are six cases in which custody has been awarded to a lesbian mother.[70] The first important favorable decision came in a Michigan case; the court awarded custody of six children to two lesbian mothers who were living together. The court found that the private sexual relationship of the mothers did not detrimentally affect the children. It was the first reported case in which a court awarded custody to a gay couple and allowed them to continue to live together. In *Schuster* v. *Schuster* and *Isaacson* v. *Isaacson*, a Washington family court granted custody to lesbians on the condition that they not live together. On appeal, the Court granted full custody to the lesbian women and allowed them to live together. This was despite the mother's political activism and the publicity surrounding the children. In *Mitchell* v. *Mitchell*, a California court granted custody to a mother on the condition that she no longer associate with her lover. The case is also on appeal. In *Spence* v. *Durham*, a North Carolina court removed custody of children from their grandparents and gave it to the mother on the belief that she had "reformed" and was no longer a lesbian. In *A* v. *A*, an Oregon Supreme Court allowed a homosexual father to retain custody of his two sons because there was no proof of substantial harm to the welfare of the boys. However, the custody was granted on the condition that the family court supervise the custody. In *Hall* v. *Hall*, an Ohio court granted custody to a lesbian mother who is living with her lover.

What is the law that should be followed at a custody hearing?

In the leading case, *Stanley* v. *Illinois*,[71] involving the right of an unwed father to have custody of his children, the United States Supreme Court found that the right to the care, custody, and management of one's child is an important right, protected by the due-process clause that may not be denied without having a fair hearing that satisfies the requisites of due process. The court also held that there may not be conclusive presumptions in child-custody matters, and that it is impermissible to presume as a matter of law that all unwed fathers are incompetent parents. Similarly, although the court has not explicitly so held, it should be impermissible to presume that all lesbian mothers or gay fathers are unfit parents.

There is, however, a presumption that natural parents are fit parents, where the state seeks to take custody of the children for foster-care placement. It should follow that the burden is on the challenging person or state to show precisely how the homosexuality of the parent will detrimentally affect the child. Nonetheless, as a practical matter, the burden is largely on the gay parent to demonstrate that homosexuality is not detrimental to the children. Many judges continue to believe that children will be embarrassed or suffer emotional injury because of homosexual parents.

It may be useful in custody cases if the children and parents are examined by a qualified psychiatrist or psychologist. If possible, this should be done with the consent of the court prior to the hearing. The psychiatrist may be able to testify at the hearing that the parent is a stable and good parent and that the children will not be adversely affected by exposure to a homosexual parent or the parent's lover.

A common question asked of doctors at the hearing will be whether it seems likely that the child will be a homosexual if he or she continues to live or visit with the gay parent (which the court ordinarily would find to be a negative result, given society's disapproval). Also the doctor will be asked whether the child is overly anxious about the parent's homosexuality in terms of being embarrassed or distressed by it. Finally, in the most ignorant of situations the doctor will probably be asked whether the child will be molested by either the parent or the parent's gay friends.

All of these questions may be answered favorably for the gay parent by the examining doctor. However, there are certain doctors who are more expert than others on the questions of the developments of children's sexual orientation and the adjustments the children make to their parents' homosexuality. These doctors believe that a child's sexual orientation is determined by age 4½ to 6 and that exposure to homosexual parents will not influence that de-

velopment after that age. Prior to that age, it is believed
that there are innumerable environmental as well as
physiological (in certain instances) causes for homosexual
orientation. Having homosexual parents is certainly not a
conclusive nor even a primary contributing reason, for homosexual orientation. It is also commonly believed by
many experts and by homosexuals that homosexual orientation is almost impossible to reverse. Therefore, exposure
to gay parents would not impede such a reversal. It would
simply make a gay child more adjusted to his or her sexuality by seeing an adult homosexual who can lead a
happy normal life.

You should try to have a doctor who actually has done
research and study in this area to be the examining psychiatrist. Because it is obvious that these witnesses cannot be
present at every trial, other doctors who are familiar with
and who ascribe to these beliefs should be contacted. A
list of such expert witnesses is being compiled by local gay
organizations and especially lesbian organizations. It is
well known that we can fill huge libraries with what we
don't know about human sexuality. Therefore, it is not
surprising that no research has been done to date on the
effects of lesbian mothers or gay fathers on their children.
An attempt is being made by doctors to fund a research
project of this sort to provide conclusive evidence for
court custody battles. However, such research will take a
long time, and in the meanwhile we must rely on the research and theories of a few informed doctors.

The myth about homosexuals molesting children, however, has been researched, and it has been proved that it is
less likely for gay men to molest children than heterosexuals and even less likely for lesbian women to do so.[72]

It is certainly possible that because of the overwhelming
positive reinforcement and importance put on heterosex-
uality in this society, children will be embarrassed by their
parents' homosexuality. However, if a balancing test is
done, it may be shown that it would be more of a trauma
for the child to be separated from its parent and be deprived of the parent's love and affection than be embarrassed by the parents' homosexuality. Many doctors

believe that it is in the best interests of the child not to be separated from either parent's love (especially at a young age) because that trauma is most long lasting. It is unlikely that the child will be completely disassociated from the gay parent in any case; therefore, the embarrassment might come at a later time, even if the child is separated from its parent.

Is there a right for you to live with your gay lover while you have custody of your children or your children are visiting you?

As noted eariler, permission to do so was granted in only three known gay custody cases, in *State* v. *Brown*, *Schuster* v. *Schuster*, *Isaacson* v. *Isaacson*, and *Hall* v. *Hall*. An argument may be made that the right of privacy guarantees you the right to cohabit with whomever you desire as long as it cannot be shown that such a living arrangement is detrimental to your children. Therefore, the challenging party should be prepared to show how the living arrangement will be detrimental before your right of privacy may be invaded.

In the state of California an argument may be made that homosexuals are being denied equal protection of the laws if they are not allowed to cohabit with a lover when having their children with them. In a recent California decision, *In re the marriage of Russo and Russo*,[73] the Court of Appeals reversed a lower court ruling that had removed a child from its home and held that a mother's admitted indiscretion (cohabiting with a young man) did not necessitate changing custody since the child was well adjusted and content. The denial of equal protection may be claimed in any state in which a similar decision has been reached concerning heterosexual parents and their children.

Are you compelled to testify about the details of your sexual activities?

In custody cases the court is entitled to have information regarding all aspects of the parents' behavior in order to ascertain whether such behavior is in the best interests of the child. Despite the latitude given family courts in collecting such information, you may be protected from providing detailed information regarding your sexual activities. First, if sodomy is a crime in the state in which you reside, you may be able to refuse to answer any questions about your sexual activity on the grounds that it might incriminate you. Second, the constitutional right of privacy prevents inquiries into private sexual activities unless there is a compelling state interest to do so. The right of sexual privacy is a fundamental right that the government may not deny without such a state interest.[74] Third, you should not be compelled to answer questions concerning your private sexual activities unless the state or the challenging person first shows how those activities may affect the welfare of your child. Similarly, in employment cases, a number of courts have refused to allow the state to deny employment or to ask intimate questions of homosexuals unless it is first shown that there is some rational nexus between private sexual activities and the ability to perform the job.[75]

What are the constitutional arguments that may be asserted to gain custody for gay parents?

The right of parents to raise their children has been deemed by the Supreme Court to be "essential,"[76] a "basic civil [right],"[77] and "far more precious ... than property rights."[78] Rights protected by the due-process clause may be abridged by governmental action only if such interference is reasonably related to a legitimate state purpose.[79] The only legitimate justification the state may have for interfering with the parent-child relationship is to protect the welfare of the child. If the state attempts to remove a child from the home because of parental conduct, it has the burden of proving that the conduct renders the parent "so unfit as to endanger the child's welfare."[80]

The state's removal of custody may also constitute an unjustifiable invasion of a parent's constitutionally protected right of privacy,[81] whether that right is derived from the Ninth Amendment to the Constitution,[82] from the "penumbras" of the First, Third, Fourth, Fifth, and Ninth

Amendments,[83] or from the "liberty" protected by the
Fourteenth Amendment.[84] The state may be argued to violate a parent's right to privacy if it makes private sexual
conduct the focus of a dependency hearing without a
demonstration that such conduct adversely affects the children. Moreover, it has been held that association with persons within the home is an activity constitutionally protected by the right to privacy.[85] One court has stated that "official inquiry into a person's private sexual habits does violence to his constitutionally protected zone of privacy."[86]
Even if a state agency is legally empowered to investigate
private conduct, it may not expand the scope of its inquiry
so that it unnecessarily intrudes into a person's private
life.[87]

Adoption and Foster Care

May a gay person adopt a child?

The laws of several states permit a single person to be
an adoptive parent, and such laws do not expressly prohibit adoption by gays. Adoption of children by gays is,
however, still controversial. The court must find that the
best interests of the child will be served by the adoption.
If the question of fitness arises, the gay person should insist that a hearing be held on the question. Expert psychiatric testimony should be obtained, and a psychiatric evaluation of the child should be made to determine whether
the homosexuality of the potential parent would have any
adverse effect on the child.

May a gay person qualify as a foster parent?

In a number of states such as New York and Washington, there have been recent efforts to permit gay people to
become foster parents to children who are gay in orientation. Some gay organizations have been working with child
welfare and placement agencies to permit such arrangements. Check with your local gay organization or child-
welfare agency for information.

NOTES

1. See M. Wetherbee, *Same Sex Singles and the Right to Marry via Statutory Interpretation and Evolving Equal Protection* (1972), for a discussion of these loopholes and state-by-state citations to the marriage laws.
2. *E.g.,* Minn. Stat. Ann. § 517.08.
3. *E.g.,* Minn. Stat. Ann. § 517.18.
4. California Civil Code § 4213.
5. *Reynolds* v. *United States,* 98 U.S. 244 (1879).
6. *Baker* v. *Nelson,* 291 Minn. 310, 191 N.W. 2d 185 (Minn. Sup. Ct. 1971)
7. *Knight and Jones* v. *Hallahan,* Ky. (Ky. Ct. of Appeals, Nov. 9, 1973).
8. *Singer* v. *Hara,* 1879-I, Ct. of App. of Wash. (June, 1974).
9. Any contract that would have been void *ab initio* if performed in a state or country does not have to be recognized by the state or country.
10. *See generally* "The Legality of Homosexual Marriage," 82 *Yale L.J.* 573 (1973).
11. The First Amendment, as construed by the Supreme Court, includes a number of other rights, among them the right to engage in free and private associations. *Williams* v. *Rhodes,* 393 U.S. (1968); *NAACP* v. *Alabama,* 357 U.S. 449 (1958). Most right of association cases to date have dealt with association for political purposes, although in *Griswold* v. *Connecticut,* 381 U.S. 479, 484 (1965), Justice Douglas refers to marriage as an "association."
12. *Griswold* v. *Connecticut,* 381 U.S. 479 (1965); *Eisenstadt* v. *Baird,* 405 U.S. 438 (1972).
13. *Roe* v. *Wade,* 410 U.S. 113 (1973).
14. Walter Barnett, *Sexual Freedom and the Constitution,* Albuquerque: Univ. of New Mexico Press (1973).
15. *Loving* v. *Virginia,* 388 U.S. 1 (1967).
16. Note, "Developments in the Law—Equal Protection," 82 Harv. L. Rev. 1065 (1969); Karst, "Invidious Discrimination: Justice Douglas and the Return of the Natural Law—Due Process Formula," 16 *U.C.L.A. L. Rev.* 716, 739–46 (1969).
17. *Frontiero* v. *Richardson,* 411 U.S. 677 (1973).
18. Resolution of the American Psychiatric Association issued December 15, 1973.
19. A. Karlen, *Sexuality and Homosexuality,* New York: W.W. Norton (1971) 572–606; Report of the Committee on Homosexual Offenses and Prostitution 17, 25-30 (1957) [Wolfenden Report].
20. Barnett, *Sexual Freedom and the Constitution, supra* note 5.

21. *Loving* v. *Virginia, supra,* note 6.
22. *In re Greenleaf's Estate,* 169 Kan. 22, 217 P. 2d 275 (1950); *Troha* v. *Sneller,* 169 Ohio St. 397, 159 N.E. 2d 899 (1959).
23. *In re Moorehead's Estate,* 289 Pa. 542, 137 A. 802 (1927); *Fricke* v. *Fricke,* 257 Wis. 124, 42 N.W.2d 500 (1950).
24. *Otis* v. *Spencer,* 102 Ill. 622, 630 (1882).
25. *Rice* v. *Gove,* 22 Pick. (Mass.) 158 (1839).
26. *Frank* v. *Carter,* 219 N.Y. 35, 113 N.E. 549 (1916).
27. *Wansmaker* v. *Weaver,* 176 N.Y. 75, 68 N.E. 135 (1903).
28. II *American Law of Property,* Part 6, Chapter II.
29. *Id.,* Part 6, Chapter I.
30. *Id.,* Part 6, Chapter III.
31. *Id.,* Part 7.
32. *See, e.g.,* New York Estates, Powers and Trusts Laws, § 4-1.1.
33. *Delafield* v. *Parish,* 25 N.Y. 9 (1862).
34. *Irvine* v. *Greenway,* 220 Ky. 388, 295 S.W. 445 (1927).
35. *Marx* v. *McGlynn,* 88 N.Y. 371 (1882).
36. *Jones' Estate,* 18 D. & C. 2d 581 (Pa.) (1959).
37. *Marx* v. *McGlynn, supra.*
38. *Matter of Brand,* 185 App. Div. 139, 173 N.Y.S. 169 (1918); *Matter of Dunn,* 184 App. Div. 393, 171 N.Y.S. 1056.
39. *Matter of Fleischmann,* 176 App. Div. 788, 163 N.Y.S. 426 (1917); *Matter of Jeffrey,* 129 App. Div. 792, 114 N.Y.S. 667.
40. *Matter of Brand, supra.*
41. *See, Matter of Kauffman,* 14 App. Div. 2d 411, 221 N.Y.S. 2d 601 (1961); 20 App. Div. 2d 464, 247 N.Y.S. 2d 664 (1964); *aff'd* 15 N.Y. 2d 825, 257 N.Y.S.2d 941, 205 N.E.2d 864 (1965).
42. *Cross* v. *National Fire Ins. Co.,* 132 N.Y. 133, 30 N.E. 390.
43. New York Insurance Law, § 146(2).
44. Coleman, *Unmarried Person's Bill of Rights,* Report to the Law Student Division of the American Bar Association (Jan. 1973).
45. *Id.* at 9.
46. *Id.* at 10.
47. *Gilpin, et al* v. *Schenck, Superintendent of Insurance of State of New York* (S.D.N.Y., filed January 24, 1974).
48. *See generally,* Richards, *Single* v. *Married Income Tax Returns under the Tax Reform Act of 1969,* 48 Taxes 301 (1970).
49. H.R. 2701, S.650 Sponsors Sen. R. Packwood (R. Oregon), Sen. J. Tower (R. Texas).
50. Internal Revenue Code § 1.

51. *Id.* at § 2 (b); See, IRS Form 1040—Filing Status § § 2b & 5b for head of household deductions that may be applicable to two gays living together.
52. *Id.* at § 2056.
53. *Id.* at § 2503(b).
54. *Id.* at § 2513.
55. *Id.* at § 2521.
56. *See generally The Catalogue for Federal Domestic Assistance* (Office of Management and Budget, Washington, D.C.) (7th ed. 1973), for a guide to what federal benefits are available.
57. 42 U.S.C. § 402; 42 U.S.C. § 417; 42 U.S.C. §§ 501-03; 42 U.S.C. §§ 601-10; 7 U.S.C. § 2012(e); 42 U.S.C. §§ 381, 1351 *et seq.*; 7 U.S.C. § 2012(e) (3) (e).
58. 413 U.S. 528 (1973).
59. 42 U.S.C. §§ 601–10.
60. *King* v. *Smith,* 392 U.S. 309 (1968).
61. *Lewis* v. *Martin,* 397 U.S. 552 (1970).
62. *Solman* v. *Shapiro,* 300 F. Supp 409 (D. Conn.) *aff'd,* 369 U.S. 5 (1969).
63. *Fhurley* v. *Vanlore,* 365 F. Supp. 186 (1973).
64. *Goldberg* v. *Kelly,* 397 U.S. 254 (1970).
65. 42 U.S.C. § 402(d).
66. *Craig* v. *Gardner,* 299 F. Supp. 247 (D.C. Tex.) (1969).
67. Internal Revenue Code § 151.
68. For example, in Illinois (S.H.A. Ch. 38, § 11-10); Pennsylvania (18 C.T.S.A., § 4302); North Carolina (Gen. St. N.C. § 14-178); Texas (Tex. C. Ann. Fam. Code § 2.21); New Hampshire and Mississippi sexual relations between adopted child and parent are considered to be incest.
69. *Nadler* v. *Supreme Court,* 255 Cal. App.3d 1045, 100 Cal. Rptr.; *Bennett* v. *Clemens,* 196 S.E.2d 842 (S.C. Ga. 1973); *Hoffower* v. *Hoffower,* No. 376-144 (Oregon) Cir. Ct. of Ore., 4th Judicial Dist.; *In re Tammy F,* L.A. Ct. of Appeals, First App. Dist., Div. Two, No. 1 Civ. 32648.
70. *Spence* v. *Durham,* 198 S.E. 2d 537 (1973), *Schuster* v. *Schuster,* No. D36868, Supr. Ct. Washington for King County (Dec. 22, 1972); *Isaacson* v. *Isaacson,* No. D36867, Supr. Ct. Washington for King County, (Dec. 22, 1972); *People* v. *Brown,* 49 Mich. App. 358 (1973); *Mitchell* v. *Mitchell,* Supr. Ct. of California, Santa Clara County; *A* v. *A,* 514 P.2d 358 (Ore. App. 1973); *Hall* v. *Hall,* No. 55900 Ct. of Common Pleas, Licking County, Ohio (Aug. 1974).
71. *Stanley* v. *Illinois,* 405 U.S. 645 (1972).
72. P. Gebhard, J. Gagnon, W. Pomeroy and C. Christensen, *Sex Offenders* (1965), De Francis, *Protecting the Child Victim of Sex Crimes by Adults* (1969).

73. *In re the Marriage of Russo and Russo,* 1 civ. 2888, Div.
    1, 1st App. Dist. (Nov. 11, 1971).
74. *Roe* v. *Wade,* 410 U.S. 113 (1973).
75. *Norton* v. *Macy,* 417 F.2d 1161 (D.C. Cir. 1969).
76. *Meyer* v. *Nebraska,* 262 U.S. 390 (1923).
77. *Skinner* v. *Oklahoma,* 316 U.S. 535 (1942).
78. *May* v. *Anderson,* 345 U.S. 528 (1953).
79. *Pierce* v. *Society of Sisters,* 268 U.S. 510 (1924); *Meyer*
    v. *Nebraska,* 262 U.S. 390 (1923).
80. *Washburn* v. *Washburn,* 49 Cal. App. 2d 581, 588, 122
    P.2d 96, 100 (1942).
81. *Griswold* v. *Connecticut, supra.*
82. *Id.* at 486-89 (Goldberg, J. concurring).
83. Id. at 484 (Douglas, J.).
84. Id. at 499-502 (Harlan, J., concurring).
85. *Fisher* v. *Snyder,* 346 F. Supp. 396 (D. Neb. 1972).
86. *In re Labady,* 326 F. Supp. 924, 927 (S.D.N.Y. 1971).
87. *Eisenstadt* v. *Baird,* 405 U.S. 438 (1972).

IX

Gays and the Criminal Law

It is too little understood, even at this late date, that there is absolutely nothing unlawful in being a homosexual. Homosexuality, defined as the condition of being sexually and emotionally oriented primarily toward persons of the same sex, is a status or condition of being. As such, it cannot constitutionally be made a crime.[1]

Homosexual orientation, just as heterosexual orientation, may or may not lead to specific sexual acts, and at least one court has recognized that there is no basis for the assumption that homosexuals are predisposed to commit a prohibited sexual act.[2] Further, in almost every state that still makes certain types of sexual conduct illegal, there are nonetheless various sexual acts that can be lawfully engaged in between members of the same sex. In seven states, any form of private sexual conduct between consenting adults of the same sex is lawful.

Some courts, however, continue to indulge the popular myth that "in order to be a homosexual, the prohibited [i.e., illegal] act must have at some time been committed or at least presently contemplated,"[3] and it is still probably true that despite some significant advances in gay rights in recent years, the popular mind thinks of gay people as necessarily being in violation of the law.

While this assumption is not an accurate one, it is nevertheless true that the laws of most states still criminalize many of the specific sexual acts that can be engaged in between persons of the same sex. (See Appendix 1, which has a compilation of all the laws by state, applicable to adult gay sexual activities). Of course, most of these laws also penalize the same conduct when it occurs between members of the opposite sex, but the generalized

societal stigma for engaging in such acts does not attach
to straights as it does to gays, nor do straights suffer the
discrimination that flows from the popular presumption
that gay people are in violation of these provisions.

In addition to provisions concerning sexual conduct,
there are other provisions of the criminal laws that are often enforced against gays, such as loitering and solicitation
laws and sex-offender registration requirements, which will
also be discussed in this chapter.

**Do legal authorities believe that consensual sexual con-
duct in private between adults should be criminalized?**

No, quite the contrary. In 1955 the Model Penal Code,
a proposed penal code recommended to the states by the
prestigious group of legal scholars of the American Law
Institute, recommended that all sexual practices not involving force, adult activity with minors, or public conduct
be excluded from the criminal law.[4] In 1957, a specially
appointed study committee in Great Britain issued a report, known as the Wolfenden Report, recommending that
private adult homosexual conduct be decriminalized.[5] In
1973, the American Bar Association passed a resolution
urging the states to repeal all laws that made criminal any
form of consenting sexual conduct between adults in
private.[6]

**Have any states followed the recommendations of these
legal authorities and removed criminal penalties for private consensual sexual activity between adults?**

Yes. Eight states have repealed their consensual sodomy laws. Those states are California*, Colorado, Connecticut, Delaware, Hawaii, Illinois, Ohio, and Oregon.
The Supreme Court of Florida has declared that state's
sodomy law unconstitutional.[7] Florida still, however, has a
prohibition against "unnatural and lascivious acts with
another person,"[8] which has been interpreted to cover acts
formerly prohibited by the sodomy provision.[9] The Massachusetts Supreme Court has ruled that a statute prohibiting
unnatural and lascivious acts that had been used to prose-

*Effective January, 1976.

cute acts of sodomy and oral copulation does not apply to
private sexual conduct between consenting adults.[10]

**What type of sexual conduct between gay persons is
permitted in the seven states that have repealed their sodomy laws?**

Any form of private consensual sexual conduct among
adults is permitted in these states, including oral or anal
intercourse.

**Is sexual conduct in public places legal in the states that
have repealed their consensual sodomy statutes?**

No. Persons engaging in consensual sexual conduct in
public places in these states are still subject to arrest under
other general statutes prohibiting lewd, indecent, or disorderly conduct in public places.

**In the 42 states that have not repealed the prohibitions
against consensual sodomy, what type of private consensual sexual activity is legal between gay people.**

In almost all of these states, both oral and anal intercourse are prohibited, either under the wording of the
statutes themselves, or as they have been interpreted by
the courts. In Maine, however, it has been held that anal
penetration must be shown to convict.[11]

The statutes prohibiting sodomy generally do not prohibit other acts of mutual sexual gratification such as
mutual masturbation, and such acts would be legal in these
states either between persons of the same or the opposite
sex. In Indiana, however, the statute itself prohibits aiding
any person under 21 to commit masturbation,[12] and the
general language of the statute has been held to prohibit
any "unnatural" sexual gratification that tends to corrupt
the morals.[13]

Also, a few states, such as Maryland, have statutes in
addition to the sodomy statutes that prohibit "unnatural or
perverted sexual practices."[14]

Such provisions, while arguably unconstitutional, could,
at this stage in the development of the law on gay rights,
probably still be used to arrest gay people for any form of

mutual sexual activity. What you should do if arrested for violating any of these statutes will be discussed later in this chapter.

Under what types of statutes are gay people subject to being arrested for activities in public places?

Generally, there are three classes of statutes under which gay people are arrested for activities in public: sodomy statutes or other statutes dealing with sexual conduct; statutes prohibiting solicitation for prohibited sexual conduct; and loitering or disorderly-conduct statutes.

Sexual conduct in public, whether between gays or straights, is illegal. While straights who are apprehended engaging in sexual activity in public will often be charged with disorderly conduct or lewd behavior and may frequently escape with just a warning, gays are likely to be charged, in addition to disorderly conduct, with violation of sodomy statutes in the 43 states retaining those statutes if their conduct comes within the particular statute.

What do solicitation statutes prohibit?

Some states and municipalities have statutes or ordinances that prohibit solicitation of—that is, requesting another person to engage in—conduct that is itself prohibited by law. Thus, where prostitution is illegal, solicitation for prostitution is also usually prohibited.

With respect to gay people, solicitation for the purposes of engaging in sexual conduct prohibited by statute is often made a crime. See Appendix 1 for a compilation of these laws in the various states.

Do solicitation laws exist in states that have repealed prohibitions on consensual sodomy?

Some of the seven states that have decriminalized consensual sodomy nevertheless retain statutes prohibiting solicitation for such acts. These statutes are subject to legal attacks on the grounds that where the conduct itself is legal, it cannot be illegal to ask someone to participate in it.

What are loitering statutes?

Loitering statutes generally prohibit being or remaining

in a public place for no apparent purpose or being in a place for an illegal purpose. Such statutes are subject to legal attack as too vague to inform a person of what conduct is prohibited where they fall into the first category— prohibiting loitering for no apparent purpose.[15] Where they fall into the second category, such as New York's prohibition on loitering for the purpose of "deviate sexual intercourse,"[16] the prosecutor must be able to prove that you were loitering for the illegal purpose.

Even if the case cannot ultimately be proved, however, gay people are still harassed by being arrested under such statutes, frequently in popular cruising places.

What should a gay person do who is arrested for an offense related to gay activity?

He should not resist arrest, but he should also not volunteer any information or admit to any conduct to the arresting officer or other police officers who may question him about what he was doing. You are not required to give any information other than your name and address. You should refuse to discuss the case further until you have had a chance to talk to a lawyer. If you do not know one who you could talk to about such a case, you should contact either a local or state gay organization or the local or state branch of the ACLU for assistance, or a legal aid or public defender's office.

If charged with an offense related to gay sexual conduct, should you ever agree to plead guilty to a lesser offense such as disorderly conduct?

The question of whether to ever agree to "cop a plea," that is, to agree to enter a guilty plea to a lesser offense if offered by the prosecutor or the court in order to avoid a trial and possible conviction on a greater offense, is always a decision that can only be made after the client and his lawyer have carefully evaluated all the facts, including not just the charge itself and the likelihood or not of a conviction, but also such things as the possible effect of various dispositions of the case on one's employment or occupational status. If one is innocent and the arrest is groundless, the decision becomes even more difficult because one never is happy to accept any conviction that is not justified. The question is usually one of proof, and even if one is innocent, he must consider whether a dishonest police officer, for example, would be likely to lie about what he actually saw in order to obtain a conviction, and whether the judge or jury would be likely to accept the police officer's version of the facts.

Of course, even if one is guilty of violating a particular statute, but wishes to contest the constitutionality of the statute, he could only do this by pleading not guilty on the grounds that the statute is unconstitutional. This would most likely be seriously considered in cases in which the sodomy statutes are involved, as these statutes will be challenged more and more frequently in the next few years on the grounds of invasion of privacy, denial of equal protection, and vagueness, although when *public* conduct is involved, such challenges are not likely to be successful. But constitutional challenges are also possible to solicitation and loitering statutes, particularly in states in which the underlying conduct for which one solicits or loiters is itself legal. Such a challenge case may, however, involve publicity and may also result in a conviction if it is unsuccessful. One contemplating such a challenge must be willing to accept these possible consequences.

What are some of the factors one should consider in determining whether to agree to a guilty plea to a lesser offense?

The primary thing one must consider is the type of record that would be established by a conviction on the original charge and what effect such a record might have on one's future, as opposed to the type of record that would be created by a plea to a lesser offense, and the likelihood of a conviction on the original charge.

Other factors are whether one has any previous arrests on the same or other charges and how a judge is likely to view them; what penalties are possible on each charge; what publicity might be involved in defending the original charge, and what effect it would have on you; and what the time involved in defending against the charge would be.

A key consideration is whether or not one is a member of a licensed trade or profession and what the effect of the possible alternate dispositions would be on one's license. In some states, for example, sodomy is classified as a felony, and conviction of a felony in some licensed professions can mean loss or suspension of one's license. In such a case, one should consider carefully with one's attorney the likelihood of conviction, and if it seems likely, acceptance of a profferred misdemeanor charge may be the wisest course.

Similarly, some licenses may be revoked or suspended as a result of conviction of an offense involving "moral turpitude." In such a case, the classification of a crime as a felony or misdemeanor is less important than whether it could be construed as one involving moral turpitude. Thus, if one is arrested for soliciting homosexual conduct, in the current state of things, a licensing body may well try to construe this as an offense involving moral turpitude. The possibility is considerably lessened by cases holding that engaging in homosexual conduct does not, for example, make one unfit to obtain a license to practice law[17] or to be a teacher,[18] but these more tolerant views are not yet universally adopted. Thus, when one is charged with, for example, soliciting for homosexual conduct and offered a chance to plead guilty to a charge of, for example, disorderly conduct, an offense with no sexual connotations, the above factors should be considered. Also to be considered is whether a conviction under a particular charge would require registration under "sex offender" statutes in jurisdictions that have them, such as California.

If you decide to contest a charge and plead not guilty, should you seek a jury trial?

This will depend on an evaluation of the facts and the charge by you and your lawyer, a consideration of what is known about the attitudes of the judge likely to try the case, and a consideration of the attitudes toward gay peo-

ple of members of the local community from which jurors
would come. If a jury trial is chosen, prospective jurors
should be questioned by the defense attorney (in jurisdictions in which this is permitted) to determine their attitudes toward gay people. Jurors who reveal prejudice
should be challenged for cause.

**If you win your case, or if charges against you are dis-
missed, can you remove the record of your arrest?**

Some states have specific statutory provisions for obtaining any fingerprints and photographs made if charges
are dismissed or if you are acquitted. Some states have
provisions for "expunging" or removing an arrest record.
Even when there are no specific statutory provisions for
such relief, however, courts are sometimes willing to order
a record expunged after a dismissal or acquittal upon motion by the defendant. The possibility should be discussed
with your attorney.

**What should you do if someone attempts to blackmail
you because you are gay or because you engaged in gay
sexual activity?**

If you do not know a lawyer you can discuss it with,
contact the local gay organization or ACLU branch. They
will often have opened channels of communication with
the police department that would make reporting of any
such attempt easier. Stall the would-be blackmailer for
time until you can contact one of the above groups and
arrange to contact the police. It is almost never advan-
tageous to pay off since the demands frequently simply
continue and even increase.

NOTES

1. *See Robinson* v. *California,* 370 U.S. 660 (1962). *One Eleven W. & L., Inc.* v. *Division of Alcoholic Beverage Control,* 50 N.S. 329, 235 A.2d 12 (1917); *Rittenour* v. *District of Columbia,* 163 A.2d 558 (D.C. Mun. App. 1960). See also Report of the Committee on Homosexual Offenses and Prostitution Presented to Parliament by the Secretary of State for the Home Department and the Secretary of State for Scotland by Command of Her Majesty, ¶18 (1957) (hereinafter "The Wolfenden Report").
2. *People* v. *Giani,* 145 C.A.2d 539, 302 P.2d 813 (1956).
3. *Gay Activists Alliance* v. *Lomenzo,* 66 Misc.2d 456, 320 N.Y.S. 2d 994, 997 (S.Ct. Albany Co. 1971), *rev'd* 38 A.D.2d 981, 329 N.Y.S. 2d 181 (3rd Dep't 1972), *aff'd* 31 N.Y.2d 965, 341 N.Y.S.2d 108 (1973).
4. Model Penal Code, Sec. 207.5(1) Comment (Tent. Draft No. 4 1955).
5. The Wolfenden Report, *supra* note 1.
6. 42 U.S.L.W. 2098 (August 14, 1973).
7. *Franklin* v. *State,* 257 So.2d 21 (Fla. 1971).
8. Fla. Stat. Ann. §800.02.
9. *Franklin* v. *State, supra* note 7.
10. *Commonwealth* v. *Balthazar,* 318 N.E. 2d 478 (Mass. S. Ct. 1974).
11. *State* v. *Viles,* 161 Me. 28, 206 A.2d 539 (1965).
12. Ind. Stat. Ann. § 10-4221 (1956).
13. *Young* v. *State,* 194 Ind. 221, 141 N.E. 309 (1923).
14. Md. Ann. Code Art. 17 §554 (1971).
15. *People* v. *Berck,* 32 N.Y.2d 567, 347 N.Y.S.2d 33, 300 N.E. 2d 411 (1973).
16. N.Y. Penal Law §240.35 (3) (McKinney's 1967).
17. Matter of Kimball, 33 N.Y.2d 586, 347 N.Y.S.2d (1973).
18. *Morrison* v. *State Board of Education,* 1 Cal. 3d 214, 461 P.2d 375, 82 Cal. Rptr. 175 (1969). *See also, Burton* v. *Cascade School District,* 5-12 F. 2d 8-50 (9th Cir. 1975).

X

The Rights of Transvestites and Transsexuals

Although transvestites and transsexuals are often not homosexual in orientation, it is appropriate that a chapter regarding the problems of such persons be included in a book on gay rights since the legal and factual issues are closely related.

What do the terms "transsexual" and "transvestite" mean?

Gender identity is the awareness of oneself as male or female. It is a basic component of personality that is extremely difficult to change.[1] The transsexual has a gender identity opposite to that of his or her actual physical anatomy, and dressing in clothes of the opposite sex and appearing to the world as a member of the opposite sex are essential parts of the transsexual's gender identity.[2] Transvestites, who are usually male, wear some or all the clothing of the opposite sex for occasional personal gratification, but not out of a psychological identification with the sex.[3]

Although psychiatrists and psychologists persist in the attempt, they have been uniformly unsuccessful in "curing" transvestites and transsexuals.[4] The patients do not wish to be "cured" in the sense of reversing their gender identity or changing their personal habits, but they often seek psychiatric help because society will not accept them for what they are.[5] Transsexuals have, however, been helped by sex-reassignment surgery and hormone therapy, which harmonizes anatomical sex with psychological gender identification.

147

May transsexuals and transvestites be legally arrested for crossdressing in public?

Yes. Anticrossdressing ordinances exist in many cities,[6] and according to a recent survey, state laws in Arizona, California, Colorado, Idaho, Nevada, Oklahoma, Oregon, Texas, Utah, and Washington make crossdressing criminal.[7] In many jurisdictions, impersonating, or masquerading as, a member of the opposite sex is made criminal by vagrancy or disorderly-conduct laws.[8] For example, it is unlawful in New York to congregate in a group while "disguised by unusual or unnatural attire or facial alteration."[9] Such statutes and ordinances may, however, raise significant constitutional issues.

In Denver and Miami anticrossdressing ordinances have been repealed.[10] Since regulation of crossdressing is typically left to municipalities, you should check local laws to ascertain what conduct is now prohibited.

How did crossdressing laws originate?

Wearing the clothing of the opposite sex was forbidden by the Jewish religion as part of an early code of sexual morality.[11] Joan of Arc was considered a heretic partly because she dressed as a man in violation of spiritual law.[12] New York's former crossdressing statute outlawed the appearance in public by individuals wearing disguises or with painted faces.[13] That statute was adopted in the nineteenth century in response to the actions of farmers who, during antirent riots, murdered law-enforcement officers while disguised as Indians or wearing dresses.[14] The general legislative purpose of such statutes is said to be to prevent the efforts of criminals to avoid recognition or to perpetrate frauds.[15]

Are crossdressing laws constitutional?

To date, two courts have found crossdressing laws to be unconstitutional. A federal district court in Toledo, Ohio, has ruled that the Toledo crossdressing law violates the Fourteenth Amendment to the Constitution because it denies due process and equal protection.[16] In Chicago, a local court has declared unconstitutional an ordinance forbidding crossdressing.[17] Constitutional challenges are pending in state courts with regard to the crossdressing ordinances of St. Louis[18] and Denver.[19]

Crossdressing ordinances may be argued to be unconstitutional for a number of reasons. First, it may be argued that they violate the individual's right to privacy. As defined by the Supreme Court, the right of privacy may more accurately be called the right of personal autonomy—the freedom to make certain individual decisions free from unwarranted governmental intrusion.[20] Several of the United States Courts of Appeals have recognized that students have a constitutional right to govern their personal appearance and have struck down school dress and hair-grooming codes.[21]

Second, crossdressing ordinances may be said to be unconstitutional because they punish for what the defendant is rather than for what he does. As noted above, it appears that transvestites and transsexuals feel compelled to wear clothing of the opposite sex. Crossdressing ordinances make criminal what may be an involuntary act.[22] In *Robinson* v. *California*, the Supreme Court held that a state may not punish a defendant merely because he is a narcotics addict.[23] Lower federal courts and state courts have held, with respect to vagrancy laws, that a state may not punish a defendant merely because he is an unemployed person without visible means of support.[24]

A third constitutional line of attack would challenge crossdressing laws on the basis that they are impermissibly vague. When the meaning of a penal law is unclear, the statute violates the constitutional right of due process.[25]

What may transvestites and transsexuals do to protect themselves from arrest and conviction?

Some transsexuals have successfully resisted conviction under crossdressing laws on nonconstitutional grounds. For example, a Columbus, Ohio, male transsexual was arrested for appearing in public in feminine dress, but the court dismissed the case because the defendant had "an irresistible impulse" to dress in the clothing of the opposite sex. The court drew an analogy to the "temporary insanity"

defense used in other criminal cases.[26] In Texas, a transsexual avoided conviction on the ground that a state
statute outlawing the public wearing of a disguise in such
a way as to hide identity was inapplicable to him because,
although he was dressed in female clothing, his identity
was known to the arresting officer.[27] These defenses would
be useful for transvestites as well as transsexuals.

Precautionary measures may be taken to avoid arrest.
Transsexuals who desire sex-reassignment surgery are often required to live in the proposed sex role for as much
as one year before the operation will be performed. Such
a person should carry a card or letter from his or her doctor stating that crossdressing is required for medical treatment. State and county health departments may provide
official letters of confirmation to transsexuals who present
an affidavit from a physician.[28] The San Francisco Police
Department's Center for Special Problems will issue identification cards allowing transsexuals to crossdress. The Erickson Educational Foundation, 4047 Hundred Oaks Avenue, Baton Rouge, Louisiana, will also issue such cards.
The cards do not guarantee that transsexuals will not be
prosecuted for crossdressing, but they will help to establish
that crossdressing is not done to defraud or to cause a
disorder.[29]

**If a transsexual is imprisoned for crossdressing or some
other crime, may he or she be incarcerated with prisoners
of the opposite psychological sex?**

Yes. There are no reported cases dealing with postoperative transsexuals, probably because the issue of their correct sexual identity would not ordinarily arise. As to pre-
operatives, however, the usual inclination of prison officials
is to group anatomical males with males and anatomical
females with females despite any psychological trauma or
physical danger that may be created for the transsexual. It
has been reported, however, that the Men's House of De-
tention in New York City separates transvestites and
transsexuals from the general prison population for their
own protection.[30] An appellate court in Illinois reduced the
sentence of a preoperative transsexual to probation be-

cause the defendant "would have difficulty adjusting to the masculine environment," and incarceration would not have encouraged rehabilitation.[31] In the Illinois case, a psychiatrist testified regarding the harmful consequences of sending the prisoner to an all-male prison.

Is sex-reassignment surgery for transsexuals legal in the United States?

Yes. Although surgery designed to coordinate a person's physical anatomy with his or her psychological gender identity is not universally accepted by the medical profession,[32] it is not illegal. Physicians formerly pointed at the "mayhem" statutes, which outlaw maiming or disfiguring the body, as a reason for not performing sex-conversion surgery. The mayhem laws originated in England and were intended to prevent men from dismembering themselves or others in order to avoid military service.[33] Those laws arguably are not applicable to medical sex conversion, however, since the crime requires a specific intent to maim, and surgery designed to benefit the patient psychologically may be said not to have such an intent.[34] In any event, such surgery is not performed with relative frequency. The first gender-identity clinic, performing sex-reassignment surgery, was established at Johns Hopkins Hospital in Baltimore in 1966.[35] By June 1973 there were 18 clinics or private surgeons in the United States performing the operation.[36]

Physicians who perform sex-reassignment surgery commonly require the transsexual to be screened by psychiatrists, undergo hormone treatment, and live as the desired sex for up to one year.[37] Given the fundamental and irreversible nature of the surgical transformation, such screening procedures are wise to assure that the individual has considered the decision to undergo the operation with sufficient care.

Will health insurance or the government pay for sex-reassignment surgery?

Sometimes. Blue Cross will pay for sex change operations if at least eleven months have elapsed since the policy was purchased. Preoperative treatment must be performed on an outpatient basis, and the hospitalization benefits do not include a period of convalescence.[38] Other insurance programs provide only partial coverage. Since individual policies differ, it is important to examine your policy and to make inquiries to the insurer to determine the exact scope of coverage.

Every state except Arizona and Alaska has a medical-assistance program for needy persons. Those programs will pay for surgery, however, only if it is "medically necessary." They exclude operations that are purely cosmetic.[39] In New York State, however, a recent decision extended the right to Medicaid payments for transsexual operations.[40] Although there appear to be no specific rules regarding sex-reassignment surgery, if a physician states that the operation is a medical necessity, a transsexual who cannot afford to pay for the operation may be able to obtain financial assistance. Transsexuals have in fact received such assistance in some cities, but welfare officials have not yet been willing to provide standardized procedures.

Once sex-reassignment surgery is completed, does the transsexual have the right to full legal recognition of his or her new sex?

The law will officially change a person's sex for the purpose of obtaining social security benefits, and will permit a change of name. But not all jurisdictions will permit a transsexual to change the sex designation on his or her birth certificate, or to marry in the new sex.

Dr. Harry Benjamin, an expert regarding transsexualism, has stated:

> After [sex-reassignment surgery] has been done and we are dealing with a fait accompli, it should be made as easy as possible for the patient to succeed in his or her new life. And the legal recognition of this new life is a very essential part indeed.[41]

The achievement of legal recognition of the postoperative sex is not, however, usually made easy.

The sex designation on one's birth certificate is the key

to legal establishment of sex for most purposes, including
obtaining marriage licenses, passports, and insurance policies. Two states, Illinois and Louisiana, have statutes that
provide that postoperative transsexuals may be issued new
birth certificates.[42] Thirteen other states—Alabama, California, Colorado, Hawaii, Iowa, Maryland, Minnesota,
New Jersey, North Carolina, Pennsylvania, Virginia, Tennessee, and Texas—permit a change of sex designation
through administrative regulations or practice.[43] Statutes
regarding birth records permit either "amendments" or
"corrections." A correction statute is limited to the correction of errors on the original certificate. Subsequent events
such as sex-reassignment surgery may not be considered to
be corrections. Amendment statutes permit the record-
keeping agency to make changes based on events that occur after birth. Minnesota has such an amendment statute,
and the State Board of Health has undertaken to issue
new birth certificates with new names to postoperative
transsexual patients referred by University of Minnesota
surgeons.[44]

In contrast, the New York City Board of Health has
consistently refused to change sex designations on birth
certificates, and the courts have thus far refused to over-
rule the board. A state court concluded in 1965 that it
lacked authority to order a change of sex on the birth certificate of a transsexual who had undergone surgery and
assumed the name and role of a female because, under
principles of administrative law, it could not overturn an
agency's ruling unless it was shown to be "arbitrary."[45] In
making its ruling, the board had consulted a committee of
the New York Academy of Medicine. The committee recommended no change of sex because:

1. Male-to-female transsexuals are still chromosomally
males while ostensibly females;
2. It is questionable whether laws and records such as
the birth certificate should be changed and thereby used as
a means to help psychologically ill persons in their social
adaptation.... The desire of concealment of a change of
sex by the transsexual is outweighed by the public interest
for protection against fraud.[46]

The committee's reasoning has been the subject of criticism.[47] A New York court, disclaiming any power to order the physical alteration of a birth certificate, has nonetheless proposed an alternative rule for the legal determination of sex:

> Where, however, with or without medical intervention, the psychological sex and anatomical sex are harmonized, then the social sex or gender of the individual should be made to conform to the harmonized status of the individual and, if such conformity requires changes of a statistical nature, then such changes should be made.[48]

The court rejected the chromosomal test for sex, noting that an individual's psychological identity is more significant than "the results of a mere histological section or biochemical analysis."[49] The court suggested that it may be misleading for an individual who has the physical appearance of a female and who comports herself socially as a female to have a birth certificate with a sex designation of "male."[50]

The current practice of the New York City Bureau of Records and Statistics is evidently to issue a new birth certificate to a postoperative transsexual, with a new name but with no identity as to sex.[51] The omission of sex identity denies transsexuals the legal recognition of their new sex, which doctors believe to be necessary for satisfactory postoperative adjustment.[52] Additionally, the lack of sex designation may cause problems for a postoperative transsexual that wishes to marry.

Under the common law, a person may use any first name he or she prefers as long as there is no intent to defraud.[53] Courts have agreed to make name changes official for postoperative transsexuals on the ground of "psychological gratification."[54] A change of name does not of itself, however, legally change a person's sex.

To receive social security benefits that are designated by sex, such as widow's benefits and optional retirement for females at age 62, the Social Security Administration requires a legal opinion and doctor's affidavit if the applicant's sex is other than that shown on the original social-security card.

· The Passport Office relies on the name and sex indicated on a person's birth certificate in issuing passports. Transsexuals who were born in jurisdictions that refuse to change sex designations on birth certificates will thus not be able to obtain new passports to correspond with their new sex.[55]

The California Division of Motor Vehicles will issue a license to a transsexual, pre- or postoperative, in the sex of choice, upon receipt of a letter from the individual's physician.

The Supreme Court has held that the right to marry is a fundamental civil right.[56] If a preoperative transsexual were to marry another person of the same anatomical sex, society would probably consider it to be a homosexual marriage, which is not currently recognized as legal in this country.[57] If a postoperative has secured a new birth certificate, or if he or she marries in a state that does not require proof of sex, marriage will not be a problem. Many transsexuals have in fact married in the new sex.[58] A transsexual who does not reveal the fact of sex reassignment to the prospective spouse, however, runs the risk of having the marriage annulled on grounds of fraud.[59] In New Jersey, a family court found that a transsexual woman could collect support from the husband. She married the husband after the operation.[60]

In an English case, the marriage between a male transvestite and a male-to-female postoperative transsexual was annulled because the wife was not legally considered a woman.[61] The court took the view that a chromosomal male born with normal sex organs is always a male and held that the law would not recognize a person's psychological sexual orientation and would also ignore any surgical intervention.

With respect to marriages entered into in the preoperative sex role, many clinics recommend that a divorce be obtained prior to sex-reassignment surgery.[62] In a New Jersey case, a wife was granted a divorce on the grounds of "extreme cruelty" because her husband's "dress, manner, occupational interests and associations [were] all designed to enhance his feeling of being a woman."[63] Some transsexuals continue to live with their spouses after surgery as "sisters" or "brothers."[64] In Colorado a court granted custody rights to a postoperative male who had been the natural mother of the children.[65]

May employers discriminate against persons who are transsexuals or transvestites?

A transvestite or transsexual who is discriminated against by a government employer may be able to assert a constitutional equal-protection claim similar to that sometimes asserted by government workers accused of homosexual conduct.[66] If the employer cannot show a connection between transvestism or transsexualism and job performance, it may be held to be impermissible to deny equal-employment opportunities. The same principle would be true of a transsexual who seeks to return to his or her job after surgery. Any claim that the job is not suitable for a person of the transsexual's new sex may permit a claim of sex discrimination.[67] A case now on appeal in the New Jersey state courts challenges the dismissal of a male-to-female transsexual music teacher because she had undergone sex-reassignment surgery.[68]

The 1964 Civil Rights Act and other federal statutes prohibit discrimination on the basis of sex by most employers.[69] Charges may be filed with the agency given responsibility for enforcement of the act, the Equal Employment Opportunity Commission (EEOC). Charge forms may be obtained by writing to the commission in Washington, D.C.

May transvestites or transsexuals be denied custody of their children or the right to visit their children?

Probably not, at least judging the few available cases. Transvestites and transsexuals who are denied custody or visitation rights may argue that there is no necessary relationship between a person's sexual orientation and his or her fitness as a parent.[70] The courts are, however, given very wide discretion to decide what is in the best interest of the child. A transvestite father in Albany, New York, is currently challenging his former wife's denial of his visitation rights.[71] A female-to-male transsexual in Colorado, who had adopted the male role in preparation for sex-reassignment surgery, was able to retain custody of children despite a legal challenge by her former husband.[72]

NOTES

1. Paul, "The Current Status of the Change of Sex Operation," J. Nervous and Mental Disease 460, 467 (1968).
2. Transsexualism and Sex Reassignment 487 (R. Green & J.
   Money, eds. 1969) [hereafter Green and Money].
3. Id.; Bowman & Engle, "Sex Offenses: The Medical and
   Legal Implications of Sex Variations," 25 Law & Contemp.
   Prob. 292, 305 (1960).
4. Stoller, *Sex and Gender* 249 & 241 (1968); Holloway,
   Transsexuals—Their Legal Sex, 40 Univ. of Colo. L. Rev.
   282, 283 (1968). Dr. Richard Green recommends behav-
   ior-modification therapy for children with atypical sexual
   identity in order to avoid the social problems which face
   the transsexual adult. Green, *Sexual Identity Conflict in
   Children and Adults,* New York: Basic Books, Inc. (1974)
   245.
5. Stoller, *supra* note 4, at 241.
6. *E.g.,* Columbus, Ohio (Columbus Municipal Code §
   2343.04), Saint Louis, Missouri (§ 788.010 of the Revised
   Code of 1960, Vol. 2 of the City of St. Louis) and Houston, Texas (Code of Ordinances, City of Houston, § 28-
   42.4 (1972)). The Houston ordinance makes it "unlawful
   for any person to appear on any public street, sidewalk, al-
   ley or other public thoroughfare dressed with the designed
   intent to disguise his or her true sex as that of the opposite sex."
7. Erickson Educational Foundation, "Legal Aspects of
   Transsexualism" 3 (1971) [hereafter EEF].
8. Sherwin, *Legal Aspects of Male Transsexualism,* in Green
   & Money, *supra* note 4, at 420.
9. N.Y. Penal Law § 240.35(4) (McKinney 1967) reads in
   part as follows:

   A person is guilty of loitering when he: 4. Being
   masked or in any manner disguised by unusual or
   unnatural attire or facial alteration, loiters, remains
   or congregates in a public place with other persons
   so masked or disguised. . . .

10. See EEF newsletter, Fall 1973.
11. Comment, "Transsexualism, Sex Reassignment Surgery and
    the Law," 56 Cornell L. Rev. 963, 964 (1971) [hereafter
    Comment].
12. Id.
13. Former § 887(7) of N.Y. Penal Law.
14. See *People* v. *Archibald,* 58 Misc. 2d 862, 864, 296 N.Y.S.
    2d 834, 837 (Sup. Ct. 1968) (dissenting opinion).

15. *Cf.* Sherwin, *supra* note 8 at 419.
16. *Flanigan* v. *Blay,* ——F. Supp. ——(N.D. Ohio, Sept. 24, 1973).
17. *City of Chicago* v. *Oscar Baldres,* See New York *Post,* Sept. 21, 1973.
18. *City of Saint Louis* v. *Goldstein Johnson,* appeal pending (Mo. Sup. Ct.).
19. *Sower* v. *City of Denver,* appeal pending (Colo. Sup. Ct.) The City of Denver repealed its crossdressing ordinance subsequent to the convictions in this case.
20. See, *Roe* v. *Wade,* 410 U.S. 113 (1973) and *Eisenstadt* v. *Baird,* 405 U.S. 438, 453-54 (1972).
21. See, *e.g., Bishop* v. *Colaw,* 450 F. 2d 1069 (8th Cir. 1971), *Richards* v. *Thurston,* 424 F. 2d 1281 (1st Cir. 1970), and *Breen* v. *Kahl,* 419 F. 2d 1034 (7th Cir.) *cert.* denied 398 U.S. 939 (1969).
22. See Comment, 21 Syracuse L. Rev. 307, 311 (1969).
23. 370 U.S. 660 (1962).
24. *E.g., Goldman* v. *Knecht,* 295 F. Supp. 897 (D. Colo. 1969) and *Alegata* v. *Commonwealth,* 231 N.E. 2d 201 (Mass. 1967).
25. See *Papachristou* v. *Jacksonville,* 405 U.S. 156, 165 ff. (1972).
26. *Columbus* v. *Zanders,* 26 Ohio Misc. 144, 266 N.E. 2d 602 (1970). *U.S.* v. *Collins* 17 Cr. L. 2013 (D.C. Supr. Ct., Apr. 2, 1975) where solicitation arrest of transsexuals was found unconstitutional.
27. *Garcia* v. *State,* 444 S.W. 2d 847 (Tex. Crim. App. 1969).
28. EEF, *supra* note 7 at 3.
29. Comment, *supra* note 11 at 971 (1971).
30. New York *Times* Magazine, 2/17/74 at 19.
31. *People* v. *Steadman,* 3 Ill. App. 1045, 280 N.E. 2d 17.
32. See Holloway, *supra* note 4 at 286.
33. See Comment, *supra* note 11 at 987.
34. *Id.* See Holloway, *supra* note 4 at 284.
35. Holloway, *supra* note 4 at 284.
36. Letter from Erickson Educational Foundation, June, 1973.
37. Holloway, *supra* note 4 at 284; Comment, *supra* note 11 at 973–74.
38. EEF, *supra* note 7 at 10.
39. *E.g.,* N.Y. Soc. Serv. Law §365-a (McKinney Supp. 1973) provides that medical assistance means "care, services and supplies which are necessary to prevent, diagnose, correct or cure conditions in the person that cause acute suffering, endanger life, result in illness or infirmity, interfere with his capacity for normal activity, or threaten some significant handicap."

40. *Denise R.* v. *Sugarman,* 364 N.Y.S. 2d 537 (March 3, 1975). The state is appealing.
41. Quoted in Comment, *supra* note 11 at 971.
42. Ill. Ann. Stat. Ch. 111 1/2 §73-17 (Smith-Hurd Supp. 1973); La. Rev. Stat. Ann. § 40:336 (Supp. 1974).
43. *Id.,* 50 Misc. 2d at 382-83, 270 N.Y.S. 2d at 322.
44. *Id.* at 997.
45. *Anonymous* v. *Weiner,* 50 Misc. 2d 380, 270 N.Y.S. 2d 319 (Sup. Ct. 1966).
46. *Id.,* 50 Misc. 2d at 382–83, 270 N.Y.S. 2d at 322.
47. *E.g., Alexander,* Family Law, 18 Syracuse L. Rev. 383, 394 (1966).
48. *In re Anonymous,* 57 Misc. 2d 813, 816, 293 N.Y.S. 2d 834, 837 (Civ. Ct. 1968).
49. *Id.,* 57 Misc. 2d at 817, 293 N.Y.S. 2d at 838.
50. *Id.*
51. See *Hartin* v. *Director of Bureau of Records and Statistics,* 75 Misc. 2d 229, 347 N.Y.S. 2d 515 (Sup. Ct. 1973).
52. Comment, *supra* note 11 at 975.
53. 65 C.J.S. Names § 11(1).
54. *In re Anonymous,* 64 Misc. 2d 309, 314 N.Y.S.2d 668 (Civ. Ct. 1970).
55. Comment, *supra* note 11 at 1001.
56. *Loving* v. *Virginia,* 388 U.S. 1, 12 (1967).
57. See chapter on Family Law.
58. Comment, *supra* note 11 at 1003.
59. Concealment of sterility is a ground for annulment in many states. 4 Am. Jur. 2d Annulment of Marriage §14.
60. *In the Matter of M.T.* v. *J.T.,* D—1476-74.
61. *Corbett* v. *Corbett (otherwise Ashley),* [1970] 2 W.L.R. 1306, 2 All E.R. 33 (P.D.A.).
62. EEF, *supra* note 7, at 10.
63. *P.* v. *P.,* 121 N.J. Super. 368, 297 A. 2d 202 (1972).
64. See New York *Times,* Oct. 23, 1973, p. 42.
65. *Christian* v. *Randall,* — Colo. — (Nov. 13, 1973).
66. See chapter on rights to employment.
67. See, *Reed* v. *Reed,* 404 U.S. 71 (1971) and *Frontiero* v. *Richardson,* 411 U.S. 677 (1973).
68. *Crossman* v. *Bernardsville Board of Education,* A1832-72, (Superior Ct. of N.J., Appellate Division, appeal pending).
69. 42 U.S.C. &2000e et seq (1970).
70. See chapter on family law.
71. *Koss* v. *Koss* (Family Court, Albany, N.Y.) (pending).
72. EEF Newsletter, Fall 1973.

Appendix

1. American Laws Applicable to Consensual Adult Homosexual Acts

State	Statute	Offense	Status	Penalty
ALABAMA	*Sodomy* Ala. Code tit. 14§42 14§106	attempt generally; applicable to indictment for sodomy crime against nature	misd. felony	NTE* 6 mos. and/or $500 2–10 yrs.
	Indecent Exposure 14§326(1)	indecent exposure	misd.	NTE 12 mos. and/or $500
	Vagrancy 14§437 & 14§438	vagrancy; persons who loaf, loiter, live in idleness or immorality held unconstitutional—298 F. Supp. 260	misd.	NTE 12 mos. hard labor and/or $500
	Sex Offender Registration 15§448	applies to persons convicted of sodomy, crime against nature	felony	1–5 yrs. and/or $1,000 (for failure to comply)

* Not to exceed.

State	Statute	Offense	Status	Penalty
	Sexual Psychopath §§434 to §§442	mental disorder coupled with commission of sex offenses		commitment to state institution
ALASKA	Indecent Exposure Alaska Stat. §11.40.080	indecent exposure and exhibition	misd.	3 mos.–1 yr. or $50–500
	Sodomy §11.40.120	sodomy	felony	1–10 yrs.
	Solicitation §11.10.070(1)	soliciting a felony	felony	NTE 3 yrs. and/or $3,000
	(2)	soliciting a misd.	misd.	NTE 6 mos. and/or $500
	Vagrancy §11.60.210	idle or dissolute persons; loitering	misd.	10–25 days and/or $20–250
	Disorderly Conduct §11.45.030	disorderly conduct; disturbing the peace	misd.	NTE 6 mos. and/or $300

ARIZONA	Disorderly Conduct A.R.S. §13-371	disturbing the peace by offensive conduct	misd.	NTE 2 mos. or $200
	Indecent Exposure §13-531	willful and lewd exposure	misd.	NTE 6 mos. and/or $300
	Sodomy §13-651	crime against nature	felony	5–20 yrs.
	Lewdness §13-652	lewd or lascivious acts in an un-natural manner	felony	1–5 yrs.
	Vagrancy §13-993	vagrancy; loitering near public toilet (if previous conviction of sex offense)	misd. / felony	NTE 6 mos. and/or $300 / NTE 5 yrs.
	Sex Offender Registration §13-1271 to §13-1274	failure to register as sex offender	misd.	NTE 6 mos. and/or $300
ARKANSAS	Sodomy Ark. Stat. §41-813	sodomy or buggery		1–21 yrs.

State	Statute	Offense	Status	Penalty
	Disorderly Conduct			
	§41-1415	vulgar exhibition	misd.	$20–200
	§41-1426	loitering for purpose of committing immoral act	misd. (1st off.)	3–6 mos. and/or $500–1,000
			felony (subsequent offense)	2–5 yrs.
	§41-1432	creating disturbance in public	misd.	NTE 6 mos. and/or $500
	Indecent Exposure			
	§41-2701	indecent exposure; obscene exhibition	misd.	$50
	Lewdness			
	§41-3202	prostitution; lewdness; lewd solicitation	misd. (1st off.)	30 days–3 mos. and $50–100
			(sub. off.)	3 mos.–6 yrs. and $100–250
	Loitering			
	§41-1125	loitering about school or public place nearby	misd.	NTE 6 mos. and/or $500
CALIFORNIA	Sodomy Cal. Penal Code			
	§220	assault to commit sodomy	felony	1–20 yrs.
	§286	sodomy or crime against nature	felony	NLT* 1 yr.

§286(1)	sodomy, acting in concert by force or violence	felony	5 yrs.-life
Lewdness §288a	sex perversion; oral copulation	misd. or felony	NTE 1 yr. (county jail) NTE 15 yrs. (state prison)
§288b	oral copulation, acting in concert by force or violence	felony	5 yrs.-life
Sex Offender Registration §290	failure to register as sex offender	misd.	NTE 6 mos. and/or $500
Indecent Exposure §314(1)	lewd conduct and indecent exposure	misd. (1st off.) felony (subsequent offense)	NTE 6 mos. and/or $500 NLT 1 yr.
§314(2)	procures or assists another to indecent exposure	misd.	NTE 6 mos. and/or $500
Disturbing the Peace 415	disturbing the peace	misd.	NTE 6 mos. and/or $500

*Not less than.

State	Statute	Offense	Status	Penalty
	Disorderly Conduct			
	§647(a)	soliciting or engaging in lewd or dissolute conduct; prostitution;	misd.	NTE 6 mos. and/or $500
	(b) (c)	loiters about public toilet with lewd intent		
	Loitering			
	§647b	loitering near adult school	misd.	NTE 6 mos. and/or $500
	§653g	loitering about school or public place	misd.	NTE 6 mos. and/or $500
	Public Indecency			
	§650½	outraging public decency	misd.	NTE 6 mos. and/or $500
	Sterilization			
	§2670	authority to asexualize recidivists		
COLORADO	*Sodomy*			
	Colo. Crim Code §40-3-404	deviate sexual intercourse by imposition	class 4 felony	1–10 yrs. and/or $2,000–3,000
	§40-3-407	sexual assault	class 1 misd.	6 mos.–1 yr. and/or $500–5,000

Solicitation §40-7-201 & -202	solicits act of deviate sexual intercourse for consideration	class 3 misd.	NTE 6 mos. and/or $50–700
§40-7-208	furnish facility for deviate sexual intercourse for pecuniary gain	class 2 misd.	3 mos.–1 yr. and/or $250–1,000
Public Indecency 40-7-301	indecent exposure; deviate and sexual intercourse in public; lewd exposure	petty offense	NTE 6 mos. and/or $500
Disorderly Conduct §40-9-106	coarse and offensive gesture or display	petty offense	NTE 6 mos. and/or $500
Loitering §40-9-113	loitering for the purpose of prostitution or deviate sexual intercourse	petty offense	NTE 6 mos. and/or $500
Sodomy §40-3-410	deviate sexual intercourse with person under 21 and over whom offender has supervision	class 5 felony	1–5 yrs. and/or $1,000–1,500
CONNECTI-CUT			
Sodomy C.G.S.A. §53a-65	deviate sexual intercourse defined—anal & oral	decriminalized	decriminalized 7/1/72

State	Statute	Offense	Status	Penalty
	§53a-71	sodomy (nonconsensual)	misd. class A	NTE 1 yr./$1,000
	§53a-75	sodomy by forcible compulsion; incapability of consent	felony class B	NTE 20 yrs./$10,000
	§53a-77	sodomy with one incapable of consent or under age 16	felony class C	NTE 10 yrs./$5,000
	Solicitation			
	§53a-82	sexual contact with another in return for a fee	misd. class A	NTE 1 yr./$1,000
	§53a-83	patronizing a prostitute	misd. class A	NTE 1 yr./$1,000
	§53a-84	sex of parties involved in engaging or soliciting a prostitute is immaterial		
	Disorderly Conduct			
	§53a-182	offensive or disorderly conduct	misd. class C	NTE 3 mos./$500
	Loitering			
	§53a-185	loitering on or about school grounds	misd. class C	NTE 3 mos./$500
	Public Indecency			
	§53a-186	sexual conduct, lewd exposure or conduct in public	misd. class B	NTE 6 mos./$100

DELAWARE

Offense	Description	Classification	Penalty
Sodomy Del. Code Ann. 11-766	nonconsensual	felony C	2–20 yrs. + fine by court
Sodomy	if serious harm	felony B	3–30 yrs. + fine by court mandatory 3 yr.
Sexual Misconduct 11-762(b)	deviate sexual intercourse with person less than 16 yrs. old & actor at least 4 yrs. older	class E felony	NTE 7 yrs. + fine by court
Indecent Exposure 11-768		class B misd.	NTE 6 mos./$500
Lewdness 11-1341		class B misd.	NTE 6 mos./$500
Public Indecency Defined 11-1356			

State	Statute	Offense	Status	Penalty
DISTRICT OF COLUMBIA	*Disorderly Conduct* D.C.C.E. §22-1107	disorderly conduct; obscene gestures	misd.	NTE 90 days and/or $250
	§22-1112	lewd, obscene, or indecent acts	misd.	NTE 90 days and/or $300
	§22-1121	offensive disorderly conduct	misd.	NTE 90 days and/or $250
	§22-3111	disorderly conduct; public buildings or grounds	misd.	$50
	Solicitation §22-2701	soliciting prostitution or immoral and lewd acts	misd.	NTE 90 days and/or $250
	Vagrancy §22-3302 & 3304	vagrancy	misd.	NTE 90 days and/or $300
	Sodomy §22-3502	sodomy	felony	NTE 10 yrs. and/or $1,000
	Sexual Psychopath §22-3503 to 3511	sexual psychopaths commitment		

FLORIDA			
Lewdness F.S.A. §796.07	lewdness, prostitution, assignation	misd. 2nd degree	NTE 60 days and/or $500
§798.02	open & gross lewdness, lascivious behavior	2nd degree	NTE 60 days and/or $500
Sodomy §800.01	crime against nature	felony 2nd deg.	NTE 15 yrs. and/or $10,000
§800.02	unnatural & lascivious acts	misd. 2nd deg.	NTE 60 days and/or $500
Indecent Exposure §800.03	indecent exposure	misd. 1st degree	NTE 1 yr. and/or $1,000
Loitering §856.021	loitering	misd. 2nd degree	NTE 60 days and/or $500
GEORGIA			
Sodomy Ga. Code Ann. §26.1001 & 1006	attempt to commit sodomy sodomy	felony felony	1-10 1-20

State	Statute	Offense	Status	Penalty
			felony	1–20 or life
	Solicitation §26.2002	aggravated sodomy		
	§26.2003	solicitation of sodomy	misd.	NTE 1 yr. and/or $1,000
	Indecent Exposure §26.2011	public indecency; lewd exposure	misd.	NTE 1 yr. and/or $1,000
	Disorderly Conduct §26.2610(d)	indecent & disorderly conduct	misd.	NTE 1 yr. and/or $1,000
	Loitering §32-9925	loitering on premises of public or private school	misd.	NTE 1 yr. and/or $1,000
HAWAII	Indecent Exposure §738		petty misd.	NTE 30 days and/or $500
	Open Lewdness §1217	any lewd act in a public place	petty misd.	NTE 30 days and/or $500
	Disorderly Conduct §711-1101	offensively coarse gesture or display. If intent to cause substantial harm	petty misd.	NTE 30 days and/or $500

	offensively coarse gesture or display	violation	NTE $500
IDAHO			
Indecent Exposure Idaho Code			
§18-4101	indecent exposure and obscenity	misd.	NTE 6 mos. and/or $300
§18-4104	obscene live conduct in a public place	misd.	NTE 6 mos. and/or $300
§18-4105	public display of offensive sexual material including genitals	misd.	NTE 6 mos. and/or $300
§18-4107	conspiracy to commit above	misd.	NTE 6 mos. and/or $300
§18-4109	a violation of §§18-4104, 4105 for 3d offenders within 2 yrs.	misd.	NTE 5 yrs. and/or $5,000
Disturbing the Peace			
§18-6200	disturbing the peace—offensive conduct	misd.	NTE 6 mos. and/or $300
Sodomy			
§18-6605	crime against nature	felony	NLT 5 yrs.

State	Statute	Offense	Status	Penalty
	Solicitation §18-5613	loitering for the purpose of soliciting sensual activity, including homosexual & deviate relations	misd.	NTE 6 mos. and/or $300
ILLINOIS	Solicitation S.H.A. ch. 38 §8-1	solicitation of an offense		NTE maximum for offense solicited
	Sodomy §11-2	deviate sexual intercourse defined —oral or anal intercourse		
	Indecent Exposure §11-9	public indecency, indecent exposure, deviate sexual conduct in public	class A misd.	NTE 1 yr. and/or $200
	Prostitution §11-14	deviate sexual conduct for money	class A misd.	NTE 1 yr. and/or $200
	Solicitation §11-15	solicitation for prostitution	class A misd.	NTE 1 yr. and/or $200

Disorderly Conduct §26-1(a)(1)	disorderly conduct; breach of the peace	class C misd.	$500
Sexual Psychopath §105-1	sexually dangerous persons defined		
§105-8	if found sexually dangerous then committed + director of corrections becomes guardian		
§105-9	if application showing recovery—hearing—if so found then to be discharged		
INDIANA			
Disorderly Conduct Ind. Stat. Ann. §10-1510	disorderly conduct; offensive behavior	misd.	NTE 180 days and/or $500
Indecent Exposure §10-2801	public indecency	misd.	NTE 6 mos. and/or $300–500
Sodomy §10-4221	crime against nature	felony	2–14 yrs. and/or $100–1,000

State	Statute	Status	Penalty	Offense
IOWA	*Sodomy* I.C.A. §705.1&2	sodomy	felony	NTE 10 yrs.
	Lewdness §724.1 §725.1	life of prostitution or lewdness open & gross lewdness; indecent exposure	felony misd.	NTE 5 yrs. NTE 6 mos. or $200
	Solicitation §724.2	soliciting for carnal knowledge	felony	NTE 5 yrs. and/or $1,000
KANSAS	*Sodomy* K.S.A. §21-3505	oral or anal copulation	misd. class B	NTE 6 mos. and/or $1,000
	§21-3506	aggravated sodomy	felony class B	5 yrs.–life and/or $10,000
	Lewdness §21-3508	lewd & lascivious behavior, indecent exposure	misd. class B	NTE 6 mos. and/or $1,000
	Disorderly Conduct §21-4101	disorderly conduct	misd. class C	NTE 1 mo. and/or $500

KENTUCKY			
Loitering §21-4108	loitering with intent to solicit for immoral act	misd. class C	NTE 1 mo. and/or $500
Solicitation §21-3110(21)	"solicitation" defined—to commit a crime		
Indecency Ky. Rev. Stat. §435.105(2)	indecent or immoral practices with another	felony	1–5 yrs.
Sodomy §436.050	sodomy or buggery	felony	2–5 yrs.
Lewdness §436.075	prostitution, lewdness, assignation	misd.	NTE 1 yr. and/or $200
Vagrancy §436.520	vagrancy; loitering	misd. (1st offense)	NTE 30 days and/or $10
		(sub. offense)	NTE 60 days
Disorderly Conduct §437.016	disorderly conduct—obscene gestures	misd.	NTE 6 mos. and/or $500

State	Statute	Offense	Status	Penalty
	Loitering §437.017(b)	loitering for purposes of soliciting or commiting a jewd or sexual act	misd.	NTE 15 days
LOUISIANA	*Sodomy* LSA-RS 14:89	crime against nature	felony	NTE 5 yrs. and/or $2,000
	Disturbing the Peace 14:103	disturbing the peace	misd.	NTE 90 days and/or $100
	14:103.1(2)	disturbing the peace—indecent proposals	misd.	NTE 4 mos. and/or $200
	14:104	maintaining a place for immoral sexual purposes	misd.	NTE 6 mos. and/or $500
	Indecent Exposure 14:106	indecent exposure; lewdness; solicitation	misd.	NTE 6 mos. and/or $100–500
	Vagrancy 14:107(7)	vagrancy; loitering around public places	misd.	NTE 6 mos. and/or $200

	Solicitation—Breach of the Peace 14:34.1(2)	aggravated battery resulting from breach of the peace; indecent proposals toward another	felony	NTE 10 yrs.
MAINE	*Sodomy* 17M.R.S.A. §1001	crime against nature	felony	1–10 yrs.
	Indecent Exposure §1901	wanton and indecent exposure	misd.	NTE 6 mos. and/or $25
	Lewdness §2151	open, gross, lewd or lascivious behavior	felony	NTE 5 yrs. and/or $300
	§3051 §3050	prostitution, lewdness, assignation defined—any indecent or obscene act	felony	NTE 3 yrs.
	Public Indecency §3758	lascivious speech or behavior in public places	misd.	NTE 30 days and/or $100
MARYLAND	*Sodomy* §553	sodomy	felony	1–10 yrs.

State	Statute	Offense	Status	Penalty
	§554	unnatural or perverted sexual practice	felony	NTE 10 yrs. and/or $1,000
	Lewdness Md. Ann. Code Art. 27 §§15, 16 & 17	prostitution, lewdness, assignation, solicitation	misd.	NTE 1 yr. and/or $500
	Disturbing the Peace §122	indecent exposure, solicitation, disorderly conduct	misd.	$5–50
	§123	disorderly conduct, disturbing the public peace	misd.	NTE 60 days and/or $50
	§124	disorderly conduct on another's property	misd.	$1–25
MASSACHU-SETTS	*Lewdness* M.G.L.A. c.272. §16	open & gross lewdness; lascivious behavior	felony	NTE 3 yrs. or $300
	Solicitation §26	solicitation—resorting to restaurants or taverns for immoral purpose; engaging in immoral acts	misd.	NTE 1 yr. and/or $25–500

Sodomy §34 §35	crime against nature unnatural & lascivious acts	felony felony	NTE 20 yrs. NTE 5 yrs. and/or $100–1,000
Disorderly Conduct §53	offensive or disorderly conduct; lewd, wanton and lascivious per- sons; indecent exposure	misd.	NTE 6 mos. and/or $200
Vagrancy §66	vagrancy	misd.	NTE 6 mos.
MICHIGAN			
Sexual Delinquency M.C.L.A. §750.10a	sexually delinquent person—repet- itive or compulsive acts	(definition only)	
Sodomy §750.85	assault with intent to commit sod- omy or gross indecency	felony	NTE 10 yrs. or $5,000
§750.158	crime against nature	felony	NTE 15 yrs.
Disorderly Conduct §750.167 & .168	indecent or obscene conduct in public; loitering	misd.	NTE 90 days and/or $100

State	Statute	Offense	Status	Penalty
	Lewdness §750.335	open and gross lewdness; lascivious behavior	misd.	NTE 1 yr. or $500
	Indecent Exposure §750.335a	indecent exposure	misd.	NTE 1 yr. or $500
	Gross Indecency §750.338	gross indecency between male persons	felony	NTE 5 yrs. or $2,500
	§750.338a	gross indecency between female persons	felony	NTE 5 yrs. or $2,500
	Solicitation §750.448	soliciting for prostitution or any lewd or immoral act	misd.	NTE 90 days and/or $100
	§750.449	admitting or place for purpose of prostitution, lewdness, or assignation	misd.	NTE 90 days and/or $100
	§750.450	aiding and abetting above offenses	misd.	NTE 90 days and/or $100
	§750.451	second offenders (above)	misd.	NTE 1 yr. and/or $500
		third & subsequent offenders	felony	NTE 2 yrs.

MINNESOTA	*Sexual Psychopaths* §720.301 to .310	sterilization of mental defectives, moral degenerates and sexual perverts		
	Disorderly Conduct M.S.A. §609.72	disorderly conduct	misd.	NTE 90 days and/or $300
	Vagrancy §609.725	vagrancy; loitering	misd.	NTE 90 days and/or $300
	Sodomy §609.293.5	consensual sodomy	gross misd.	NTE 1 yr. and/or $1,000
	Solicitation §609.32	soliciting acts of prostitution or sodomy	gross misd. or felony	NTE 1 yr. and/or $1,000 NTE 5 yrs. and/or $5,000

State	Statute	Offense	Status	Penalty
	Lewdness & Indecent Exposure §617.23	indecent exposure; gross lewdness or lascivious behavior	misd.	NTE 10 days or $5
	Criminal Defamation §609.765	anything which exposes a person or group, class or association to hatred, contempt, ridicule, degradation, etc.	gross misd.	NTE 1 yr. and/or $1,000
MISSISSIPPI	Indecent Exposure Miss. Code Ann. §97-29-31	indecent exposure	misd.	NTE 6 mos. and/or $500
	Lewdness §97-29-49 & -53	prostitution, solicitation, lewdness, assignation	misd.	NTE 6 mos. and/or $200
	Sodomy §97-29-59	unnatural intercourse, crime against nature	felony	NTE 10 yrs.
	Disorderly Conduct §97-35-3	disorderly conduct—obscene gestures, indecent proposals	misd.	NTE 4 mos. and/or $200
	§97-35-13	disturbance in a public place	misd.	NTE 6 mos. and/or $500

	§97-53-15	disturbance of public peace	misd.	NTE 6 mos. and/or $500
	Vagrancy §97-35-37 & -39	loitering; persons leading immoral life		10–30 days
MISSOURI	*Disturbing the Peace* V.A.M.S. §562.240	disturbing the peace	misd.	NTE 1 yr. and/or $1,000
	Lewdness §563.150	open gross lewdness, lascivious behavior, public indecency	misd.	NTE 1 yr. and/or $1,000
	Sodomy §563.230	crime against nature	felony	NLT 2 yrs.
	Vagrancy §563.340	loitering; vagrancy		NLT 20 days and/or $20
MONTANA	*Indecent Exposure* Mont. Rev. Code Ann. §94-3603	indecent exposure	misd.	NTE 6 mos. and/or $500

State	Statute	Offense	Status	Penalty
	Sodomy §94-4118	crime against nature	felony	NLT 5 yrs.
	Vagrancy §94-35-248	vagrancy; idle, dissolute, lewd persons		NTE 90 days
	Unlawful Assembly §94-35-242 and 243	two or more persons together for an immoral act	misd.	NTE 6 mos. and/or $500
NEBRASKA	*Disturbing the Peace* Neb. Rev. Stat. §28-818	wilfully disturbing the peace	misd.	3 mos. or $100
	Sodomy §28-919	crime against nature	felony	NTE 20 yrs.
	Indecent Exposure §28-920	indecent exposure	misd.	90 days or $100
	§28-920.01	indecent exposure: procuring, aiding, counseling	misd.	NTE 6 mos. and/or $50–500
	Vagrancy §28-1119	vagrancy	misd.	3 mos. or $5
	Sexual Psychopath §28-929	debauching minor; sexual psychopath examination	misd. or felony	NTE 6 mos. and/or $500 1–5 yrs.

NEVADA

Statute	Offense	Classification	Penalty
§29-2901 to 2907	sexual psychopaths—commitment		
Sodomy Nev. Rev. Stat. §201.190 and 193	crime against nature	felony	1-6 yrs.
Lewdness §201.210	open or gross lewdness	(1st off.) gross misd. (sub. off.) felony	NTE 1 yr. and/or $1,000 1-6 yrs.
Indecent Exposure §201.220	indecent or obscene exposure	(1st off.) gross misd. (sub. off.) felony	NTE 1 yr. and/or $1,000 1-6 yrs.
Solicitation & Vagrancy §207.030	solicitation of lewd or dissolute conduct; loitering about public toilet	misd.	NTE 6 mos. and/or $500
§207.270	loitering about schools	misd.	NTE 6 mos. and/or $500
Sex Offender Registration §207-151 to 157	failure to register as sex offender	misd.	NTE 6 mos. and/or $500

State	Statute	Offense	Status	Penalty
NEW HAMPSHIRE	*Sodomy*			
	632:2(I)	sodomy by force	felony	NLT 7 yrs. NTE 15
	632:2(II)	consensual	misd.	NTE 1 yr. and/or $1,000
	632:2(III)	bestiality	misd.	NTE 1 yr. and/or $1,000
	Indecent Exposure + Lewdness			
	645:1	act of gross lewdness		
	Disorderly Conduct			
	644:2	disorderly conduct	violation-probation, cond., uncond. discharge, fine, misd. if persists	NTE 1 yr. and/or $1,000
	Loitering			
	644:6	failure to give reasonably credible account of conduct + purposes	violation-probation, cond., uncond. discharge, fine, misd. if persists	NTE 1 yr. and/or $1,000

NEW
JERSEY

Lewdness N.J.S.A. 2A:115-1	open lewdness, public indecency, carnal indecency in private	misd.	NTE 3 yrs. and/or $1,000
Solicitation 2A:133-2	solicitation for prostitution, lewdness, assignation	misd.	NTE 3 yrs. and/or $1,000
2A:170-5	soliciting unlawful sexual or indecent acts	misd.	NTE 3 yrs. and/or $1,000
Sodomy 2A:143-1	sodomy; crime against nature	high misd.	NTE 20 yrs. and/or $5,000
Disorderly Conduct 2A:170-1	disorderly person with unlawful purpose	misd.	NTE 6 mos. and/or $500
2A:170-4	disorderly persons	misd.	NTE 6 mos. and/or $500
Sexual Psychopath Act 2A:164-3	upon conviction of sex crime defendant committed NTE 60 days in Diagnostic Center. If on report of Diagnostic Center Court feels commitment is proper, then NTE		

State	Statute	Offense max. sentence of crime for which defendant was convicted	Status	Penalty
NEW MEXICO	*Sodomy* N. Mex. Stat. Ann. §40A-9-6	sodomy	felony (3rd degree)	2–10 yrs. and/or $5,000
	Indecent Exposure §40A-9-8	indecent exposure	petty misd.	NTE 6 mos. and/or $100
	Disorderly Conduct §40A-20-1	indecent and disorderly conduct	petty misd.	NTE 6 mos. and/or $100
	Vagrancy §40A-20-5	vagrancy; loitering	petty misd.	NTE 6 mos. and/or $100
NEW YORK	*Sodomy* N.Y. Penal Law §130.38	consensual sodomy	class B misd.	NTE 3 mos. and/or $500

Solicitation §230.05	soliciting sexual conduct for a fee	violation	NTE 15 days and/or $250
Loitering §240.35(3)	loitering for deviate sexual purposes	violation	NTE 15 days and/or $250
Disorderly Conduct §240.20	disorderly conduct; obscene gestures	violation	NTE 15 days and/or $250
Lewdness §245.00	public lewdness; indecent exposure	class B misd.	NTE 3 mos. and/or $500
NORTH CAROLINA *Sodomy* N.C. Gen. Stat. §14-177	crime against nature	felony	discretionary
Lewdness §14-198	lewd woman within 3 miles of colleges & boarding schools	misd.	$50 or 30 days
Disorderly Conduct §14-275.1	disorderly conduct; loitering	misd.	$50 cr 30 days

State	Statute	Offense	Status	Penalty
NORTH DAKOTA	Sodomy §12-22-07	sodomy-forced	felony	NTE 10 yrs.
	Vagrancy §12-42-04(5)	lewd, wanton, & lascivious behavior	misd.	NTE 1 yr. and/or $100
	Sodomy §12.1-20-12	intent to arouse or gratify sexual desire	misd.	NTE 1 yr. and/or $1,000
	Disorderly Conduct §12.1-31-01(3)	making obscene gesture	misd.	NTE 30 days and/or $500
	Solicitation §12.1-31-01(6)	for purposes of sexual contact	misd.	NTE 30 days and/or $500
OHIO	Sexual Imposition Ohio Rev. Code Ann. §2907.06	sexual imposition (nonconsensual)	misd. 3rd degree	NTE 60 days and/or $500
	Solicitation §2907.07(B)	offensive solicitation	misd. 1st degree	NTE 6 mos. and/or $1,000

§2907.24	solicitation of sexual activity for hire	misd. 3rd degree	NTE 60 days and/or $500
Public Indecency §2907.09	indecent exposure or sexual conduct in public	misd. 4th degree	NTE 30 days and/or $250
Disorderly Conduct §2917.11	disorderly conduct; offensive gestures or display	misd. 4th degree	NTE 30 days and/or $250
	if persisting after warning		NTE 6 mos. and/or $1,000
Habitual Sex Offender §2950.01 and	2 or more convictions of sex offense (1st off.)	misd. 1st degree	NTE 6 mos. and/or $1,000
§2950.99	(subs. off.)	felony 4th degree	6 mos.–5 yrs. and/or $2,500
OKLAHOMA Disturbing the Peace 21 Okla. Stat. Ann. §22	grossly disturbing the peace; outraging public decency; injury to public morals	misd.	NTE 1 yr. and/or $500

State	Statute	Offense	Status	Penalty
	Sodomy §886	crime against nature	felony	NTE 10 yrs.
	Indecent Exposure §1021	lewd and indecent exposure	felony	30 days–10 yrs. and/or $10–100
	Lewdness §1029 to 31	lewdness, prostitution, assignation	misd.	30 days–1 yr.
	Vagrancy §1141 and 1142	vagrancy—idle persons; loitering	misd.	NTE 30 days and/or $10–100
OREGON	*Disorderly Conduct* ORS §166.025	disorderly conduct—obscene gestures in public	class B misd.	NTE 6 mos. and/or $500
	Loitering §166.045	loitering near a school or in a public place	class C misd.	NTE 30 days and/or $250
	Prostitution §167.007	deviate sexual intercourse for a fee	class A misd.	NTE 1 yr. and/or $1,000
	Sodomy §163.385	sodomy with person under 16	class C felony	NTE 5 yrs. and/or $2,500

	§163.445	deviate sexual conduct with unmarried person under 18	class C misd.	NTE 30 days and/or $250
	Solicitation §163.455	soliciting deviate sexual intercourse; accosting for deviate purposes	class C misd.	NTE 30 days and/or $250
	Public Indecency §163.465	indecent exposure; deviate sexual intercourse in public	class A misd.	NTE 1 yr. and/or $1,000
PENNSYLVANIA	*Sodomy* 18 C.P.S.A. §3123	involuntary deviate sexual intercourse	felony 1st degree	NTE 20 yrs. and/or $2,500
	§3124	voluntary deviate sexual intercourse	misd. 2nd degree	NTE 2 yrs. and/or $5,000
	Indecency §3126	indecent assault offensive to another	misd. 2nd degree	NTE 2 yrs. and/or $5,000

State	Statute	Offense	Status	Penalty
	Indecent Exposure §3127	indecent exposure	misd. 2nd degree	NTE 2 yrs. and/or $5,000
	Disorderly Conduct §5503	disorderly conduct; obscene gestures	misd. 3rd degree	NTE 1 yr. and/or $2,500
	Loitering §5506	malicious loitering at night	misd. 3rd degree	NTE 1 yr. and/or $2,500
	Lewdness §5901	open lewdness	misd. 3rd degree	NTE 1 yr. and/or $2,500
	Solicitation §5902	loitering in public for sexual activity	misd. 3rd degree	NTE 1 yr. and/or $2,500

RHODE ISLAND	*Sodomy* R.I. Gen. Laws Ann. §11-10-1	crime against nature	felony	7–20 yrs.
	Solicitation §11-34-5	loitering for purpose of soliciting lewdness, unlawful intercourse or indecent acts	felony	NTE 5 yrs.
	Vagrancy §11-45-1	idle, disorderly, lewd, wanton, or lascivious persons; indecent behavior in public	misd.	NTE 1 yr.
SOUTH CAROLINA	*Lewdness* S.C. Code §16-409 & 411	lewdness, prostitution, assignation	misd. (1st off.)	**NTE 30 days or $100**
			(2nd off.)	NTE 90 days and/or $250
			(3rd off.)	6 mos.–3 yrs. and/or $1,000
	Sodomy §16-412	buggery	felony	5 years and/or $5,000 mandatory

State	Statute	Offense	Status	Penalty
	Indecent Exposure §16-413	indecent exposure	misd.	discretionary
	Disorderly Conduct §16-558	public disorderly conduct	misd.	NTE 30 days or $100
	Vagrancy §16-565	persons leading idle, disorderly life	misd.	NTE 30 days or $100
SOUTH DAKOTA	Disturbing the Peace S.D. Comp. Laws Ann. §22-13-1	wilfully, grossly disturbing the peace	misd.	NTE 1 yr. and/or $500
	Disorderly Conduct §22-13-5 §22-13-6	disorderly conduct (unincorp. town) disorderly conduct (township)	misd. misd.	$5-10 1-10 days
	Vagrancy §22-13-12 & -13	loafers, loiterers, idle or immoral persons not working	misd.	NTE 30 days and/or $100
	Loitering §22-13-14	loitering	misd.	NTE 10 days or $25
	Sodomy §22-22-21	crime against nature	felony	NTE 10 yrs.

Offense / Citation	Description	Classification	Penalty
Lewdness §22-23-1	leading life of lewdness; prostitution	misd. (1st off.) (2nd off.) (3rd off.)	$10–25 NTE 30 days and/or $25–100 NTE 5 yrs.
Indecent Exposure §22-24-1 §22-24-2	indecent exposure procuring indecent exposure	misd. misd.	NTE 1 yr. and/or $500
Public Indecency §22-24-6	outraging public decency; injury to public morals	misd.	NTE 1 yr. and/or $500
TENNESSEE *Sodomy* Tenn. Code Ann. §39-07	crimes against nature	felony	5–15 yrs.
Disorderly Conduct §39-1209 & -1210	disturbance of, loitering near female schools	misd. (1st off.) (sub. off.)	$5–50 NTE 10–30 days and $10–50
Loitering §39-1211	loitering on public school grounds	misd. (1st off.) (sub. off.)	$20–100 $50–100

State	Statute	Offense	Status	Penalty
	Lewdness §39-3501 to -3505	prostitution, assignation, lewdness	misd. (1st off.) (2nd off.) (3rd off.)	NTE $50 NTE 30 days and/or $50 NTE 12 mos. and/or $500
	Vagrancy §39-4701 & -4702	vagrancy; loitering without visible means of support	misd.	10 days–1 yr. and/or $5–25
	Disturbing the Peace §39-1213	disturbing the peace—indecent or offensive conduct	misd. (1st off.) (sub. off.)	NTE 30 days and $20–200 NTE 90 days and $50–500
TEXAS	*Sodomy* V.T.C.A. Penal Code §21.04	deviate sexual intercourse (non-consensual)	felony 2nd degree	2–20 yrs. and/or $100
	§21.06	homosexual conduct; deviate sexual intercourse	class C misd.	NTE $200

Lewdness §21.07	sexual or deviate sexual intercourse or contact in public	class A misd.	NTE 1 yr. and/or $200
Indecent Exposure §21.08	indecent exposure	class C misd.	NTE $200
Disorderly Conduct §42.01	offensive gesture or display in public; indecent exposure	class C misd.	NTE $200
UTAH			
Sodomy §76-5-403(1)	sodomy	class B misd.	NTE 6 mos. and/or $299
(2)	sodomy–nonconsensual	felony 2nd degree	1–15 yrs. and/or $1,000
Disorderly Conduct §76-9-102	disorderly conduct; obscene gestures in public	infraction (or) class C misd.	NTE 90 days and/or $299
Indecent Exposure & Lewdness §76-9-702	gross lewdness; indecent exposure	class B misd.	NTE 6 mos. and/or $299

State	Statute	Offense	Status	Penalty
	Loitering §76-9-703	loitering	class C misd.	NTE 90 days and/or $299
	Sex Offender Act §77-49-1 to §77-49-8	If mental illness, then commitment for life. Parole only upon certification of recovery by hospital superintendent. (definition)		
VERMONT	*Disorderly Conduct* 13 V.S.A. §1026	disorderly conduct	misd.	NTE 60 days and/or $500
	Lewdness §2601	gross lewdness; lascivious behavior	felony	NTE 5 yrs. or $300
	§2631 & 2632	prostitution, lewdness, assignation	misd. (1st off.) felony (sub. off.)	NTE 1 yr. or $100 NTE 3 yrs.
	Sodomy §2603	fellatio	felony	1–5 yrs.

VIRGINIA			
Vagrancy §3901 & 3902	vagrancy	misd.	NTE 6 mos. or $100
Lewdness Code of Va. §18.1-193	open and gross lewdness and lasciviousness	misd. (1st off.) (sub. off.)	$50–500 / 6–12 mos.
§18.1-197 & -199	prostitution, lewdness, assignation, illicit intercourse	misd.	NTE 12 mos.
Solicitation §18.1-200 to -202	commitment of persons convicted of soliciting for immoral purposes		
Sodomy §18.1-212	crime against nature	felony	1–3 yrs.
Indecent Exposure §18.1-236	indecent exposure	misd.	NTE 12 mos. and/or $1,000
Disorderly Conduct §18.1-253.1 & -253.2	disorderly conduct	misd.	NTE 12 mos. and/or $1,000

State	Statute	Offense	Status	Penalty
WASHING-TON	*Indecent Exposure* RCWA 9.79.080(2)	indecent or obscene exposure	felony	(penitentiary) NTE 20 yrs. (jail) NTE 1 yr.
	Sodomy 9.79.100(2)	sodomy	felony	NTE 10 yrs.
	Lewdness 9.79.120	open or gross lewdness; indecent exposure	gross misd.	NTE 1 yr. and/or $1,000
	Solicitation 9.79.130	solicitation of minor for immoral purposes	gross misd.	NTE 1 yr. and/or $1,000
	Vagrancy 9.87.010(6)	vagrancy—lewd, disorderly or dissolute persons	misd.	NTE 6 mos. or $500
	Sexual Psychopaths 71.06.010 71.06.040 71.06.060 71.06.091	definitions generally hospital detention for observation commitment length of commitment—until in opinion of supt. of institution he is "safe to be at large"		NTE 90 days

WEST VIRGINIA			
	Lewdness W. Va. Code §61-8-4	open & gross lewdness and lasciviousness	misd. (1st off.)	NLT 6 mos. and $50
			(sub. off.)	6–12 mos.
	Sodomy §61-8-13	sodomy	felony	1–10 yrs.
	Indecent Exposure §61-8-28	obscene or lewd exposure	misd.	NTE 30 days and/or $20–100
	Loitering §61-6-14(a)	loitering on school property	misd. (1st off.)	NTE 30 days and/or $100
			(sub. off.)	NTE 1 yr. and/or $500
WISCONSIN	*Sodomy* W.S.A. §944.17	sexual perversion; sodomy	felony	NTE 5 yrs. and/or $500

State	Statute	Offense	Status	Penalty
	Lewdness §944.20	indecent acts; indecent exposure, lewd and lascivious behavior	misd.	NTE 1 yr. and/or $500
	Solicitation §944.30	prostitution—act of sexual perversion for value	misd.	NTE 1 yr. and/or $500
	Disorderly Conduct §947.01	indecent and disorderly conduct	misd.	NTE 90 days or $200
	Vagrancy §947.02	vagrancy; loitering	misd.	NTE 6 mos.
WYOMING	*Lewdness* Wyo. Stat. Ann. §6-90, 91, 93	prostitution, lewdness, assignation	misd. felony	(jail) 4 mos.–1 yr. or (reformatory) 1–3 yrs.
	Sodomy §6-98	crime against nature	felony	NTE 10 yrs.
	Public Indecency §6-102	indecent exposure	misd.	NTE 3 mos. and $100
	Breach of the Peace §6-114	breach of the peace	misd.	NTE 30 days and/or $50

Vagrancy §6-221, 222	vagrancy—persons leading immoral lives	misd.	NTE 3 mos. and $100
Persons convicted of sex crimes			
§7-348	persons convicted upon pleading guilty to the above statutes		court shall order a mental examination
§7-351	if examiner's report shows compulsive behavior accompanied by violence or age discrepancy so as to make convicted person an adult aggressor		out patient treatment or commitment
§7-356	commitment NTE max. sentence for crime of which person is convicted except in case of indecent exposure, commitment for which NTE 1 yr.		

2. Statutory Provisions Affecting the Licensing of Gays

The following is a list of occupations subject to licensing restrictions. The type of restriction is indicated by the numbers 1, 2 and 3 according to state statutory provisions:

"1"—Indicates a statutory provision that refers to a criminal offense as grounds for denying a license.

"2"—Indicates a statutory provision that conditions the granting of a license on the applicant's possessing good moral character.

"3"—Indicates a statutory provision that conditions the granting of a license on the applicant's possessing good moral character and not having a criminal record.

* Source: National Clearinghouse on Offender Employment Restrictions, *Law, Licenses and the Offender's Rights to Work: A Study of State Laws Restricting the Occupational Licensing of Former Offenders A-1 through A-13 (1973).*

OCCUPATION

#	Occupation	TOTAL	ALA.	ALASKA	ARIZ.	ARK.	CAL.	COL.	CONN.	D.C.	DEL.	FLA.	GA.	HAWAII	IDAHO	ILL.	IND.	IOWA
1	Abstractor	3		2									2					
2	Accountant (or CPA)	48	2	2	2	2	2	2	2	2	2	2	2	2	2	3	3	2
3	Agricultural Chemical Applicator	1				1												
4	Agricultural Produce—Broker	1											2					
5	Agricultural Produce—Dealer	2				3							2					
6	Agricultural Processor	1											2					
7	Agricultural Produce—Merchant	1											2					
8	Aircraft Broker	1	2															
9	Aircraft Pilot	2																
10	Alcoholic Beverage—Dealer	9					2	1	3								1	
11	Alcoholic Beverage—Employee	7					1		1								1	
12	Alcoholic Beverage—Manufacturer	6					3	1	3									
13	Alcoholic Beverage—Retailer	8					3	1	3								1	
14	Alcoholic Beverage—Transporter	1																
15	Amusement Operator	1												2				
16	Animal Dealer	1																
17	Apprentice	1						2										
18	Architect	42	2	2					3	2	2	2	2	2	2	3	3	2
19	Artificial Inseminator	2													3			
20	Artist Manager	1				2												
21	Astrologer	1												2				
22	Attorney	51	2	2	2	2	2	2	2	2	2	2	3	2	2	2	2	2
23	Auctioneer	10							2		2							
24	Auctioneer—Livestock	1																
25	Automobile Dismantler	1				3												

	KAN.	KY.	LA.	ME.	MD.	MASS.	MICH.	MINN.	MISS.	MO.	MONT.	NEB.	NEV.	N.H.	N.J.	N.M.	N.Y.	N.C.	N.D.	OHIO	OKLA.	ORE.	PA.	R.I.	S.C.	S.D.	TENN.	TEXAS	UTAH	VT.	VA.	WASH.	W. VA.	WIS.	WYO.
1												2																							
2	2	2	2	2	3	2	2		2	2	2	2	2	2	3	2	2	2	2	2		2	2	2	2	2	2	2	3	2	3	2	2	2	2
3																																			
4																																			
5																																			
6																																			
7																																			
8																																			
9												2		2																					
10									3						1		1						3												
11										1					1		1					1													
12										3					1		1																		
13										3					1		1																		
14										3																									
15																																			
16																											3								
17																																			
18		2	2		2	2	2	2	2	2		2	2		2	2	2	3	2	2	2	3	2	2	2	2	2	2	2	2		2	2	2	2
19											2																								
20																																			
21																																			
22	2	2	3	2	2	2	2	2	3	2	2	2	3	2	2	2	2	2	2	2	2	2	2	2	2	2	2	3	2	2	2	2	3	2	2
23		2		2										3			2			2		2	2				2								
24													1																						
25																																			

No.	Occupation	Count	Values
26	Babcock Test Operator	1	2
27	Barber	47	2 3 3 3 2 2 2 2 3 3 3 3 3 2
28	Barber Apprentice	8	2 2 3 3
29	Barber Instructor	6	2 1 3 3
30	Barber Manager/Owner	12	2 2
31	Barber School	1	3
32	Beautician	29	3 2 3 3 3 3 3 3 3
33	Beauty Culturist	1	
34	Beauty School	2	
35	Beauty Shop Owner	12	2
36	Beer Retailer/Wholesaler	1	3
37	Billiard Operator	3	3 2
38	Bingo Operator	1	
39	Bioanalytical Lab Operator	2	3
40	Biochemist	1	
41	Boiler Inspector	1	
42	Bondsman (Bail)	11	3 3 3 3 2
43	Boxer/Wrestler	6	2
44	Boxing Promoter	2	2
45	Broker—Business Chance	1	
46	Broker—Insurance	18	2 3 3 3 2 2 3 3 3
47	Broker—Investment	1	
48	Broker—Personal Property	1	2
49	Broker—Real Estate	46	3 3 2 2 2 3 2 2 2 2 3 3 3
50	Broker—Savings and Loan	1	2
51	Broker—Surplus Line Insurance	9	2 3 2 3
52	Burial Association Agent	1	2
53	Business School Operator	2	3
54	Butcher	1	

```
26
27 2 3 3 2 2   3 2 3 2 1 3 3   3 2 2 3 3 3 3 2 3 2 2   2 3 2 2 2 2 2 2 3 2
28                     3       2       3                           2
29             2 2
30   3               2         2       3 2           3             2 2 2 2
31
32 2 3     2         3         3 2   3           2 2   2 2   1 2 3 2 3   2 3 3
33                                                     2
34                           2                         2
35 3       2   2 3                   3   2           3       1   2 2     2
36
37             2
38                                       3

39                                   3
40                             2   3
41             2
42                         1       3 3     3           3         2
43 1                               2                     2 2     3
44                                                       2
45     2
46 2   2   2 2 2           2               2   3   2
47                                                                           1

48
49 2 2 2 3 2 2   3 3 3 2   3 2 3 3   3 3 3 2 3 2 2 2 2 2 2 2 2 3 2 2 3 2 2

50

51       2             2               3 3       1

52
53 1
54                               2
```

OCCUPATION

#	Occupation	TOTAL	ALA.	ALASKA	ARIZ.	ARK.	CAL.	COL.	CONN.	D.C.	DEL.	FLA.	GA.	HAWAII	IDAHO	ILL.	IND.	IOWA
1	Cattle Dealer	3					2											
2	Cemetery Salesman	3				2								3				
3	Chauffeur	12			1											3		2
4	Check Casher/Seller	9			2	2												
5	Child Day Care Operator	3																
6	Chiropodist	36		2	3	2	2	3	2		2	3			2	3		
7	Chiropractor	43	1	3	3	3	2	3	2	2	3	3	3	3	2	3	3	3
8	Cigarette Dealer	1																
9	Cigarette Manufacturer	1																
10	Civil Engineer	1																
11	Cleaning Plant Operator	1																
12	Clinical Chemist	1						3										
13	Clinical Lab Director	1						3										
14	Clinical Lab Technologist	2						3			2							
15	Coal Mine Examiner	1																
16	Collection Agent	15	3	3		3	3	3						1	1		3	
17	Commercial Driving School	1		2														
18	Commission Merchant	1																
19	Contractor (Builder)	1																
20	Correspondence School Rep.	1																
21	Cosmetologist	24	3	2		2	2	2	3		2		2		3			
22	Cosmetology Instructor	3						2							3			
23	Cotton Classer	1	2															

	KAN.	KY.	LA.	MD.	ME.	MASS.	MICH.	MINN.	MISS.	MO.	MONT.	NEB.	NEV.	N.H.	N.J.	N.M.	N.Y.	N.C.	N.D.	OHIO	OKLA.	ORE.	PA.	R.I.	S.C.	S.D.	TENN.	TEXAS	UTAH	VT.	VA.	WASH.	W. VA.	WIS.	WYO.
1															2	3																			
2								2																											
3		2						1		3	2				3		2		2				1		2	2									
4						2			2			3		3			2		2															2	
5									2									2																2	
6	3	3	3			2	3	3	3		3	2		2		3		2	3	2	3	3	3	2	2		3	2	3	3	2	3		2	2
7	3	2			3	3	3	1	1		2	3	3		2	3	3		3	2		2	3	3	2		2	3	3	3	3	3		3	2	2
8								2																											
9																																		3	
10		2																																	
11							1																												
12																																			
13																																			
14																																			
15										2																									
16					2						2	3		3					3														3	2	
17																																			
18							2																												
19						2																													
20						2																													
21	2		3		2		2		3	2	2	3				2		2		3			2		3	3				3					
22							3																												
23																																			

#	Occupation																		
24	Dairy Product Distributor	2			2			2											
25	Dairy Product—Buyer/Processor	3		2		2		2											
26	Day Care Operator	2																	
27	Dealer—Livestock/Poultry	2																	
28	Dealer—Tobacco/Soft Drink	2																	
29	Debt Adjustor	2			3		2												
30	Debt Management Business	1																	
31	Dental Hygienist	48	3 2 2 2 2 3	2 2 2 2 2 3 1 2 3														
32	Dental Specialist	1																	
33	Dentist	47	3 2 2 2 2 1	2 2 2 2 1 3 3 3 3														
34	Detection of Deception Examiner	1																	
35	Detective Agent	2																	
36	Detective Agency Operator	1																	
37	Disposal Plant Operator	1						2											
38	Distilling Certificate Broker	1																	
39	Dog Racing	1					3												
40	Driver	2																	
41	Driving Instructor	8																	
42	Driving School Operator	2																	
43	Drug Dealer/Wholesaler	3																	
44	Dry Cleaning	1																	
45	Egg Dealer	1																	
46	Electrician	2			2														
47	Electrical Worker	1			2														
48	Electrologists	10		2 2					3									
49	Electrology Instructor	1		2															
50	Elevator Craftsman/Helper	1			2														
51	Elevator Inspector	1																	
52	Embalmer	46	2	2 3 2 2 2		3 3 2 3 3 3 3												
53	Emigrant Agent	2					3												

```
24

25
26                    2              2
27                         3              1

28                            2         2
29

30                                              3
31 3 2 2 2 2 2 2 2 2 2 3 2 2 2 2 3 3 2 2 2 2 2 2 2 2 2 2   1 2 2 2 2 3   2
32   2
33 3   3 2 2 2 2 2 2 3 2 3 2 2 2 3 2 3 2 2 2 2 2   2 2 2 3 3 2 2 2 3   2

34   3
35                                        3           3
36                                     2
37

38                                  2
39
40                    2
41 2 2    2           2                2           2       3     1
42   2                2                                          3
43      3                                              2         2
44   1

45                                                 2
46                  2
47
48      2 2        2    3         3 3          3
49
50
51                                        2
52 3 3 3 1 3 3 3 3 2 3   3 2 2 3 2 2 3 2 3 3 3   2 3 3 3 3 2 3 3 3 2 3 2 2
53                                                        2
```

#	OCCUPATION	TOTAL	ALA.	ALASKA	ARIZ.	ARK.	CAL.	COL.	CONN.	DEL.	D.C.	FLA.	GA.	HAWAII	IDAHO	ILL.	IND.	IOWA
1	Employment Agency Operator	11	2	2		2	2		2							3	2	
2	Engineer	43	2	2	2		2	3		2	3	2	2	2	2	3	1	2
3	Engineer in Training	2																
4	Escrow Agent	1			2													
5	Explosives Dealer	2					2							1				
6	Explosives Manufacturer/ Distributor	2																
7	Explosives Handlers	1																
8	Exterminator	4		2								2	1	2				
9	Farm Product Broker	1																
10	Farrier	1																
11	Feeder Swine Dealer	2														1	3	
12	Financial Planner	1														3		
13	Finger Weaver	1		2														
14	Firearms Dealer	1																
15	Fishing Boat Operator	1										1						
16	Florist	1														2		
17	Foreign Exchange Dealer	1														1		
18	Forester	3																
19	Fortune Teller	1																
20	Fraternal Society Agent	1													2			
21	Frozen Foods Dealer	1																
22	Fumigator	1													1			
23	Fund Raiser	1																
24	Funeral Director	45			2	3	2	1	3	1		3	3	2	3	3	3	
25	Fur Dealer/Breeder	1																

	KAN.	KY.	LA.	ME.	MD.	MASS.	MICH.	MINN.	MISS.	MO.	MONT.	NEB.	NEV.	N.H.	N.J.	N.M.	N.Y.	N.C.	N.D.	OHIO	OKLA.	ORE.	PA.	R.I.	S.C.	S.D.	TENN.	TEXAS	UTAH	VT.	VA.	WASH.	W. VA.	WIS.	WYO.
1						2			3											2						3									
2	2	3	2	2		2	2	2	2	2	2	2		2	2	2	2	2		2	3	2		2	2	2	2		2	2	2	2	2	2	2
3							2				2																								
4																																			
5																																			
6									3				1																1						
7										1																									
8	1																																		
9										2																									
10								2																											
11																																			
12																																			
13																																			
14																3																			
15																																			
16																																			
17																																			
18				2														2				2													
19																																2			
20																																			
21																		2																	
22																																			
23			2																																
24	3	3	3	1	3		3	3		3	3	3	2	2	2	2	2	3	2	3	3	3	3	2	3	3	3	3	3	2	3	3	2	3	2
25																				2															

26	Gambling Operator	1					
27	Game Breeder	3	2				2
28	Game Warden	1					
29	Geologist	1		2			
30	Guard	5					
31	Guide	4	3			2	
32	Guide (Hunting, Fishing)	1		2			
33	Guide Outfitter	1					3
34	Gun Dealer	1				2	
35	Gunsmith	1					
36	Hairdresser	12	2		2		
37	Hairdressing Instructor	1			2		
38	Harbor Pilot	7	2			2	2
39	Hawker	3					
40	Hearing Aid Dispensor	10		3			
41	Hearing Aid Fitter	2					
42	Healing Arts Practitioner	1					
43	Home Improvement Salesman	1					
44	Homeopath	1					
45	Horsemeat Processor	1					3
46	Horse Racing	6					3
47	Horse Racing Personnel	2					
48	Horse Shoer	1					2
49	Horse Trainer	1					
50	Hospital Operator	1		2	2		
51	Hunting Guide	1		2			
52	Hypertrichnologist	1			3		

26					2												
27									2								
28										2							
29																	
30		3							3	2		3				1	
31				2													2
32																	
33																	
34																	
35		1															
36	2 2	2		2		2	3 2	2						2 3			
37																	
38						2			2			2 2					
39		2			2				2								
40	2		3		2		2		2	2	3	2			2		
41	2									3							
42		2															
43	2																
44		3															
45																	
46	3				2	1 3		3									
47					2			3									
48																	
49				1													
50																	
51																	
52																	

OCCUPATION	TOTAL	ALA.	ALASKA	ARIZ.	ARK.	CAL.	COL.	CONN.	DEL.	D.C.	FLA.	GA.	HAWAII	IDAHO	ILL.	IND.	IOWA
1 Industrial Alcohol	1																
2 Inhalation Therapist	1			3													
3 Insurance Adjustor	15			2		2						3	3				
4 Inspector	1																
5 Insurance Agent/Broker	42	3	2	3	2	3	2		2				3	1	3	2	2
6 Insurance Agent—Fire	1	2															
7 Insurance Agent—Life	3																2
8 Insurance Agent—Life and Health	2	2										2					
9 Insurance Counselor	1												3				
10 Insurance Manager	1																
11 Insurance Rater	1																
12 Investment Agent	5																
13 Jockey	1																
14 Journeyman (Limited)	1							2									
15 Junk Dealer	4					2											
16 Junk Yard Operator	1																
17 Labor Agent	1																
18 Landscape Architect	6								2	1		2	2				
19 Land Surveyor	32	2		2		2		2				2	2	3	2	1	
20 Lightning Rod Salesman	2																
21 Limburger Cheese Maker	1																
22 Limited Contractor	1						2										

WYO.
WIS.
W. VA.
WASH.
VA.
VT.
UTAH
TEXAS
TENN.
S.D.
S.C.
R.I.
PA.
ORE.
OKLA.
OHIO
N.D.
N.C.
N.Y.
N.M.
N.J.
N.H.
NEV.
NEB.
MONT.
MO.
MISS.
MINN.
MICH.
MASS.
MD.
ME.
LA.
KY.
KAN.

```
 1                                1
 2
 3        2  2      3   2  3          2      3 3  2        2
 4                                                          2
 5 5 2 2    2 2 2 2 2.  3 2 3 3    3 2   2 3 2 3 3    2 2 1 2 2 2 3 2 2 2 3
 6
 7   2                    2

 8
 9
10                                        2
11
12  1              2          3           2              1
                   1
13                 1
14
15         2                  1                          2
16

17                                        2
18                              2                          2
19 2 2      2    2 2   2 2 2  2 2 2 2 2    3    2 2 2    2 2 2 3 2 2
20      2              2
21                                                        2
22
```

23	Live Poultry Dealer	1									
24	Livery Service	1			2						
25	Livestock Dealer	7							2	3	
26	Livestock Producer	1									
27	Loanmaker	5									
28	Lobbyist	1									
29	Lodging Housekeeper	1			2						
30	Logscaler	1						3			
31	Manicurist	22	3	2 2 2		3	3 2 2 3				
32	Marine Diver	1									
33	Marine Pilot	1	2								
34	Marriage Counselor	2		3							
35	Masseur	12		3		2 3	2				
36	Medical Lab Technician	1									
37	Medical Technician	2 2				2					
38	Merchant Truck Man	1									
39	Midwife	16	2		2	2 2 2		3 3			
40	Milk Handler/Dealer	3									
41	Milk Plant Manager	1									
42	Milk Tester/Weigher	1									
43	Mine Foreman	4	2	2							
44	Mine Inspector	7		2				2			
45	Mineral, Oil, and Gas Broker	1	3								
46	Mobile Home Salesman	1									
47	Money Lender	1									
48	Money Order Vendor/Forwarder	3		2							
49	Mortgage Broker	1			2						
50	Mortician	1									
51	Hand Carrier Vehicle Operator	1									
52	Motor Club Agent	2					3				

```
23                                                          2
24
25                        1      3  12              1
26 1
27       2                             2 2 2 2
28            2
29
30

31 3 3     2 3  2    2 2  3            2        3      3 3 3
32   1
33
34                    3
35         2   2 3   3 2  3    3              2
36                 1
37
38                    2
39   3  2  3       2  3 2    2    3              2  2
40 2              2   2
41                    2
42                    2
43                    2  2
44 2          2                        2    2       2

45
46            2
47               2
48               2
49
50         3

51 2
52         2
```

OCCUPATION

	TOTAL	ALA.	ALASKA	ARIZ.	ARK.	CAL.	COL.	CONN.	D.C.	DEL.	FLA.	GA.	HAWAII	IDAHO	ILL.	IND.	IOWA
1 Motor Common Carrier	1							2									
2 Motor Vehicle Dealer	12				3						2	1	1				
3 Motor Vehicle Operator	12					2					2	3	1				
4 Motor Vehicle Salesman	5												1				
5 Motor Vehicle Used Parts Dealer	1									3							
6 Naturopath	7		3	2	1			2									
7 Nurse— Practical/Vocational	48	2	3	3	3	2	2	2	2	3	2	2	3	3	3	2	
8 Nurse— Professional/Registered	49	2	3	3	3	3	2	2	2	2	2	2	2	3	3	2	3
9 Nurse—Psychiatric	1																
10 Nurse— Psychiatric Technician	2			3	3												
11 Nursing Home Administrator	14	2						2			3	2			3		
12 Nursing Home Operator	1																2
13 Nurseryman	3			2	2												
14 Nursery Stock Dealer	1																
15 Obstetrician	1																
16 Operating Engineer	1							2									
17 Ophthalmic Dispenser	4																
18 Optician	11	2		3	3			2				2	3	3			
19 Optician—Assistant	1							2									
20 Optician— Assistant Mechanical								2									
21 Optician—Mechanical	1							2									
22 Optometrist	49	2	2	2	2	3	1	2	2	3	2	3		2	3		2
23 Orthopedist	1																
24 Osteopath	44	2	2	2	3	1	3	3	2	2	3	3	1	3	3	3	2

	KAN.	KY.	LA.	ME.	MD.	MASS.	MICH.	MINN.	MISS.	MO.	MONT.	NEB.	NEV.	N.H.	N.J.	N.M.	N.Y.	N.C.	N.D.	OHIO	OKLA.	ORE.	PA.	R.I.	S.C.	S.D.	TENN.	TEXAS	UTAH	VT.	VA.	WASH.	W.VA.	WIS.	WYO.
1																																			
2		2	2											1	1		2								2	3								3	
3		2	2					1						3	3	2	2		1						2	3			2						
4		2		1				1						1																					2
5																																			
6																									3						3	3			
7	3	3	2	3	3	3	2	3	3	2		2	3	2	3	3	3	2	3	2	3	3	2	2	2	2	2	3	2	2	3	3	2	2	3
8	3	3	3	2	3	3	3	2	3	3		3	3	3	3	3	2	3	2	3	3	3	2	2	2	2	3	3	3	3	3	2	2	3	2
9								3																											
10																																			
11		2												2	2		3				2	2					2	2							2
12																																			
13																									2										
14							2																												
15																																	3		
16																																			
17	2													3	3	2																			
18							1																				2	2	2						
19																																			
20																																			
21																																			
22	2	3	3	1	2	2	3	2	3	3	2	3	2	3	3	3	2	2	2	3	2	2	3	2	2	2	2	3	2	2	2	2	3	3	3
23																			3																
24	2	3		3	3	2	2	3	2	3	2	3	3			3	3			3	1	2	3	3	2	3	2		3	3	3	2	3		1

#	Occupation		
25	Pawnbroker	11	2222
26	Peddler	1	
27	Pedicurist	1	3
28	Pest Control	7	22 222
29	Petshop Owner/Dog Dealer	1	1
30	Pharmicist	47	2 3 2 3 3 3 2 3 2 2 2 3 3 3 3
31	Photographer	2	2
32	Physical Therapist	47	3 3 3 3 3 3 3 2 3 3 3 3 2 2 3 3
33	Physician	50	2 2 3 3 1 3 2 3 2 3 3 2 3 3 3 3
34	Pilot—Ship	2	
35	Plumber	10	2 2 2 1
36	Podiatrist	26	3 2 2 3 3 2
37	Polygraph Examiner	1	
38	Poultry Technician	1	
39	Priest (for marriage)	1	
40	Private Investigator	25	3 3 2 3 3 3 3 3
41	Product Wholesaler	1	
42	Professional Planner	1	
43	Psychiatric Technician	1	1
44	Psychologist	40	3 2 3 3 3 2 2 3 3 3 3 3
45	Public Adjustor	1	
46	Public Service Operator (Motor Veh.)	1	2
47	Public Weigher	2	2 2
48	Radiologist	1	
49	Real Estate Salesman/Broker	45	3 3 2 2 2 3 2 2 2 3 3 3 3
50	Recreation Hall Operator	1	
51	Remittance Agent	1	2

```
25    2                        2
26                                2       2      2 2 2
27                                                     2
28 1

29                                        3
30 2 2 2 2 2   3 3 2 3 2 3 3 3 2 3 2 1   2 3 2 2 2 2 2 3   3 3 2 2 2 2 2 2
31      2
32 3 3 3 3 3 3   3 3 3 3 3 3 2 3 3 2 3 3 3 3 3   3 2 2 2 2 2 3 3 2 3 2
33 2   3 2 2 2 3 3 2 3 3 3 2 2 3 3 2 2 3 2 3 2 3 3 3 2 3 2 3 3 3 3 2 3 2 2
34           2                                          2
35    2     2 2                  2                        2 2
36 3 3   2 2 3 3       3   2 3 3 2       2         2 2 3 3   3   2   2 2
37                            3         3                3
38                                            2
39    2
40 2           3 1 3       3 3   2 3 3 2 1 3     3   2     3     3     3
41                       2
42                              2
43
44 2 2 3 3 2 2 2   3   3 3 2 3 2 3 2 3 3   2 3   3 2   3   3 3   2 3 3 3
45                              3
46
47


48                                        2

49 2 2 2 3 2 2   3 3 3 2   3 2 3 3   3 3 3 2 3 2 2 2 2 2 2 2 2 3 2 2 3 2 2
50          3
51
```

OCCUPATION

#	OCCUPATION	TOTAL	ALA.	ALASKA	ARIZ.	ARK.	CAL.	COL.	CONN.	DEL.	D.C.	FLA.	GA.	HAWAII	IDAHO	ILL.	IND.	IOWA
1	Retail Drugs	1							2									
2	Roentgenologist	1	2															
3	Safety Deposit Box Agent	1																1
4	Sanitarian	14					2		2			3	2	2	2			
5	School Bus Driver	4			3													
6	Second Hand Dealer	3							2			2						
7	Second Hand Dealer—Auto	2																
8	Securities Agent/Broker/Salesman	34	1			3	1		1	3	1	2	3	2	1	1	1	2
9	Seller of Checks and Money Orders	1		2														
10	Septic Tank Cleaner	1																
11	Ship Pilot	1																
12	Ship Port Pilot	1												2				
13	Shorthand Reporter	7				2	2							2				
14	Small Loan Lender	6	2				2		2									
15	Social Worker	6					3								3			
16	Solid Fuel Weigher	1																
17	Sprinkler Irrigation Fitter	1																
18	Steam Engineer	1									2							
19	Stevedores	1										2						
20	Structural Pest Controller	2				1												
21	Surveyors	2																

	KAN.	KY.	LA.	ME.	MD.	MASS.	MICH.	MINN.	MISS.	MO.	MONT.	NEB.	NEV.	N.H.	N.J.	N.M.	N.Y.	N.C.	N.D.	OHIO	OKLA.	ORE.	PA.	R.I.	S.C.	S.D.	TENN.	TEXAS	UTAH	VT.	VA.	WASH.	W. VA.	WIS.	WYO.
1	1																																		
2	2																																		
3																																			
4			1					2												3					3						2	3	2	2	
5														2							2														1
6			2																																
7						2							2																						
8			1		3	1							3	1	1	1		3	3				3	2	1	1	2	1	2	1	1	1	2	1	
9																																			
10		2																																	
11								2																											
12																																			
13	2																2		2												2				
14																						2			2		2								
15																				2			1				3					3			
16						2																													
17																																	2		
18																																			
19																																			
20																							3												
21			2					2																											

22	Tattoo Artist	1			2		
23	Taxidermist	1					
24	Taxi Driver	1		2			
25	Teacher	28 2	3 2	2 2	1 2		
26	Television Repairman	1				3	
27	Television Technician	1					
28	Ticket Broker	1					
29	Transportation Broker	1					
30	Tree Expert	1			3		
31	Tree Surgeon	2					
32	Undertaker	1		3			
33	Used Car Dealer	1					
34	Vendor	4	2	2 2 2			
35	Veterinarian	47 2 2 2 3 3 2	2 2 3 2 2 2 3 3 2				
36	Warehouseman	1 2					
37	Watchmaker	11			3 2		
38	Watchman	5					
39	Water Maker	1		2			
40	Water Treatment Plant Operator	1					
41	Water Well Contractor	1					
42	Weatherman	2					
43	Weighmaster	5	2				
44	Well Driller/Contractor	2		3			
45	X-Ray Technician	3					

```
22
23                                              2
24
25   2   2 2 3   2 2 2 2 2       1     2 1 3 2   1 3 2 2 2   3   2
26
27        2
28                                       2
29                                               2
30
31      2                 2
32
33                                                            3
34
35 2 3 2   3 3 2 2 2 3 3 3 3 2 3 2 2 3   3 2 2 2 1 3 2 3 3 2 2   2 2 1 2
36
37  2 2     2 2              3 2   2           3         2
38       3   2 2          3    3 2     2       3         2
39
40                                       2
41                  2
42              2   1
43                   2   2       2       2
44                            2
45                  2 2   2
```

3. Joint Domicile Agreement

WHEREAS, the parties hereto have expressed to each other feelings of love and affection, and

WHEREAS, each party hereto has a desire to enter into a relationship with the other whereby a home and family may be established, and

WHEREAS, the parties hereto recognize that the creation of such a relationship involves not only the feelings of the parties, each to the other, but considerations of property and financial security, and

WHEREAS, each of the parties hereto is personally of the same biological sex (optional—may be permitted), and

WHEREAS, the laws of the jurisdiction in which this Joint Domicile Agreement is being executed do not recognize the right of persons of the same sex to enter into what is traditionally termed a "marriage," and

WHEREAS, the parties hereto reject as unacceptable to themselves the terms imposed by law unto the parties undertaking such a relationship in the traditional manner, and

* The outline of this proposed agreement was prepared by Michael Miller, Esq., general counsel for the National Committee for Sexual Civil Liberties and general counsel for the Mattachine Society of New York.

WHEREAS, the parties hereto believe in the legitimacy of their intended relationship despite the failure of the law to personally recognize it as such, and

WHEREAS, it is the intent of the parties hereto to establish a relationship between themselves which expresses their binding and enforceable intentions and promises,

NOW, THEREFORE, in consideration of the mutual promises and covenants herein, the parties hereto agree as follows: (the following matters must be considered as clauses structured to express the agreement of the parties with respect thereto)

1. Real property.
2. Personal property.
3. Income from property.
4. Income from labor.
5. Right to manage property.
6. Right to manage income.
7. Right to terminate agreement (including grounds and arbitration).
8. Choice of domicile.
9. Use of names.
10. Fidelity issue.
11. Housework.
12. Sexual relationship.
13. Affection.
14. Duty of financial support.
15. Public anouncement.
16. Disclaimers and waivers of all rights and duties created by law.
17. Children.
    a. Duties.
    b. Custody.
    c. Names.
18. Property before agreement.
19. Property after agreement.
20. Property acquired by gift or inheritance.
21. Mutual wills.

22. Sharing of expenses.
23. Bank accounts.
24. Pooling arrangements of salary and accruals.
25. Education.
26. Loans (a) intra-spousal (b) third-party.
27. Taxes.
28. Birth control (including abortion).
29. Amendments and renegotiation.
30. Finite term and renewals.
31. Effect of elicit sex laws.
32. Periodic (or initial) VD tests.

4. A Gay Bibliography

Task Force on Gay Liberation
Social Responsibilities Round Table
American Library Association

THIRD REVISION—JANUARY 1974

This carefluly compiled non-fiction bibliography emphasizes materials that support a positive view of homosexuals and homosexuality.

Books

Abbott, Sidney and Love, Barbara. SAPPHO WAS A RIGHT-ON WOMAN. Stein and Day, 1972, cloth and paper eds.

Aldrich, Ann, TAKE A LESBIAN TO LUNCH. Manor (formerly Macfadden-Bartell), 1972, paper orig, out of print but reprint due Summer 1974.

Altman, Dennis. HOMOSEXUALITY: OPPRESSION AND LIBERATION. Outerbridge (dist. by Dutton), 1974. Also Avon paper ed.

Bailey, Derrick S. HOMOSEXUALITY AND THE WESTERN CHRISTIAN TRADITION. Longmans Green, 1955, out of print.

Barnett, Walter. SEXUAL FREEDOM AND THE CONSTITUTION. Univ. of New Mexico Press, 1973.

Bell, Arthur. DANCING THE GAY LIB BLUES. Simon & Schuster, 1971.

Benson, R.O. IN DEFENSE OF HOMOSEXUALITY. Julian Press, 1965, out of print. Also Ace paper ed. titled WHAT EVERY HOMOSEXUAL KNOWS, out of print.

* The bibliography was prepared by and published with the permission of the Task Force on Gay Liberation and Social Responsibilities Round Table, American Library Association, c/o Barbara Gittings, Box 2383, Philadelphia, Pennsylvania 19103.

Churchill Wainwright. HOMOSEXUAL BEHAVIOR AMONG
    MALES. Hawthorn, 1967, out of print. Also Spectrum/Pren-
    tice-Hall paper ed.
Clarke, Lige and Nichols, Jack. I HAVE MORE FUN WITH
    YOU THAN ANYBODY, St. Martin's, 1972.
Cory, Donald Webster. THE HOMOSEXUAL IN AMERICA.
    Greenberg, 1951, out of print.
Fisher, Peter. THE GAY MYSTIQUE: THE MYTH AND
    REALITY OF MALE HOMOSEXUALITY. Stein & Day,
    1972, cloth & paper eds.
Ford, Clellan S. and Beach, Frank. PATTERNS OF SEXUAL
    BEHAVIOR. Harper & Row, 1951, cloth & paper eds.
Freedman, Mark. HOMOSEXUALITY AND PSYCHOLOGI-
    CAL FUNCTIONING. Brooks/Cole (div. of Wadsworth),
    1971, paper orig.
Gearhart, Sally and Johnson, William R. (eds.). LOVING
    WOMEN/LOVING MEN: GAY LIBERATION AND
    THE CHURCH. Glide Publications, 1974 (Spring), cloth &
    paper eds.
Hart, H.L. LAW, LIBERTY AND MORALITY. Stanford
    Univ. Press, 1963, cloth & paper eds.
Hoffman, Martin. THE GAY WORLD: MALE HOMOSEX-
    UALITY AND THE SOCIAL CREATION OF EVIL. Ba-
    sic Books, 1968, out of print. Also Bantam paper ed.
Hyde, H. Montgomery. THE LOVE THAT DARED NOT
    SPEAK ITS NAME. Little, Brown, 1970, out of print.
Jay, Karla and Young, Allen (eds.). OUT OF THE CLOS-
    ETS: VOICES OF GAY LIBERATION. Douglas Books,
    1972, cloth & paper eds., dist. by Quick Fox, 33 W. 60th St.,
    NYC, NY 10023.
Johnston, Jill. LESBIAN NATION: THE FEMINIST SOLU-
    TION. Simon & Schuster, 1973. Also Touchstone paper ed.
    in Spring 1974.
Kinsey, Alfred C. et al. SEXUAL BEHAVIOR IN THE HU-
    MAN FEMALE. Saunders, 1953. Also Pocket Books paper
    ed.
Kinsey, Alfred C. et al. SEXUAL BEHAVIOR IN THE HU-
    MAN MALE. Saunders, 1948.
Martin, Del and Lyon, Phyllis. LESBIAN/WOMAN. Glide
    Publications, 1972. Also Bantam paper ed.
Miller, Merle. ON BEING DIFFERENT: WHAT IT MEANS
    TO BE A HOMOSEXUAL. Random House, 1971. Also
    Popular Library paper ed.
Murphy, John. HOMOSEXUAL LIBERATION: A PER-
    SONAL VIEW. Praeger, 1971, out of print.
Oberholzer, W. Dwight (ed.). IS GAY GOOD? ETHICS,
    THEOLOGY AND HOMOSEXUALITY. Westminster
    Press, 1971, paper orig.

Perry, Troy and Lucas, Charles L. THE LORD IS MY SHEP-
    HERD AND HE KNOWS I'M GAY. Nash, 1972. Also
    Bantam paper ed.
Pittenger, W. Norman. MAKING SEXUALITY HUMAN.
    Pilgrim/United Church Press, 1970.
Richmond, Len and Noguera, Gary (eds.). THE GAY LIBER-
    ATION BOOK. Ramparts Press, 1973, cloth & paper eds.,
    illus.
Szasz, Thomas S. THE MANUFACTURE OF MADNESS: A
    COMPARATIVE STUDY OF THE INQUISITION AND
    THE MENTAL HEALTH MOVEMENT. Harper & Row.
    1970. Also Delta paper ed.
Teal, Donn. THE GAY MILITANTS. Stein & Day, 1971.
Tobin, Kay and Wicker, Randy. THE GAY CRUSADERS.
    Paperback Library, 1972, paper orig., illus.
Tyler, Parker. SCREENING THE SEXES: HOMOSEXUAL-
    ITY IN THE MOVIES. Holt, Rinehart & Winston, 1972.
    Also Anchor/Doubleday paper ed. Both illus.
Valente, Michael F. SEX: THE RADICAL VIEW OF A
    CATHOLIC THEOLOGIAN. Bruce, 1970, paper orig.
Weinberg, George. SOCIETY AND THE HEALTHY HO-
    MOSEXUAL. St. Martin's, 1972. Also Anchor/Doubleday
    paper ed.
Weltge, Ralph W. (ed.). THE SAME SEX: AN APPRAISAL
    OF HOMOSEXUALITY. Pilgrim/United Church Press,
    1969, paper ed.

Articles

Prices given are for prepaid orders.

Connexion, May 1973. Articles by Sally Gearhart, "The Les-
    bian and God the Father"; John Preston, "Gay, Proud and
    Christian"; Rodger Harrison, "No Smog in Irvine"; Norman
    De Puy, "God's Gays." (United Ministries in Higher Educa-
    tion, Rm. 708, 3 W. 29, NYC, NY 10001, issue 25¢.)
"Government-Created Employment Disabilities of the Homosex-
    ual." *Harvard Law Review,* June 1969, 1739–1751.
Green, Richard. "Homosexuality as a Mental Illness." *Interna-
    tional Journal of Psychiatry,* Vol. 10, No. 1, March 1972,
    77–98. (International Journal Press, 59 4th Ave., NYC, NY
    10003, issue $4.) [See also J. Marmor article.]
Guttag, Bianca. "Homophobia in Library School." In: West,
    Celeste and Katz, Elizabeth (eds.). REVOLTING LI-
    BRARIANS. Booklegger Press, 1972, paper orig., illus.
    (Book $2 prepaid from Booklegger Press, 72 Ord St., San
    Francisco, CA 94114.) [See also S. Wolf article.]

"Homosexual Doctors: Their Place and Influence in Medicine Today." *Medical World News,* Vol. 15, No. 4, Jan. 25, 1974, 41–51. (Available at most medical libraries.)

"Homosexuals—To Cure, Not Convert." *Medical Dimensions,* Vol. 1, No. 1, March 1972. (MBA Enterprises, 555 Madison Ave., NYC, NY 10022, 25¢.)

Hooker, Evelyn. "The Adjustment of the Male Overt Homosexual." *Journal of Projective Techniques,* Vol. 21, 1957, 18–31. Also in: Ruitenbeek, Hendrik M. (ed.). THE PROBLEM OF HOMOSEXUALITY IN MODERN SOCIETY. Dutton, 1963.

Johnson, Eric W. "Homosexuality—Being 'Gay'." In: LOVE AND SEX IN PLAIN LANGUAGE (New Revised Edition). Lippincott, 1974. Also Bantam paper ed. April 1974. [Grades 7–12.]

Kameny, Franklin E. "Gay Liberation and Psychiatry." *Psychiatric Opinion.* Vol. 8, No. 1, Feb. 1971, 18–27. Also in: McCaffrey, Joseph A. (ed.). THE HOMOSEXUAL DIALECTIC. Prentice-Hall, 1972.

Kitsuse, John I. "Societal Reaction to Deviant Behavior: Problems of Theory and Method." In: Becker, Howard S. (ed.). THE OTHER SIDE: PERSPECTIVES ON DEVIANCE. Free Press (Macmillan), 1964.

Klein, Carole. "Homosexual Parents." In THE SINGLE PARENT EXPERIENCE. Walker, 1973. Also Avon paper ed.

Lerrigo, Charles. "MCC: The Church Comes Out." *New World Outlook,* New Series Vol. 33, No. 9, May 1973, 28–32. (New World Outlook, 475 Riverside Dr., NYC, NY 10027, 35¢ single copy, $3/dozen.)

"Lesbian Oppression Is . . ." *Quicksilver Times* (defunct), no date. (Reprints from National Gay Student Center, 2115 S St. NW, Wash., DC 20008, 25¢.)

LeShan, Eda J. "Homosexuality." In: NATURAL PARENTHOOD: RAISING YOUR CHILD WITHOUT A SCRIPT. Signet, 1970, paper orig.

Lyon, Phyllis and Martin, Del. "The Realities of Lesbianism." In: Cooke, J. et al. (eds.). NEW WOMEN: A MOTIVE ANTHOLOGY OF WOMEN'S LIBERATION. Bobbs-Merrill, 1970. Also Fawcett Premier paper ed.

MacDonald, A.P. et al. "Attitudes Toward Homosexuality: Preservation of Sex Morality or the Double Standard?" *Journal of Consulting & Clinical Psychology,* Vol. 40, No. 1, 1973, 161.

Marmor, Judd. "Homosexuality—Mental Illness or Moral Dilemma?" *International Journal of Psychiatry,* Vol. 10, No. 1, March 1972, 114–117. (International Journal Press, 59

4th Ave., NYC, NY 10003, issue $4.) [See also R. Green article.]

Martin, Del and Lyon, Phyllis. "Lesbian Mothers." *Ms.*, October 1973, 78–80. (Ms. Magazine, 370 Lexington Ave., NYC, NY 10017, issue $1.50.)

Martin, Del and Mariah, Paul. "Homosexual Love—Woman to Woman, Man to Man." In: Otto, Herbert A. (ed.). LOVE TODAY: A NEW EXPLORATION. Association Press, 1972. Also Delta paper ed.

McGraw, James R. "The Scandal of Peculiarity." *Christianity and Crisis*, Vol. 33, No. 6, April 16, 1973, 63–68. (Christianity & Crisis, 537 W. 121, NYC, NY 10027, 75¢.)

McNeill, John. "The Homosexual and the Church." *National Catholic Reporter*, Vol. 9, No. 38, Oct. 5, 1973, 7–8, 13–14. (National Catholic Reporter, 115 E. Armour Blvd., Kansas City, MO 64111, single copies free.)

"Should Homosexuality Be in the APA Nomenclature?" (symposium). *Amer. Journal of Psychiatry*, Vol. 130, No. 11, Nov. 1973, 1207–1216.

Smith, Kenneth T. "Homophobia: A Tentative Personality Profile." *Psychological Reports*, 1971, Vol. 29, 1091–1094.

Solomon, Joan. "Long Gays' Journey Into Light." *The Sciences*, Vol. 12, No. 8, October 1972, 6–15. (The Sciences, N.Y. Academy of Sciences, 2 E. 63, NYC, NY 10021, issue 75¢.)

"To Accept Homosexuals." Editorial in *Christian Century*, March 3, 1971, p. 3.

Wolf, Steve. "Sex and the Single Cataloguer." In: West, Celeste and Katz, Elizabeth (eds.). REVOLTING LIBRARIANS. Booklegger Press, 1972, paper orig., illus. (Book $2 prepaid from Booklegger Press, 72 Ord St., San Francisco, CA 94114.) [See also B. Guttag article.]

X, Dr. "I Am a Homosexual Physician." *Medical Opinion*, Vol. 2, No. 1, Jan. 1973, 49–58. (Medical Opinion, 575 Madison Ave., NYC, NY 10022, issue $1.25.)

Pamphlets

Prices given are for prepaid orders.

AMERICAN PSYCHIATRIC ASSOCIATION RESOLUTIONS ON HOMOSEXUALITY. Amer. Psychiatric Assn., Dec. 15, 1973. (Press release & rationale paper available free from APA Div. of Public Affairs, 1700 18th St. NW, Wash., DC 20009.)

Blair, Ralph (ed.). THE OTHERWISE MONOGRAPHS SERIES. National Task Force on Student Personnel Services and Homosexuality, 1972. 15 pamphlets, $20. (List of titles from Homosexual Community Counseling Center, 921 Madison Ave., NYC, NY 10021.)

Blamires, David. HOMOSEXUALITY FROM THE INSIDE. London: Social Responsibility Council of the Religious Society of Friends, 1973. (Friends Book Store, 302 Arch St., Phila., PA 19106, 95¢, plus p/h 30¢ single copy, 50¢ p/h 2 or more.)

Fluckiger, Fritz A. RESEARCH THROUGH A GLASS, DARKLY: AN EVALUATION OF THE BIEBER STUDY ON HOMOSEXUALITY. Privately printed, 1966. (Barbara Gittings, Box 2383, Phila., PA 19103, $1.)

HOMOSEXUALITY. SIECUS Study Guide No. 2 (Revised Ed.). Sex Information & Education Council of the U.S., 1973. (Behavioral Publications, 72 5th Ave., NYC, NY 10011, single copy $1 prepaid, $1.75 if billed; quantity discount available.)

HOMOSEXUALITY: NEITHER SIN NOR SICKNESS. *Trends* (produced by Program Agency of the United Presbyterian Church USA), Vol. 5, No. 6 July/Aug. 1973. Out of print. (Available at some Presbyterian churches. Also limited supply, $1 plus 25¢ p/h, at: Oscar Wilde Memorial Bookshop, 291 Mercer, NYC, NY 10003, and Giovanni's Room, 232 South St., Phila., PA 19147.)

Kameny, Franklin E. ACTION ON THE GAY LEGAL FRONT. Privately printed, 1974. (Natl. Gay Task Force, 80 5th Ave., NYC, NY 10011, $1.)

Lauritsen, John and Thorstad, David. THE HOMOSEXUAL RIGHTS MOVEMENT (1864–1935). Privately printed, 1973. (Oscar Wilde Memorial Bookshop, 291 Mercer, NYC, NY 10003, 50¢ plus 25¢ p/h.)

Lee, Ronald D. et al. GAY MEN SPEAK. Multi Media Resource Center ("The Yes Book of Sex" series), 1973, illus. (Multi Media Resource Center, 540 Powell, San Francisco, CA 94108, $1.95.)

Martin, Del and Lyon, Phyllis. LESBIAN LOVE AND LIBERATION. Multi Media Resource Center ("The Yes Book of Sex" series), 1973, illus. (Multi Media Resource Center, 540 Powell, San Francisco, CA 94108, $1.95.)

MOTIVE: GAY MEN'S LIBERATION ISSUE. Wash., DC: Motive, Inc., 1972. (Natl. Gay Student Center, 2115 S St. NW, Wash., DC 20008, $1.)

MOTIVE: LESBIAN/FEMINIST ISSUE. Wash., DC: Motive, Inc., 1972. (Natl. Gay Student Center, 2115 S St. NW, Wash., DC 20008, $1.)

National Institute of Mental Health. TASK FORCE ON HOMOSEXUALITY: FINAL REPORT AND BACK-

GROUND PAPERS. 1972 [Final Report section issued previously, 1969.] (Supt. of Documents, Govt. Printing Office, Wash., DC 20402, Cat. no. HE20-2402: H75/2, $1.)

National Organization for Women. N.O.W. LITERATURE—SEXUALITY AND LESBIANISM. Resolution 144 of NOW national conference, Feb. 1973. (Natl. Gay Task Force, 80 5th Ave., NYC, NY 10011, 15¢.)

PACKET OF RESOLUTIONS AND STATEMENTS RE: HOMOSEXUALITY [from church groups, the Natl. Organization for Women, professional organizations (incl. Amer. Library Assn., Amer. Psychiatric Assn., NYC Bar Assn., Amer. Anthropological Assn., Calif. Federation of Teachers), etc.]. (Natl. Gay Task Force, 80 5th Ave., NYC, NY 10011,$2.)

Parker, William. HOMOSEXUALS AND EMPLOYMENT. San Francisco: The Corinthian Foundation et al., 1970. (Council on Religion & the Homosexual, 83 McAllister, San Francisco, CA 94102, $1.)

Tripp, C.A. WHO IS A HOMOSEXUAL? Privately printed, 1966. (Barbara Gittings, Box 2383, Phila., PA 19103, 50¢.)

TWENTY QUESTIONS ABOUT HOMOSEXUALITY. Gay Activists Alliance of New York, 1972. (GAA, Box 2, Village Sta., NYC, NY 10014, $1 individuals, 50¢ institutions & non-gay organizations, 35¢ gay groups. Also bulk rates on request.)

Periodicals

Code for subscription rates: X=individual, L=libraries & institutions, G/L=gay and lesbian/feminist organizations, P=prisoners and state hospital patients.

THE ADVOCATE. Newspaper of America's homophile community. Box 74695, Los Angeles, CA 90004. Bi-weekly. X, L, & G/L, 13 issues/$4, $5 foreign; 26 issues/$7.50, $9 foreign. P, 26 issues/$3.75.

AIN'T I A WOMAN? Gay women's paper—radical. Box 1169, Iowa City, IA 52240. Approx. bimonthly. X & G/L, $5, $13 foreign. L, $20. P (women), free.

AMAZON QUARTERLY. Lesbian-feminist arts journal. 554 Valle Vista, Oakland, CA 94610. Quarterly. X & G/L, $4, $5 foreign. L, $6. P (women), free.

THE BODY POLITIC. Gay liberation journal. 139 Seaton St., Toronto, Ont., Canada M5A 2T2. Bimonthly. X, L & G/L, 6 issues/$2 Canada, $2.25 USA, $3.25 overseas airmail. P, free.

COWRIE. Lesbian/feminist. 359 E. 68, NYC, NY 10021. Irregular. X & G/L, 10 issues/$5. G/L bulk rate 30¢ ea. L, $10. P (women), free.

DIGNITY. A national publication of the gay Catholic community. 755 Boylston, Rm. 514, Boston, MA 02116. Monthly. X (except Catholic religious), L, & G/L, $10. Catholic religious, $5. P, free.

FAG RAG. A gay male publication. Box 331, Kenmore Sta., Boston, MA 02215. Quarterly. X, L, & G/L, 12 issues/$5, 50¢ ea. P, free.

FOCUS. A journal for gay women. C/o Boston DOB, Rm. 323, 419 Boylston, Boston, MA 02116. Monthly. X, L, & G/L, $5. P (women), free.

THE GAY ALTERNATIVE. Journal for gay people. 232 South St., Phila., PA 19147. Bimonthly. X & L, 10 issues/$3.50. G/L, same but will exchange. P, free.

THE GAY CHRISTIAN. A journal of Metropolitan Community Church. MCC/New York, Box 1757 GPO, NYC, NY 10001. 4–6 issues a year. X, L, & G/L, 12 issues/$5 3rd class $7 1st class. P, free through MCC prison ministry.

GAY LIBERATOR. A newspaper of gay activism. Box 631-A, Detroit, MI 48232. Monthly. X & G/L, $3, $4 outside USA, L, $10. P, free.

GAY PEOPLE AND MENTAL HEALTH. Newsletter on events & resources. Box 3592, Nicollet Sta., Minneapolis, MN 55403. Monthly. X, $6. G/L, same but will exchange. L, $12. P, free.

GAY SUNSHINE. A journal of gay liberation. PO Box 40397. San Francisco, CA 94140. Bimonthly. X, L, & G/L, 12 issues/$5, $9 1st class, $7 overseas, sample copy 50¢. Discount on bulk to G/L. P, free.

HOMOSEXUAL COUNSELING JOURNAL. Quarterly Journal to the Helping Professions. 921 Madison Ave., NYC, NY 10021. Quarterly. X, $10. L & G/L, $15. P, free.

INTERCHANGE. Magazine of the National Gay Student Center. 2115 S St. NW, Wash., DC 20008. Bimonthly. X & L, $3. G/L, same but will exchange. P, free.

JOURNAL OF HOMOSEXUALITY. Journal for the mental health & behavioral science professions. Haworth Press, 53 W. 72, NYC, NY 10023. Quarterly. X, G/L, & P, $12. L, $25. First issue Spring 1974.

IT'S TIME. Newsletter of the National Gay Task Force. NGTF, Suite 903, 80 5th Ave., NYC, NY 10011. Monthly. X & L, $15 (includes regular membership in NGTF). G/L & P, free.

LAVENDER WOMAN. A lesbian paper. Box 60206, 1723 W. Devon, Chicago, IL 60660. 8–9 issues a year. X & G/L, $3. L, $6. P (women), free.

THE LESBIAN FEMINIST. A political and arts newsletter.

Box 243, Village Sta., NYC, NY 10014. Monthly. X, L, & G/L, $3. P (women), free.

THE LESBIAN TIDE. Feminist publication by and for the rising tide of women today. The Tide Collective, 373 N. Western Ave., no. 202, Los Angeles, CA 90004. Monthly. X & G/L, $7.50. L. $10. P (women), free but donation requested.

LONG TIME COMING. Canadian lesbian/feminist newspaper. Box 161, Sta. E, Montreal, Que., Canada H2T 3A7. Monthly. X & G/L, $5. L, $7. P (women), free.

OUT. A gay magazine. Box E, Old Chelsea Sta., NYC, NY 10011. Monthly. X, L, & G/L, $6 USA & Canada, $9 foreign. (Cover price $1; G/L may buy in bulk @ 50¢ for resale.) P, free. First regular issue March 1974.

SAPPHO. The only lesbian magazine in Europe. BCM/Petrel, London WCIV 6xx, England. Monthly. X, L, G/L, & P, £4.66 sealed, £3.28 wrapper. Pay in Sterling only by International Money Order.

SISTERS. A magazine by & for gay women. 1005 Market, Suite 402, San Fran., CA 94103. Monthly. X, L, & G/L, $5, $7 Mexico & Canada, $10 overseas. P (women), free.

TRES FEMMES. Publication for women. c/o Gay Center for Social Services, 2250 B St., San Diego, CA 92102. 2–4 issues a year. X, L, & G/L, 4 issues/$3.50. Single copy $1. 10 copies same issue $9. P (women), free.

5. Antidiscrimination Laws of Minneapolis, Minnesota and East Lansing, Michigan

City of Minneapolis

Office of City Council-City Clerk
307 City Hall
Minneapolis, Minnesota 55415
Adopted: March 29, 1974

AN ORDINANCE

Amending Chap 945 of the Minneapolis Code of Ordinances relating to Civil Rights. (99-68)
The City Council of the City of Minneapolis do ordain as follows:

SEC. 1. That subdivisions (a), and (b) of Sec 945.010 of the above entitled ordinance be amended to read as follows:
945.010. Findings, Declaration of Policy and Purpose.

(a) Findings. It is determined that discriminatory practices based on race, color, creed, religion, national origin, sex OR AFFECTIONAL OR SEXUAL PREFERENCE, with respect to employment, labor union membership, housing accommodations, property rights, education, public accommodations, and public services, or any of them, tend to create and intensify conditions of poverty, ill health, unrest, civil disobedience, lawlessness, and vice and adversely affect the public health, safety, order, convenience, and general welfare; such discriminatory practices threaten the rights, privileges and opportunities OF ALL INHABITANTS OF THE CITY AND SUCH RIGHTS, PRIVILEGES AND OPPORTUNITIES are hereby declared to be civil rights, and the adoption of this Chapter is deemed to be an exercise of the police power of the City to protect such rights.

(b) Declaration of Policy and Purpose. It is the public policy of the City of Minneapolis and the purpose of this Chapter:

(1) To declare as civil rights the rights of all persons to the fullest extent of their capacities, and without regard to race, color, creed, religion, ancestry, national origin, sex OR AFFECTIONAL OR SEXUAL PREFERENCE, equal opportuni-

251

ties with respect to employment, labor union membership, housing accommodations, property rights, education, public accommodations, and public services;

(2) To prevent and prohibit any and all discriminatory practices based on race, color, creed, religion, ancestry, national origin, sex, OR AFFECTIONAL OR SEXUAL PREFERENCE, with respect to employment, labor union membership, housing accommodations, property rights, education, public accommodations, or public services;

(3) To protect all persons from unfounded charges of discriminatory practices;

(4) To effectuate the foregoing policy by means of public information and education, mediation and conciliation, and enforcement; and

(5) To eliminate existing and the development of any new ghettos in the community.

SEC 2. That subdivisions (r) and (s) of Sec 945.020 of the above entitled ordinance be amended to read as follows:

945.020. Definitions.

(r) Discrimination. "Discrimination" means any act or attempted act which because of race, color, creed, religion, ancestry, national origin, sex, OR AFFECTIONAL OR SEXUAL PREFERENCE, results in the unequal treatment or separation or segregation of any person, or denies, prevents, limits, or otherwise adversely affects, or if accomplished would deny, prevent, limit, or otherwise adversely affect, the benefit of enjoyment by any person of employment, membership in a labor organization, ownership or occupancy of real property, a public accommodation, a public service, or an educational institution. Such discrimination is unlawful and is a violation of this ordinance.

(s) AFFECTIONAL OR SEXUAL PREFERENCE. "AFFECTIONAL OR SEXUAL PREFERENCE" MEANS HAVING OR MANIFESTING AN EMOTIONAL OR PHYSICAL ATTACHMENT TO ANOTHER CONSENTING PERSON OR PERSONS, OR HAVING OR MANIFESTING A PREFERENCE FOR SUCH ATTACHMENT.

SEC 3. That Sec 945.030 of the above entitled ordinance be amended to read as follows:

945.030. Violations.

(a) Act of Discrimination. Without limitation, the following are declared to be discrimination:

(1) For an employer, because of race, color, creed, religion, ancestry, national origin, sex OR AFFECTIONAL OR SEXUAL PREFERENCE, to fail or refuse to hire; to discharge an employee; or to accord adverse, unlawful or unequal treatment to any person or employee with respect to application, hiring, training, apprenticeship, tenure, promotion, upgrading, compen-

sation, layoff, discharge, or any term or condition of employment except when based on a bona fide occupational qualification.

(2) For an employment agency, because of race, color, creed, religion, ancestry, national origin, sex OR AFFECTIONAL OR SEXUAL PREFERENCE, to accord adverse, unlawful or unequal treatment to any person in connection with any application for employment, any referral, or any request for assistance in procurement of employees, or to accept any listing of employment on such a basis, except when based on a bona fide occupational qualification.

(3) For any labor organization, because of race, color, creed, religion, ancestry, national origin, sex OR AFFECTIONAL OR SEXUAL PREFERENCE, to deny full and equal membership rights to an applicant for membership or to a member; to expel, suspend or otherwise discipline a member; or to accord adverse, unlawful or unequal treatment to any person with respect to his hiring, apprenticeship, training, tenure, compensation, upgrading, layoff or any term or condition of employment, except when based on a bona fide occupational qualification.

(4) For any person, having any interest in real property and any real estate broker or real estate agent, because of race, color, creed, religion, ancestry, national origin, sex OR AFFECTIONAL OR SEXUAL PREFERENCE, to fail or refuse to sell, rent, assign, or otherwise transfer any real property to any other person, or to accord adverse, unlawful, or unequal treatment to any person with respect to the acquisition, occupancy, use, and enjoyment of any real property.

(5) For any person engaged in the provision of public accommodations, because of race, color, creed, religion, ancestry, national origin, sex OR AFFECTIONAL OR SEXUAL PREFERENCE, to fail or refuse to provide to any person access to the use of and benefit from the services and facilities of such public accommodations; or to accord adverse, unlawful, or unequal treatment to any person with respect to the availability of such services and facilities, the price or other consideration therefor, the scope and quality thereof, or the terms and conditions under which the same are made available, including terms and conditions relating to credit, payment, warranties, delivery, installation, and repair.

(6) For any person engaged in the provision of public services, by reason of race, color, creed, religion, ancestry, national origin, sex OR AFFECTIONAL OR SEXUAL PREFERENCE, to fail or refuse to provide to any person access to the use of and benefit thereof, or to provide adverse, unlawful, or unequal treatment to any person in connection therewith.

(7) For any person, because of race, color, creed, religion,

ancestry, national origin, sex OR AFFECTIONAL OR SEXUAL PREFERENCE, to conceal or attempt to conceal any unlawful discrimination or to aid, abet, compel, coerce, incite or induce, or attempt to induce, another person to discriminate, or by any means, trick artifice, advertisement or sign, or use any form of application, or make any record on inquiry, or device, whatsoever to bring about or facilitate discrimination, or to engage in or threaten to engage in any reprisal, economic or otherwise, against any person by reason of the latter's filing a complaint, testifying or assisting in the observance and support of the purposes and provisions of this Chapter.

(8) For any person, bank, banking organization, mortgage company, insurance company, or other financial institution or lender to whom application is made for financial assistance for the purchase, lease, acquisition, construction, rehabilitation, repair, or maintenance of any real property or any agent or employee thereof to discriminate against any person or group of persons, because of race, color, creed, religion, ancestry, national origin, sex OR AFFECTIONAL OR SEXUAL PREFERENCE of such person or group of persons or of the prospective occupants or tenants of such real property in the granting, withholding, extending, modifying, renewing, or in the rates, terms, conditions or privileges of any such financial assistance or in the extension of services in connection therewith.

(9) Wherever religious organizations or bodies are exempt from any of the provisions of this ordinance such exemption shall apply only to religious qualifications for employment or residence in church owned or operated property, and such organizations shall not be exempt from any provisions of this Chapter relating to discrimination based upon race, color, ancestry, national origin, sex OR AFFECTIONAL OR SEXUAL PREFERENCE.

SEC 4. That subparagraph (1) of subdivision (d) of Sec 945.060 of the above entitled ordinance be amended to read as follows:

(d) Substantive and Procedural Power and Duties. The Commission shall:

(1) Seek to prevent and eliminate bias and discrimination because of race, color, creed, religion, ancestry, national origin, sex OR AFFECTIONAL OR SEXUAL PREFERENCE, by means of education, persuasion, conciliation, and enforcement, and utilize all of the powers at its disposal to carry into execution the provisions of this Chapter.

Passed March 29, 1974. Louis G. DeMars, President of the Council.

Approved April 4, 1974. Albert J. Hofstede, Mayor.
Attest: Lyall A. Schwarzkopf, City Clerk.

East Lansing, Michigan
City of East Lansing
410 Abbott Road

ORDINANCE NO. 325

AN ORDINANCE TO AMEND SECTIONS 1.124, 1.126 AND 1.127 OF CHAPTER 4 OF TITLE I OF THE CODE OF THE CITY OF EAST LANSING

The City of East Lansing Ordains:

Section 1. Section 1.124 of the Code of the City of East Lansing shall be amended to read:

Section 1.124. *Duties.* It shall be the duty of the Human Relations Commission to protect and to promote the concept of human dignity and respect for the rights of all individuals and groups within the community; and to promote amicable relations among all individuals and groups within the city; to assemble, analyze, and disseminate authentic and factual data relating to group and individual relationships.

It shall have the power to publish and distribute such factual material as it deems necessary or desirable and to make such investigations, studies, and surveys as are necessary for the performance of its duties. It shall also make such recommendations as it deems necessary to the City Council when adopted by an affirmative vote of six members of the Commission. The Commission shall annually report its activities to the City Council.

Section 2. Section 1.126 of the Code of the City of East Lansing shall be amended to read:

Section 1.126. *Public Policy.* It is hereby declared to be contrary to the public policy of the City of East Lansing for any person to deny any other person the enjoyment of his civil rights or for any person to discriminate against any other person in the exercise of civil rights because of religion, race, color, sex or national origin.

Section 3. Section 1.127 of the Code of the City of East Lansing shall be amended to read:

Section 1.127. *Civil Rights Defined.* Employment. The opportunity to obtain employment without discrimination because of race, color, sex, religion, or national origin is hereby recognized and declared to be a civil right. Further it shall be contrary to the public policy of the City of East Lansing for any employer, because of the age of any individual, or because of the sex of any individual, or because of the sexual beliefs or sexual orientation of any individual, to refuse to hire or otherwise discriminate against him or her with respect to hire, tenure, terms, conditions or privileges of employment unless such refusal to hire or discrimination is based on a bona fide occupational qualification.

Housing. The opportunity to purchase, lease, sell, hold, use and convey dwelling houses or dwelling units without discrimination solely because of race, color, religion, sex, or national origin is hereby recognized and declared to be a civil right.

Public Accommodations. The opportunity to enjoy full and equal accommodations, advantages, facilities and privileges of inns, hotels, motels, government housing, restaurants, eating houses, barber shops, billiard parlors, stores, public conveyances on land and water, theaters, motion picture houses, public educational institutions, in all methods of air transportation and all other places of public accommodation, amusement, and recreation, without discrimination solely because of race, color, sex, sexual orientation, religion, or national origin is hereby recognized and declared to be a civil right.

Interpretation. Nothing contained in this section shall be construed to limit the powers, duties, or responsibilities of the Human Relations Commission nor shall anything in this section be deemed in any manner to restrict the definition of civil rights to those herein defined.

6 ACLU States Affiliates

ALABAMA

Alabama CLU
POB 1972
University, Alabama 35486
(205) 758-2301

ALASKA

Alaska CLU
320 Charles St.
Fairbanks, Ak. 99701
(907) 479-7227

ARIZONA

Arizona CLU
822 A Mill Ave.
Tempe, Az 85281
(602) 966-3374

ARKANSAS

ACLU of Arkansas
P.O. Box 5045
North Little Rock, AR 72119
(501) 374-8892

CALIFORNIA

ACLU of Northern California
593 Market St.
San Francisco, Calif. 94105
(415) 433-2750

ACLU of Southern California
633 S. Shatto Place
Los Angeles, California 90005
(213) 487-1720

COLORADO

ACLU of Colorado
1711 Pennsylvania St.
Denver, Co. 80203
(303) 825-5176

CONNECTICUT

Connecticut CLU
57 Pratt St., Rm. 713
Hartford, Conn. 06103
(203) 246-7471 or 72

FLORIDA

ACLU of Florida
7210 S. Red Road
Room 213
So. Miami, Fla. 33143
(305) 373- 2052

GEORGIA

ACLU of Georgia
88 Walton St.
Atlanta, Ga. 30303
(404) 523-5398

HAWAII

ACLU of Hawaii
217 S. King St.
Suite 211
Honolulu, Hawaii 96813
(808) 524-5177
         524-7373

ILLINOIS

Illinois Division, ACLU
5 South Wabash Ave.
Suite 1516
Chicago, Ill. 60603
(312) 236-5564

INDIANA

Indiana CLU
445 North Pennsylvania St.
Suite 604
Indianapolis, In. 46204
(317) 635-4056

Calumet Chapter
POB 2521
Gary, In. 46203

IOWA

Iowa CLU
1101 Walnut St.
Des Moines, Ia. 40309
(515) 282-0923

KANSAS

Kansas CLU
3926 E. First St.
Wichita, Ks. 67208

KENTUCKY

Kentucky CLU
134 Breckenridge Lane
Louisville, Ky. 40207
(502) 895-0279

LOUISIANA

ACLU of Louisiana
606 Common St., rm. 302
New Orleans, La. 70130
(504) 522-0617

MAINE

Maine CLU
193 Middle Street
Portland, Me. 04111
(207) 774-5444

MARYLAND

ACLU of Maryland
1231 North Calvert St.
Baltimore, Md. 21202
(301) 685-6460

MASSACHUSETTS

CLU of Massachusetts
100 Franklin St.
Boston, Mass. 02108
(617) 227-9469

MICHIGAN

ACLU of Michigan
808 Washington Blvd. Bldg.
234 State St.
Detroit, Mi. 48226
(313) 961-4662

MINNESOTA

Minnesota CLU
628 Central Ave.
Minneapolis, Minn. 55414
(612) 332-1708 or 2032

MISSISSIPPI

ACLU of Mississippi
520 North President St.
Jackson, Ms. 39201
(601) 355-7495

MISSOURI

ACLU of Eastern Missouri
8011 Clayton Rd., Suite 216
St. Louis, Mo. 63117
(314) 721-1215

ACLU of Western Missouri
823 Walnut, Room 608
Kansas City, Mo. 64106
(913) 782-2500

MONTANA

ACLU of Montana
625½ Ave. "E."
Billings, Mn. 59102
(406) 656-8695

NATIONAL CAPITAL AREA, WASH., D.C.
ACLU of the National Capital Area
3000 Connecticut Ave., N.W.
Suite 437
Washington, D.C. 20008
(202) 483-3830

NEBRASKA

Nebraska CLU
POB 81455
Lincoln, Nebraska 68501
(402) 432-8091

NEVADA

ACLU of Nevada
POB 8947
Reno, Nv. 89507
(702) 784-6718

NEW HAMPSHIRE

New Hampshire CLU
3 Pleasant St., Room 7
Concord, N.H. 03301
(603) 225-3080

NEW JERSEY

ACLU of New Jersey
45 Academy St., rm 203
Newark, N.J. 07102
(201) 642-2084

NEW MEXICO

ACLU of New Mexico
510 Second St., N.W.
Albuquerque, N.M. 87101
(505) 842-1448

NEW YORK

New York CLU
84 Fifth Ave., Suite 300
New York, New York 10011
(212) 924-7800

NORTH CAROLINA

North Carolina CLU
POB 3094
Greensboro, N.C. 27402
(919) 273-1641

OHIO

ACLU of Ohio
203 E. Broad St., Suite 200
Columbus, Ohio 43215
(614) 228-8951

Greater Cleveland Chapter
2108 Payne Avenue, Rm. 825
Cleveland, Ohio 44114
(216) SU 1- 6276

Cincinnati Chapter
1717 Section Rd.
Cincinnati, Ohio 45237
(513) 631-3737

OKLAHOMA

Oklahoma CLU
POB 799
Oklahoma City, Ok. 73101
(405) 235-0946 or 427-0626

OREGON

ACLU of Oregon
309 Senator Bldg.
Portland, Or. 97204
(503) 227-3186

PENNSYLVANIA

ACLU of Pennsylvania
260 South 15th St.
Philadelphia, Pa. 19102
(215) 735-7103

Pittsburgh Chapter
237 Oakland Ave.
Pittsburgh, Pa. 15213
(412) 261-5160 Or 391-7210
X 1541

Delaware Chapter
2409 West 17th St.
Wilmington, De. 19806
(302) 654-3966

RHODE ISLAND

Rhode Island CLU
55 Eddy St., Suite 508
Providence, R.I. 02903
(401) 831-7171

SOUTH CAROLINA

ACLU of South Carolina
2016½ Green St., Rm. 3
Columbia, S.C. 29205
(803) 799-5151 or 799-3767

TENNESSEE

ACLU of Tennessee
POB 91
Knoxville, Tenn. 37901
(615) 524-1787

TEXAS

Texas CLU
600 West Seventh St.
Austin, Texas 78701
(512) 477-5849 or 4335

Houston Chapter
905 Richmond
Houston, Tx. 77006
(713) 524-5925

UTAH

ACLU of Utah
211 E. 3rd South
Salt Lake City, Ut. 84111
(801) 521-9289

VERMONT

Vermont CLU
43 State St.
Montpelier, Vt. 05602
(802) 223-6304

VIRGINIA

ACLU of Virginia
10 South 10th St.
Insurance Bldg.
Richmond, Va. 23219
(804) 644-8022

WASHINGTON

ACLU of Washington
2101 Smith Tower
Seattle, Wa. 98104
(206) 624-2180

WEST VIRGINIA

West Virginia CLU
1332 Washington Blvd.
Huntington, W.V. 25701
(304) 525-3951

WISCONSIN

Wisconsin CLU
1840 North Farwell Avenue
Room 1, Lower Level
Milwaukee, Wi. 53202
(414) 272-4032

National Chapters

IDAHO

Boise Valley Natl. Chapter,
ACLU
2312 Jean St.
Boise, Id. 83705
Office: (208) 336-0862

East Idaho Natl. Chapter,
ACLU
3810 Holly Place
Idaho Falls, Id. 83401

NORTH DAKOTA

Ward County (Minot)
National Chapter, ACLU
Political Science Division
Minot State College
Minot, N.D. 58701
(701) 838-6101

Red River Valley Natl.
Chapter
Box 5502
Fargo, ND 58102

SOUTH DAKOTA

South Dakota Chapter,
ACLU
I
POB 362
Vermillion, S.D. 57069
(605) 624-8191

WYOMING

Laramie Chapter, ACLU
Box 3282, University Station
Laramie, Wy. 82071
Office: (307) 766-4371

Regional Offices

Washington Office
410 First St., S.E.
Washington, D.C. 20003
Office: (202) 544-1681

Southern Regional Office
52 Fairlie St., N.W.
Atlanta, Ga. 30303
Office: (404) 523-2721

Mountain States Regional
Office
1330 Leyden St.
Denver, Co. 80220
Office: (303) 321-5901

Projects

Military Rights Project
The Dupont Circle Bldg.
Suite 604
1346 Connecticut Ave., N.W.
Washington, D.C. 20036
(202) 659-1138

National Prison Project
1346 Conn. Ave N.W.
Suite 1031
Washington, D.C. 20036

7. Gay Organizations

There are more than 800 gay and lesbian-feminist organizations in the United States. Listed here are national headquarters of organizations with affiliates in various states, and local groups that may provide political or legal information; they can also provide information about other groups in their areas.

Alabama

Gay Liberation
PO Box 5877
Birmingham, AL 35486

Arizona

Gay Liberation Arizona Desert (GLAD)
PO Box 117
Tempe, AZ 85281

California

Gay Community Services Center
1614 Wilshire Blvd.
Los Angeles, CA 90017
(213) 482-3062
Metropolitan Community Church—Exec. Offices
1050 South Hill St.
Los Angeles, CA 90015
(213) 748-0121

Lesbian Activist Women
1614 Wilshire Blvd.
Los Angeles, CA 90017
(213) 934-6593

Daughters of Bilitis
1005 Market Street
San Francisco, CA 94103
(415) 861-8689

Lesbian Mothers Union
1076 Guerrero St.
San Francisco, CA 94102
(415) 824-2790

Society of Individual Rights (SIR)
83 Sixth Street
San Francisco, CA 94103
(415) 781-1570

Whitman-Radclyffe Foundation
2131 Union Street
San Francisco CA 94123
(415) 346-7929

Colorado

Lesbian Task Force
c/o Marge Johnson
5720 South Pearl
Littleton, CO 80121
(303) 798-3033

Gay Coalition of Denver
PO Box 18501
Denver, CO 80218
(303) 831-8838

Connecticut

Kalos Society—Gay Liber-
ation Front
PO Box 403
Hartford, CT 06101
(203) 542-1111

District of Columbia

Gay Activists Alliance
PO Box 2554
Washington, DC 20013
(202) 462-8729

National Gay Student Center
2115 S Street NW
Washington, D.C. 20008
(201) 247-2258

Florida

Metropolitan Community
Church
P.O.B. 370963
Miami, FL 33127
(305) 758-7190

Georgia

Atlanta Lesbian Feminist
Alliance
PO Box 7684
Atlanta, GA 30309
(404) 872-5071

Gay Information Service
P.O. Box 7922
Atlanta, GA 30309
(404) 874-4400

Hawaii

Metropolitan Community
Church
P.O.B. 15825
Honolulu, HI 96815
(808) 538-7940

Idaho

North West Gay People's Alliance, Inc.
P.O. Box 8758
Moscow, ID 83843
(208) 882-1208

Illinois

Chicago Gay Alliance
PO Box 909
Chicago, Ill. 60609
(312) 664-4708

Indiana

Bloomington Gay Alliance
c/o Student Association
Room 3, IMU, Indiana Uni-
versity
Bloomington, IN 47401
(812) 332-6077

Iowa

Lesbian Alliance
c/o Women's Resource and
Action Center
3 East Market Street
Iowa City, IA 52240
(319) 353-6265

Kansas

Lawrence Gay Liberation,
Inc.
PO Box 234
Lawrence, KS 66044

Kentucky

Gay Liberation
416 Belgravia Ct.
Louisville, KY 40208

Louisiana

Erickson Educational
Foundation (Transsexuals)
1627 Moreland Ave.
Baton Rouge, LA 70808
(504) 343-2549

Metropolitan Community
Church
Box 15757
New Orleans, LA 70175
(504) 891-5443

Maine

Maine Gay Task Force
Box 4542
Portland, ME 04144

Maryland

Gay Women's Community
Center of Baltimore
3028 Greenmount Ave.
Baltimore, MD 21218

Massachusetts

Daughters of Bilitis
419 Boylston Street
Boston, MA 02116
(617) 262-1592

Dignity—National Office
(Gay Catholics)
755 Boylston St.
Boston, MA 02116

Homophile Union of Boston
419 Boylston Street
Boston, MA 02116
(617) 536-6197

Michigan

Gay Advocate's Office
Michigan Union
University of Michigan
Ann Arbor, MI 48104
(313) 763-4186

Ambitious Amazons
PO Box 811
East Lansing, MI 48823

Minnesota

Minnesota Committee for
Gay Rights
Box 4226 St., Anthony Falls
Station
Minneapolis, MN 55414
(612) 721-3738

Mississippi

Mississippi Gay Alliance
c/o Liz Landrum
PO Box 4470
Mississippi State University
State College, MS 39762
(601) 323-9699

Missouri

Gay People's Union of Kansas City
3825 Virginia
Kansas City, MO 64109
(816) 931-3579

Nebraska

Lincoln Gay Action Group
333 N. 14th Street
Lincoln, NB 68508
(402) 475-5710

Nevada

Metropolitan Community
Church
2791 Shady Lane
Las Vegas, NV 89110
(702) 452-9659

New Hampshire

Seacoast Area Gay Alliance
(SAGA)
PO Box 1424
Portsmouth, N.H. 03801

New Jersey

Daughters of Bilitis
PO Box 62
Fanwood, N.J. 07023
(201) 233-3848

Gay Activists Alliance of
N.J., Inc.
PO Box 1734
South Hackensack, New Jersey 07606
(201) 343-6402

New Mexico

New Mexico Gay People's
Union
3214 Silver, SE
Albuquerque, N.M. 87106

New York

Capitol District Gay Community Council
PO Box 131
Albany, N.Y. 12201
(518) 462-6138

Mattachine Society of the
Niagara Frontier
PO Box 975
Ellicott Sq. Station
Buffalo, N.Y. 14205
(716) 881-5335

Lesbian Feminist Liberation,
Inc.
PO Box 243, Village Station
New York, N.Y. 10014
(212) 691-5460

Gay Academic Union (national clearinghouse)
Box 1479
Hunter College, C.U.N.Y.
New York, N.Y. 10021

Lambda Legal Defense and
Education Fund, Inc.
30 Grove Street
New York, N.Y. 10014
(212) 758-1905

National Gay Task Force
80 Fifth Avenue
New York, N.Y. 10011
(212) 741-1010

North Carolina

Duke Gay Alliance
7686 College Station
Durham, N.C. 27708
(919) 684-3196

Ohio

Gay Activists Alliance
323 Ohio Union
1739 N. High St. #3
Columbus, OH 43210
(614) 422-9212

Oklahoma

Christ the King MCC
P.O. Box 60738
Oklahoma City, Oklahoma
73106
(405) 528-3100

Oregon

Portland Association for Gay
Equality
118 W. Burnside St.
Portland, Oregon 97209
(503) 227-6550

Pennsylvania

Gay Activists Alliance
PO Box 15748
Middle City Station
Philadelphia, PA 19103
(215) 387-2813

Gay Nurses' Alliance
PO Box 5687
Philadelphia, PA 19129
(215) 623-1543

Rhode Island

Kingston Gay Liberation
c/o Memorial Union
University of Rhode Island
Kingston, R.I. 02881
(401) 792-5817

South Carolina

Metropolitan Community
Church
PO Box 11181
Columbia, S.C. 29211
(803) 252-1250

Tennessee

Knoxville Lesbian Collective
2911 Jersey Avenue
Knoxville, TN 37919
(615) 523-7288

Texas

Awareness, Unity and Re-
search Assn. (AURA)
PO Box 7318
Fort Worth, TX 76111
(817) 838-2095

Daughters of Bilitis
PO Box 1242
Dallas, TX 75221
(214) 742-1947

Utah

Metropolitan Community
Church
PO Box 11607
Salt Lake City, UT 84110
(801) 531-9434

Vermont

Gay-in-Vermont
Box 3216
North Burlington Station,
Burlington, Vermont 05401
(802) 863-2496

Washington

Seattle Gay Alliance
PO Box 1170
Seattle, WA 98111
(206) 323-6969

Lesbian Mothers' National
Defense Fund
1941 Division
Enumclaw, WA 98002

Wisconsin

Gay People's Union
PO Box 90530
Milwaukee, WI 53202
(414) 271-5273

Puerto Rico

Communidad de Orgullo Gay
Apartado 5523
Puerta de Tierra
San Juan, P.R. 00906
(809) 767-7722

DISCUS BOOKS

DISTINGUISHED NON-FICTION

A SELECTION OF RECENT TITLES

DRT 7-75

DISCUS BOOKS
DISTINGUISHED NONFICTION

THEATER, FILM, AND TELEVISION

ACTORS TALK ABOUT ACTING Lewis Funke and John Booth, Eds.	15062	1.95
ACTION FOR CHILDREN'S TELEVISION	10090	1.25
ANTONIN ARTAUD Bettina L. Knapp	12062	1.65
A BOOK ON THE OPEN THEATER Robert Pasoli	12047	1.65
THE CONCISE ENCYCLOPEDIC GUIDE TO SHAKESPEARE Michael Martin and Richard Harrier, Eds.	16832	2.65
THE DISNEY VERSION Richard Schickel	08953	1.25
EDWARD ALBEE: A PLAYWRIGHT IN PROTEST Michael E. Rutenberg	11916	1.65
THE EMPTY SPACE Peter Brook	19802	1.65
EXPERIMENTAL THEATER James Roose-Evans	11981	1.65
FOUR CENTURIES OF SHAKESPEARIAN CRITICISM Frank Kermode, Ed.	20131	1.95
GUERILLA STREET THEATRE Henry Lesnick, Ed.	15198	2.45
THE HOLLYWOOD SCREENWRITERS Richard Corliss	12450	1.95
IN SEARCH OF LIGHT: THE BROADCASTS OF **EDWARD R. MURROW** Edward Bliss, Ed.	19372	1.95
INTERVIEWS WITH FILM DIRECTORS Andrew Sarris	21568	1.65
MOVIES FOR KIDS Edith Zornow and Ruth Goldstein	17012	1.65
PICTURE Lillian Ross	08839	1.25
THE LIVING THEATRE Pierre Biner	17640	1.65
PUBLIC DOMAIN Richard Schechner	12104	1.65
RADICAL THEATRE NOTEBOOK Arthur Sainer	22442	2.65

GENERAL NON-FICTION

ADDING A DIMENSION Isaac Asimov	22673	1.25
A TESTAMENT Frank Lloyd Wright	12039	1.65
THE AMERICAN CHALLENGE J. J. Servan Schreiber	11965	1.65
AMERICA THE RAPED Gene Marine	09373	1.25
ARE YOU RUNNING WITH ME, JESUS? Malcolm Boyd	09993	1.25
BLACK HISTORY: LOST, STOLEN, OR STRAYED Otto Lindenmeyer	09167	1.25
THE BOOK OF IMAGINARY BEINGS Jorge Luis Borges	11080	1.45
BUILDING THE EARTH Pierre de Chardin	08938	1.25
CHEYENNE AUTUMN Mari Sandoz	09001	1.25
THE CHILD IN THE FAMILY Maria Montessori	09571	1.25
CHINA: SCIENCE WALKS ON TWO LEGS Science for the People	20123	1.75
CLASSICS REVISITED Kenneth Rexroth	08920	1.25
THE COMPLETE HOME MEDICAL ENCYCLOPEDIA Dr. Harold T. Hyman	15214	1.95

DISCUS BOOKS
DISTINGUISHED NON-FICTION

DISCUS BOOKS

DISTINGUISHED NON-FICTION

NATURE OF POLITICS M. Curtis	12401	1.95
THE NEW GROUP THERAPIES Hendrick M. Ruitenbeek	09647	1.25
NOTES OF A PROCESSED BROTHER Donald Reeves	14175	1.95
OF TIME AND SPACE AND OTHER THINGS Isaac Asimov	24166	1.50
THE OMNI-AMERICANS Albert Murray	11460	1.50
ON CONTEMPORARY LITERATURE Richard Kostelanetz (editor)	12385	1.95
THE PARIS AND NEW YORK DIARIES **OF NED ROREM** Ned Rorem	12617	2.45
POLITICS AND THE NOVEL Irving Howe	11932	1.65
THE POWER TACTICS OF JESUS CHRIST AND **OTHER ESSAYS** Jay Haley	11924	1.65
PRISONERS OF PSYCHIATRY Bruce Ennis	19299	1.65
THE PSYCHOANALYTIC REVOLUTION Marthe Robert	08763	1.25
THE LIFE OF EZRA POUND Noel Stock	20909	2.65
THE QUIET CRISIS Stewart Udall	24406	1.75
THE ROMAN WAY Edith Hamilton	14233	1.50
RUSSIA AT WAR Alexander Werth	12070	1.65
THE SCHOOLCHILDREN: GROWING UP IN THE SLUMS Mary Frances Greene and Orletta Ryan	18929	1.65
STUDIES ON HYSTERIA Freud and Breuer	16923	1.95
THE TALES OF RABBI NACHMAN Martin Buber	11106	1.45
THINKING ABOUT THE UNTHINKABLE Herman Kahn	12013	1.65
THINKING IS CHILD'S PLAY Evelyn Sharp	11072	1.45
THOMAS WOODROW WILSON Freud and Bullitt	08680	1.25
THREE NEGRO CLASSICS Introduction by John Hope Franklin	16931	1.65
THREE ESSAYS ON THE THEORY OF SEXUALITY Sigmund Freud	11957	1.65
TOWARDS A VISUAL CULTURE Caleb Gattegno	11940	1.65
THE WAR BUSINESS George Thayer	09308	1.25
WHAT WE OWE CHILDREN Caleb Gattegno	12005	1.65
WHEN YOU SEE THIS, REMEMBER ME: **GERTRUDE STEIN IN PERSON** W. G. Rogers	15610	1.65
WILHELM REICH: A PERSONAL BIOGRAPHY I. O. Reich	12138	1.65
WOMEN'S ROLE IN CONTEMPORARY SOCIETY	12641	2.45
WRITERS ON THE LEFT Daniel Aaron	12187	1.65

Wherever better paperbacks are sold, or directly from the publisher. Include 25¢ per copy for mailing; allow three weeks for delivery.

Avon Books, Mail Order Dept.
250 West 55th Street, New York, N. Y. 10019

DISCUS BOOKS
DISTINGUISHED NON-FICTION

American Civil Liberties Union Handbooks
on The Rights of Americans

THE RIGHTS OF MENTAL PATIENTS
Bruce Ennis and Loren Siegel   10652   1.25

THE RIGHTS OF THE POOR
Sylvia Law   18754   .95

THE RIGHTS OF PRISONERS
David Rusovsky   07591   .95

THE RIGHTS OF SERVICEMEN
Robert S. Rivkin   07500   .95

THE RIGHTS OF STUDENTS
Alan H. Levine and Eve Cary   05776   .95

THE RIGHTS OF SUSPECTS
Oliver Rosengart   18606   .95

THE RIGHTS OF TEACHERS
David Rubin   07518   .95

THE RIGHTS OF WOMEN
Susan Deller Ross   17285   1.25

THE RIGHTS OF REPORTERS
Joel M. Gora   21485   1.25

THE RIGHTS OF HOSPITAL PATIENTS
George J. Annas   22459   1.50

THE RIGHTS OF GAY PEOPLE   E. Carrington
Boggan, Marilyn G. Haft, Charles Lister, John P. Rupp   24976   1.75

Wherever better paperbacks are sold, or direct from the
publisher. Include 25¢ per copy for mailing; allow three
weeks for delivery.

Avon Books, Mail Order Dept.
250 West 55th Street, New York, N. Y. 10019